The Right to Learn

The concept of the 'learning society' brings to mind access to education for all and a culture of lifelong learning. But government interventions in education such as the National Curriculum and standardised tests have only served to consolidate the connection between learning and schooling. Schools, furthermore, now have to juggle an increasingly diverse and incompatible range of tasks, providing equal opportunities while catering for individual needs and hitting academic attainment targets while preparing pupils for life in the global workplace. In this climate, what is the future for a democratic system of education?

This important book aims to encourage debate about alternative ways of providing education, and discusses how these are being practised now in Britain, Europe and the USA. Taking the issue of human rights and access as a central theme, the author examines the current state of education provision and the possibilities for its future.

This book will be of interest to specialists in education, politics and philosophy, and also to those seeking alternative ways of educating their children.

Ken Brown is an Honorary Research Fellow at the Centre for Educational Research, University of Aberdeen.

The Right to Learn
Alternatives for a learning society

Ken Brown

London and New York

First published 2002 by RoutledgeFalmer
11 New Fetter Lane, London EC4P 4EE

Simultaneously published in the USA and Canada
by RoutledgeFalmer
29 West 35th Street, New York, NY 10001

RoutledgeFalmer is an imprint of the Taylor & Francis Group

© 2002 Ken Brown

Typeset in Times by Taylor & Francis Books Ltd
Printed and bound in Great Britain by Biddles Ltd, Guildford and
King's Lynn

British Library Cataloguing in Publication Data
A catalogue record for this book is available from the British Library

Library of Congress Cataloging in Publication Data
Brown, Ken, 1942–
The right to learn : alternatives for a learning society / Ken Brown.
p. cm.
Includes bibliographical references and index.
1. Right to education–Great Britain. 2. Right to education–United
States. 3. Right to education–Europe. I. Title.
LC93.G7 B76 2002
379.2'6–21

2001045708

ISBN 0–415–23164–7 (hbk)
ISBN 0–415–23165–5 (pbk)

To Maureen, Evan and Calum

Contents

Preface

Mary Ann's personal almanac had lain forgotten in a corner of the attic for over a century: a sheaf of mottled yellow pages held loosely in a marbled binding. The handwriting was a neat italic: an assemblage of recipes for Christmas puddings and home-made stout, opiate-rich folk-medicines, shopping lists and proverbs suitable for the regulation of an uncomplicated daily life. All the spellings were correct; commas, full stops and capital letters were placed where convention requires them to be. Lists of groceries and household goods costed in pounds, shillings and pence had been added up faultlessly. Tiny numbers at the foot of each column demonstrated an ability to 'carry', using those cumbersome Imperial bases of twelve and twenty. Mary Ann was clearly literate and numerate in the 'functional' sense that recent surveys have now suggested is beyond the capabilities of nearly a quarter of the people of Britain, America and many other 'developed' countries.

On the other hand, Mary Ann was a general-purpose housemaid, the lowliest member of a lower-middle-class household in an industrialised Welsh valley town. Her ambitions seem to have been harnessed to duties typical of that calling. She had no vote until she was nearly old enough to be a grandmother. Any lifestyle choices she might have exercised, other than to marry and found a family, would have been likely to propel her further downward through the stratified society of her time. In short, she knew her place. Her command of basic 'skills' had not done for her what education had been meant to do by many of its late eighteenth-century and early nineteenth-century proponents. It had not empowered her; it had not liberated her from a relentlessly servile station in life. On the contrary, it appears to have consolidated her position as the biddable servant of a society with a Platonic nostalgia for stable rank order, founded on incontrovertible truths about the world and human destinies in it.

In 1867, a few years before Mary Ann's birth, Walter Bagehot considered the absurd idea that an accomplished gentleman, a member of the educated 'ten thousand', might engage his housemaid in intelligent conversation. He would be thought 'mad and wild' for his disregard of the geological immobility of the various social strata and their respective capabilities and limitations. Bagehot's classic work, *The English Constitution*, portrayed political leadership as a compromise between the 'efficient secret' of cabinet government, shared by a small élite, and the theatrical illusion of a ruling monarchy that satisfied the political curiosity of the uneducated masses.

That year, 1867, is significant in other ways. The Reform Act almost doubled the electorate and sowed the seeds of modern party politics. Equally significant was an amendment to the Reform Bill proposed by the radical philosopher John Stuart Mill, then a Liberal MP, for the extension of suffrage to women on equal terms with men. Although his amendment was supported by little more than eighty votes, Mill described it as his greatest parliamentary achievement. This unexpected level of support for women's rights prompted his daughter, Helen Taylor, to establish a society for female suffrage.

Mary Ann was a real person whose descendants are alive now. She was born after these revolutionary events, but too early to benefit fully from them. The humble example of her neat writing, competent spelling and careful arithmetic should prompt us to ask questions that, ironically, have become less fashionable with a mounting sense of crisis in education. Why do we educate? What are the purposes of this enormous modern enterprise? Do we educate people to fulfil determinate roles in society or to gain some kind of personal fulfilment – or both? Do we even know what new social roles might arise a few decades hence? What truths and what assumptions underpin our educational strategies? How, if at all, can we separate myth from reality in the task of introducing young people to a culture that is so complex that no single person can hope to achieve a commanding view of it?

In the following pages, I explore questions of this kind without pretending to offer categorical solutions. Indeed, my central theme is that education takes place in an atmosphere of inevitable uncertainty about ends and means. But this very lack of certainty has implications for the ways in which a society views learning and organises teaching. Two and a half thousand years ago, Plato identified education as a political activity. Educational and political systems are deeply intertwined; they can liberate or enslave according to dominant visions of the relationship between human minds and human societies – and according to the institutionalised expressions of that vision.

Acknowledgements

I am grateful to my friend John Darling for suggesting the title of this book and for his support and encouragement for the idea. I must also thank my son, Evan, for rescuing the manuscript from electronic oblivion.

1   Introduction

> There has been a tendency to treat education as the waste paper basket
> of social policy – a repository for dealing with social problems where
> solutions are uncertain or where there is disinclination to wrestle with
> them seriously.
>
> (Halsey, 1972, p. 8)

A continuing sense of crisis in the UK education system has prompted
unprecedented levels of government intervention to raise standards of
educational attainment. Scarcely a week goes by without the
announcement of another measure to tackle the widely advertised
problems in Britain's schools. Reports of disagreement or disillusionment with previous measures appear in the media almost as regularly.
Within a few weeks of his resignation after four years of controversy
as HM Chief Inspector of Schools, Chris Woodhead pronounced his
own scathing verdict on government education policy in a column in
the *Daily Telegraph* newspaper:

> No government will achieve its goals if it lurches from one initia-
> tive to another, hoping that the electorate, mesmerised by its
> hyperactivity and the slickness of its presentational skills, will have
> forgotten the solution it was proffering a month or two back.
>
> (Woodhead, 01–03–01)

Stimulated partly by unfavourable comparisons between Britain
and comparable countries, this plethora of remedial initiatives taken
by government and its agencies, however, has drawn little inspiration
from alternatives exemplified by the varying provisions for education
in other countries. Radical changes in school management structures
in recent years have been accompanied by the rhetoric of 'parent
power'. Yet centralised control has been consolidated in the state

schools system, principally through implementation of a national curriculum and standardised methods of assessment. Moreover, for most members of the public, as for most educational professionals and politicians, education and schooling are synonymous. Few proposals for raising educational standards omit that familiar mantra, 'in the classroom'.

This last point was strikingly illustrated in a foreword by Chris Woodhead to the highly controversial critique by Professor James Tooley (Tooley, 1998) of much contemporary educational research. According to Woodhead, that report was inspired partly by anxieties about research standards expressed by the eminent educationalist Professor David Hargreaves, and was sponsored by Ofsted to 'help raise standards in the classroom'. Significantly, he ignored the fact that Hargreaves' strictures embraced not only research but also UK education as a whole and its characterising features, schools and classrooms:

> Indeed, unless we dismantle and reconstruct many social institutions, including education, conceptions of 'the learning society' or 'lifelong learning' will remain pure rhetoric. The traditional 'education system' must be replaced by polymorphic educational provision – an infinite variety of multiple forms of teaching and learning.
>
> (Hargreaves, 1997a)

The contradiction implicit in these words of Woodhead and Hargreaves comprises the theme of this book; it is the question of viable alternatives to an increasingly expensive, monolithic education system that is seen by many to be failing a significant proportion of its client-group and society as a whole. The objective is not to propose utopian solutions nor to ponder the daunting task, recommended by Hargreaves, of dismantling educational institutions. It is to consider the intimations of existing alternatives in the UK and elsewhere: to identify some simple, dynamic principles that might encourage a civilised transition to that happy state, 'the learning society'.

Another recent publication by a UK government advisor suggests that cracks may be appearing in the monolith. Entitled *Learning beyond the Classroom: Education for a Changing World*, Tom Bentley's book also calls for institutional diversification to stimulate proactive learning. But a programme of this kind could not be effective as an exclusively top-down initiative; it would be more than likely to crumble into token gestures and half-measures compatible with existing institutional rigidities. Grounds for such anxiety are apparent. Concern is widespread about standards of literacy and numeracy. It seems that nearly one quarter of the people of the world's great industrial democracies are 'functionally illiterate' (*Times Educational Supplement for Scotland* (*TESS*), 11–02–00). According to some very recent research in the UK, this already depressing average includes figures for certain inner-city areas which suggest that between 30 and 40 per cent of their populations cannot read the kind of basic information contained in timetables and recipes or work out how much change they should receive in a typical corner-shop transaction (*TESS*, 12–05–01). Schoolchildren on a slightly higher rung of the educational ladder are said to have a generally poor grasp of science and mathematics. In addition to such mainstream educational problems are others concerning standards of behaviour and a proliferating youth drug-culture. Some voices express distaste for the prevalence of 'rote-learning' in schools and disaffection is widespread among professional educators, already deprived of much of their traditional autonomy by a highly specified national curriculum.

Despite all this, a relentless flow of official literature fosters the myth of the omnicompetent school, catering for the 'individual needs and aptitudes of students'; ensuring that all 'reach their full potential'. This school provides an education not only in traditional core-curriculum subjects but also in the beliefs and values of a multi-cultural society, addressing such complex social issues as adolescent sexuality, racialism and bullying. One index of the all-encompassing influence ascribed to schools by government and the general public is the periodic convocation of expert representatives to deliberate on a form of words with which teachers will convey socially acceptable attitudes about human relationships and other values to their pupils.[1] Irrespective of increasing government spending on education, a suspicion must remain that reality will differ profoundly from the myth. There is, too, the vital question of the rights of children and parents to exercise choice in, and about, education.

Education policy is increasingly dominated by a vocational emphasis that prioritises individual and collective economic efficiency as objectives. Such a view is often supported by the assertion that it is only on the basis of the production of wealth that other social goods can be realised. But it faces an obvious objection: an education orientated towards the acquisition of workplace skills might do very little to equip future generations with the intellectual resources for questioning values implicit in the organisation of wealth production. Conflation of the aims of vocational training and education is an accelerating trend that substitutes for the ideal of individual critical autonomy a servile adaptability to the caprices of a global market economy. Ostensibly, this burgeoning language of 'skills' addresses difficulties posed by rapid social, technological and economic changes that, almost by definition, are unpredictable. It might be argued that the more tightly skills are specified in the interests of 'effective' pedagogy, the less adaptable they are likely to prove; that the more desirable educational objective remains that of cultivating individual critical and creative abilities through a broad, liberal curriculum. But there are more fundamental issues concerning the realisation of liberal, democratic and egalitarian ideals that again highlight the institutional perspective. How could a centrally directed, hierarchical system of mass schooling, largely isolated as it is from society at large and from the intimacies of family and community life, adequately address the diversity of individual children's needs, aptitudes and aspirations? And how might we apportion responsibility for determining educational purpose, content and method more equitably between children themselves, their parents and the state?

These are fundamental questions concerning the rights of individual citizens that have been endorsed through explicit agreement between the governments of many western democracies, including the UK. But interpretation of these rights by individual states has varied considerably. The UK government, for instance, subscribes to a principle enshrined in Article 2, Protocol 1 of the European Convention on Human Rights and also in the Human Rights Act 1998 which came into force in October 2000. This is that 'the State shall respect the right of parents to ensure ... education and teaching in conformity with their own religious and philosophical convictions'. Acceptance of the wider implications of this Article is still qualified in the new Act, however, by the UK government's 1952 requirement for 'efficient instruction and training, and the avoidance of unreasonable public expenditure'. Apart from the controversial status of concepts of educational efficiency and cost-effectiveness, there are glaring contrasts in the extent to which different countries have anticipated or interpreted the rights in question within their legislative and policy frameworks, as expressions of the constitutional relationship between individual citizen and state. Rather than limit parental supervision of education, for example, the Dutch government insisted on the need for official financial support to ensure the exercise of that right. The Irish government endorsed the relevant section of the Convention and elaborated it by asserting the right of parents to educate children at home or in state or private schools of their own choice. Moreover, the notion of 'efficiency' espoused by the UK government is epistemologically and psychologically complex and there is a neglected legacy of debate on this issue that cannot be resolved simply by implementing assessment regimes throughout the education system. Likewise, determination of the cost-effectiveness of educational method is ultimately a political and philosophical question, linked internally to different social values and ends. After all, what price should we be prepared to pay for citizens equipped by their education to contribute positively to the future of democracy?

Insight into the complexity of these issues is furnished by some more extreme international comparisons. Experience in the USA provides a strong *prima facie* case for the claim that a wide range of typical school-age children meet or surpass standardised criteria of assessment in the absence of state involvement in – or significant expenditure on – the education process. It is estimated that between one and two million American children are now educated at home and a series of academic studies indicate significantly higher average levels of attainment in this sector than those achieved in public (state) schools and, perhaps more significantly, in private sector schools. Much the same seems to be true of putative measures of that much-vaunted but over-general concept, *socialisation*. Successive actions by American parents to secure a legal right to 'home educate' appear to have succeeded on the basis of such evidence and in 1999 the movement achieved nation-wide endorsement when the US Senate passed a resolution calling on the President to recognise 'the contribution that home-schooling families have made to the nation'.[2] If governments stipulate the criteria of sound educational performance *within* the formal education system, there must be a case for regarding identical or superior performances by those educated otherwise as one important benchmark for assessing the effectiveness of the system itself. Indeed, this and other alternatives suggest that the most basic assumptions of that system require more critical appraisal than they have so far received – and, I will argue, that the issue of educational rights and freedoms should be treated with greater respect by governments and their agencies. American disillusionment with state education is not necessarily a repudiation of the idea of schooling; a recent trend has been the development of family 'networks' to exploit learning resources and expertise in the wider community. Nor, on the other hand, is the school recognised universally as a necessary context for the effective education of children in western democracies. Government provision of distance-learning facilities in remote regions of Australia, Canada and Alaska furnishes examples which have relevance to remote rural areas in Britain and other European countries, but also more generally, as a route to educational diversification.

Arguably, the radical departure of home education reflects the paucity of alternatives within state schooling and neglect of available expertise within and outside the educational community and the ever-expanding possibilities of distance-learning through developments in information technology. Initiatives exist in the UK with the aim of reforming the education system so that state-funded schools become more diverse and responsive to citizens' rights of self-determination, models for which have been supplied by the educational policy and practice of countries like the Netherlands and Denmark.[3] Important questions are raised, however. To what extent does the idea of a 'learning society' imply an ethos of self-motivation, and where do the rights, interests and responsibilities of citizen and state intersect? Do parental rights, recognised by international agreement, conflict with those of children, also the subject of international agreements? If so, how should such conflicts be resolved and by whom? How far is recognition of greater educational autonomy on the part of citizens and their children consistent with long-standing commitments to equality of opportunity? And, of course, what evidence is there that a reformation could be achieved within the constraints of 'reasonable public expenditure'?

This book is predicated on a conviction that schooling, during the years of compulsory education, has acquired an unjustifiable aura of specialist autonomy from other areas of social and political life in which it is, nonetheless, deeply enmeshed. One apparent exception has been the growing assimilation of the aims of education to those of industry and commerce within government policies. This vocational emphasis, too, has acquired an aura of technicality through the introduction of what are described as 'generic skills'.[4] But no single definition of educational ends and means is above criticism, particularly as they are so closely connected with the diverse aspirations of the individuals and groups who make up a pluralistic society. And effective criticism involves the right to explore and evaluate alternatives. That, rather than a commitment to particular initiatives, like the home education movement, will be the rationale for drawing on research in the USA and elsewhere which suggests that various informal modes of education can be at least as effective and economical as formal state schooling – in terms defined by that formal system. Devolved control of education is also more consistent with international agreements on the rights and liberties of children and citizens. I will examine some significant contrasts in this respect between educational legislation and policy in the UK and some other European countries to identify practical opportunities for educational diversification and the extension of choice.

Thus, a theme that runs through the following pages concerns the legitimate extent of government powers in education. This is really a sub-text, though an important one, to more general questions about the scope and limits of political, moral and intellectual authority that have had far-reaching consequences in the emergence of western liberal democracy. A tradition of thought reaching back to John Locke, powerfully reinforced in the nineteenth century by John Stuart Mill, identifies individual political liberties with the liberation of human intellectual potentials and the possibility of social progress. The point which I will develop in a later chapter is that the ultimate justification of democracy is an epistemological one, a justification in terms of the nature of human knowledge and the proper conditions for its acquisition and growth. One of these conditions may be summed up as the principle that authority, political or otherwise, is legitimate only insofar as it remains open to effective challenge by those held to be subject to it. And that implies significant freedoms to experiment; to pursue varying ways of life and to value different social and moral ends.

The Danish government, for example, has been forthright in accepting the contemporary educational implications of this principle. Affirming the right of parents to state support for their own educational initiatives, as well as their right to educate their children at home, an official publication identifies this respect for civil liberties as a legacy of nineteenth-century political reform and a cornerstone of its educational legislation: '[t]here is broad agreement among the population at large and in Parliament that it cannot be left to a monopoly of public authority to lay down rules on the true way of life' (Carlsen and Borga, 1994, p. 18). On the other hand, many states formally committed by international agreement to respect educational freedoms have interpreted the right to self-determination much more restrictively. An important aim in the following pages will be to consider how this widely endorsed principle is applied in educational policies and practices and to highlight its vulnerability to alternative conventions, even in countries historically associated with the liberal democratic political tradition.

Education policy in Britain has performed a *volte-face* since the publication of the Plowden Report in 1967. Since then, successive UK governments have repudiated the 'progressive' education which that report promulgated and have introduced sweeping reforms involving highly prescriptive curricula and didactic teaching methods. Yet the educational and social problems addressed in the late 1960s are still officially acknowledged and many of the general solutions recommended by Plowden form the basis of present-day UK government education policy. This paradox raises the issue of official fallibility and the rarely acknowledged controversiality of theories that inform government policy. I argue in Chapter 2 that the limited recognition of civil rights and liberties in British education cannot be adequately defended on the grounds that a variety of alternative approaches are necessarily less effective, more costly or more socially divisive.

Chapter 3 reviews the aims of education in democratic societies and the respective rights of governments and citizens to define those aims, a question involving some consideration of the liberal, Enlightenment tradition to which I have already referred. A closely related issue is the tendency of some western governments to define the educational needs of children in terms of the perceived economic and commercial skill-requirements of society. These, I argue, are ill-defined and controversial and such deliberate prioritisation can easily subvert liberal democratic tradition. Consequently, Chapter 4 addresses the subject of international agreements on educational rights and the extent to which these authoritative declarations have been realised in educational law, policy and practice in some western democracies. Chapter 5 is concerned with the apparent tension between the rights and liberties of citizens and their children and the responsibility of the state to ensure that education is both efficient and cost-effective. A major consideration, here, is that concepts of efficiency and cost-effectiveness are internally related to moral, religious and political values as well as to notions of general social utility.

Educational means and ends cannot be distinguished in a fundamental sense, nor are they distinct from questions about the nature of knowledge, effective learning and the development of the creative and critical faculties of children. Chapter 6 consists of a brief review of some theoretical treatments of such matters. Its purpose, which is unavoidably limited, is to indicate the depth and complexity of the issues involved: to question the readiness with which government and its agencies elevate particular theoretical approaches to the status of official orthodoxies, even investing competing theories with a suggestion of heresy. But the most cherished assumptions of formal education systems are open to question. Chapters 7 and 8 examine some official and unofficial educational alternatives in an international context for the light which they may shed on effective learning and teaching. My final chapter considers opportunities for the development of a 'learning society' and the crucial importance of a liberal interpretation of educational rights and liberties if that expression is to rise above the level of rhetoric.

2 New buckets under old leaks?

> I was to learn later in life that we tend to meet any new situation by reorganising, and a wonderful method it can be for creating the illusion of progress while producing confusion, inefficiency, and demoralisation.
>
> (Attributed controversially to Gaius Petronius, ?–66 AD)

That remorseless increase in the number of educational measures by recent British governments must be even more confusing to the general public, the majority of parents included, than to the many teachers who suffer from a new affliction dubbed 'initiativitis'. Change occurs at every level, accompanied by an evolving discourse among politicians, civil servants and educators that is replete with such quasi-industrial jargon as *performance indicators, quality assurance* and *development planning*. The national curriculum, itself a radical innovation of the late 1980s, remains but has changed repeatedly in its details; literacy and numeracy hours have been more recent additions. The ideal of comprehensive state education, realised to some extent in concrete terms in the 1960s and beyond, appears to be yielding to more pragmatic enthusiasms for a degree of selection by 'aptitude' and specialised schooling, supported by private-sector involvement in the management of schools. Popularisation of the idea of 'lifelong learning' by individual people and its collective manifestation, the 'learning society', create the impression of a shift in the ownership of education from the state to the individual, though most of the developments inspired by those slogans remain harnessed to aims determined by the state and delivered by institutions securely within its control.

This condition of permanent revolution seems to offer few vantage points from which to gain an overall impression of the directions of educational development, though that depends partly on the degree of an observer's immersion in the daily minutiae of what is ever more often and tellingly described as the educational *process*. It also depends on the particular dimension of education one identifies as the most sensitive index of its relationship to the wider society. And this, of course, is fundamental because it raises questions about the very point of universal education, itself an idea of comparatively recent origin. A brief review of some recent historical developments will help to provide the beginning of an answer to this question. It will highlight the persistent character of some of the social problems which contrasting education policies have been designed to solve. Above all, it helps to bring into sharper focus some of the ancient fault lines in educational thinking about human potentials and their implications for relationships between citizen and state.

Revolution from above

In 1967 the Central Advisory Council for Education (England), chaired by Lady Plowden, published their report, *Children and their Primary Schools*. It heralded the introduction of progressive, child-centred teaching methods. The Council's terms of reference encompassed 'primary education in all its aspects and the transition to secondary education'. Nearly two hundred wide-ranging recommendations, many of which required significant increases in government expenditure and changes in the law, were presented under the heading 'The Change of Direction'. Although the report dealt with virtually all aspects of primary schooling, including buildings and equipment, size, organisation, staff training and deployment, the new orientation of educational ideals was aptly summarised in the opening words of its second chapter:

> At the heart of the educational process lies the child. No advances in policy, no acquisitions of new equipment have their desired effect unless they are in harmony with the nature of the child, unless they are fundamentally acceptable to him.
>
> (Plowden, 1967, p. 7)

Nonetheless, the history of universal education in the United Kingdom might be just as accurately summarised by the following paraphrase of that opening line: *at the heart of the educational process lies the state*. From the early nineteenth century onwards British governments began to assert a control of education which barely slackened, if at all, with the advent of progressivism. Paradoxically, government intervention in education had not only survived periods during which *laissez-faire* doctrines prevailed in economic and social affairs of the country. It was to reach an unprecedented level under successive late twentieth-century Conservative administrations, zealously committed to 'rolling back the state' through the de-regulation of other areas of national life. Central government acquired a dominance over the schools system perhaps unmatched anywhere else in the world. Although education is delivered by local education authorities, as Alan Ryan has pointed out, 'they are governed by DfEE circulars in a way that no American would think a free society could tolerate' (Ryan, 1999, p. 90).

Ryan's comment hints at a core issue in education that is rarely acknowledged in Britain. This is the problem of reconciling the collective objective of educating people for life in a free and complex democracy while at the same time respecting the fundamental rights and liberties of individual citizens that are the defining characteristics of such a society. For these fundamentals include rights of choice and self-determination in the transmission of a cultural heritage from generation to generation through education. Not only that, but the rights in question have been legally protected by the European Convention for the half-century since the demise of European totalitarianism, and are now enshrined in the law of the United Kingdom through the provisions of the Human Rights Act 1998.

Another, related, problem increases the complexity of this issue. This is the distinction that needs to be drawn between the rights of mature citizens to determine the nature of their children's education and the rights of their children to an education that meets certain collectively determined criteria of adequacy. Thus, the legislation just mentioned provides that no one shall be denied a right to education, but that the state must respect parents' rights to ensure that the education of their children is in conformity with their religious and philosophical convictions. I will consider the differences of interpretation between Britain and some neighbouring countries on this question of citizens' rights *vis-à-vis* the state in more detail in later chapters. It would be wrong to suggest that there is an unambiguous categorical distinction to be drawn here. Education is quite fundamentally about the integration of individuals within their culture. I shall claim, however, that the particular nature of that connection is of pivotal importance for the liberal democratic tradition. My present argument is simply that radical changes in the direction of state education in Britain, and indeed America, have been driven far more by periodic official decisions about educational effectiveness and social utility than by constitutional desiderata of the kind just outlined.

Much of the inspiration for the idea of child-centred teaching derived from psychological research and learning theory rather than from an abstract conception of the rights of children to individualised treatment. Perhaps a more accurate way of putting this is to say that the conception of individual children's educational rights implicit in the Plowden Report was contingent on its judgment about the most appropriate psychological theory of children's learning and development. When the child-centred tradition was finally and decisively repudiated by government and its agencies it was on the putative grounds of collective social and economic efficiency. Not only were concepts of individual educational rights and liberties eclipsed by demands of this kind but learning was tacitly redefined according to a different standard: the measurement of performance on a variety of officially pre-specified tasks. One of the most explicit, brief statements of this philosophical reorientation was the government's negative response in 1988 to some Scottish proposals to introduce features of child-centred teaching to the secondary school curriculum, recorded by Darling (1994, p. viii). The recommendations, it was claimed, were grounded in the psychology of the individual child, but 'a society where enterprise and competition must be increasingly valued ... must be a main determinant of what schools teach'.

It is ironic, perhaps, that a de-regulated economy was thought to require intensified regulation of the education system, but such apparent ideological inconsistencies should not divert attention from another feature of conflict between progressivism and the policies which replaced it. That is that the drive for child-centred education, based on a universalising psychological theory of the child, was itself the product of a highly centralised decision-making system. However, there are prior questions about the nature and sources of the epistemic authority invoked in the course of deciding these matters: for educational rights and freedoms are directly implicated. From both historical and philosophical perspectives they are integral to the development of knowledge in individuals and in their communities. They are not merely abstractions to be given concrete expression and legitimised according to a prevailing consensus on the collective interests of society.

Admittedly, a principal concern of the Plowden Report was to enlist the support of parents and communities and by its very nature progressivism was sensitive to individual difference. But there is an irony here, too. The monolithic structure of state education could not accommodate a theory that valued diversity and innovation without large measures of standardisation. Civil rights and liberties were thus accorded an important but almost incidental place in the deliberations recorded by the Plowden Report. Parental involvement was conceived as ancillary to the main educational task. Fears that parent–teacher associations might interfere with that task were allayed by reassurances that 'the head and the teachers had complete control where professional matters were concerned' in those cases regarded by the schools inspectorate as having outstandingly good relationships with parents (Plowden, 1967, paras 107–20). Although divided on the question of religious education, the committee had felt it necessary to recommend that parents should be informed of their statutory right to withdraw their children from acts of worship and religious education (*ibid.*, para. 577). They acknowledged the provisions of the European Convention concerning parents' rights of choice about their children's education. This was interpreted narrowly, however, as the desirability of permitting choice between local authority schools. But these are not necessarily the same kinds of choice, as the alternative of state-funded independent educational initiatives by parents in the Netherlands and Denmark demonstrates.

In other respects, however, the Plowden Committee's conclusions were heavily indebted to one particular theory of child development for which they felt there was substantial empirical support: that of Jean Piaget and his Genevan School. Then, within a relatively short time, that theory itself became extremely controversial. The central conclusions in the report were publicly repudiated by government and its agencies on the basis of alleged educational ineffectiveness. Meanwhile, a small élite of educational philosophers including Dearden, Hirst and Peters articulated the theoretical rationale for yet another change of direction that was to encompass primary and secondary levels of the UK education system.

Counter revolution

In October 1999, Chris Woodhead, then Chief Inspector of Schools for England and Wales, attributed much under-performance among British children to a former 'excess of child-centredness' in education when he was interviewed during a popular BBC radio programme.[1] In this and similar ways, the general public was familiarised with a seismic shift which had taken place in educational thinking, mainly under Conservative governments, during the preceding two decades. Child-centredness had become associated with a sentimental liberalism ill-suited to an increasingly competitive world which prioritised the sharply honed survival skills of the entrepreneur. The new change of direction had been comprehensive, as Darling pointed out:

> Today we again have a government that aims to limit the power of the teaching profession and also to limit the critical study of education. It has already created both the climate and the framework within which every teacher must now think and work: both climate and framework are inimical to the child-centred tradition.
>
> (Darling, 1994, p. 110)

These words provide an edifying sub-text to Woodhead's sweeping and debatable generalisation. They are indicative of the vulnerability of the United Kingdom education system to political control from the centre. Indeed, it is hardly an exaggeration to say that the dominant influence of the state in British education had been the one thing that remained unchanged for more than a century and a half, irrespective of whether prevailing government ideologies inclined towards the interventionist or the *laissez-faire*. Child-centred education can be described plausibly as a myth that inspired many educationalists working within an institutional framework that was essentially inhospitable to it.

There are cogent objections to the simplistic disjunction between present-day, centrally directed education policy and what is implied (in Woodhead's words, for example) to be a homogenous, discredited method of the past. One is that despite major contrasts between education policies immediately prior to the 1980s and those of the more recent past, the position of the teacher has been that of a subordinate in a hierarchical system. 'Progressivism' and 'child-centredness' became watchwords of the post-Plowden era, but it remains questionable to what extent the meanings attached to these terms by their authors retained their theoretical specificity in their downward progress through that educational hierarchy. In fact, it seems likely that a typical classroom response to trickle-down theory was an unstable amalgam of both traditional and progressive teaching methods, often without much critical awareness of any clear distinction between them.

From the start, child-centred education was hostage to the assumption that the practical implications of an entire body of research can be communicated effectively through a process of institutional management that rarely engages the majority of teachers in constructive, ongoing dialogue. It is scarcely surprising that for many of them the most concrete, lingering imagery of the era of progressivism concerns a redeployment of classroom furniture. For many parents the concept of 'learning by discovery' is convincingly parodied by critics who recall children scraping aimlessly in sandpits or hurling plastic bricks around the classroom. Arguably, the ideal of an education which starts with the epistemic, emotional and social needs of individuals is in any case over-ambitious in the context of classrooms consisting of one teacher, possibly an assistant, and between twenty and thirty children of like ages from varied backgrounds. But this is a criticism of the organisational means of delivering education rather than of the principle in question.

Some shortcomings of the official belief that new ideas can 'cascade' down intact to the classroom level are underlined by the complexity and increasing controversiality of this once-influential research in 'genetic epistemology' by Piaget and his colleagues. The Plowden Report described that approach as in accordance with 'what is generally regarded as the most effective primary school practice, as it has been worked out empirically'. On the other hand, it considered Piagetian thought 'not easy to understand' and 'almost impossible to express other than in technical terms'. The opacity of the theory, its disputed pedagogical implications, not to mention philosophical refutations of its central tenets advanced by critics like Noam Chomsky, Dennis Phillips and Robert Ennis,[2] must raise doubts about the consistency of 'child-centred' classroom practices commonly attributed to its influence. As a result, adverse criticisms of educational progressivism as a whole tend to be indiscriminate attacks on a range of activities that reflected different theoretical commitments and levels of understanding. For the purposes of the present argument the salient point concerns the institutional context. It is that the change of direction in British education signalled by the Plowden Report became the policy of a system of administration that embodied few, if any, mechanisms for teachers to participate actively in the interpretation and criticism of the principles that inspired it, or of some notable alternatives. This was even truer of the position of parents whose influence for good or ill on the educational prospects for their children was acknowledged and addressed by the report itself.

A further objection to the implied disjunction between traditional and progressive educational methods concerns the paucity of evidence for claims about the superiority of more traditional, didactic teaching. This is compounded by the lack of clarity about precisely which varieties of classroom activity exemplified 'progressive' methods and which others were properly regarded as more 'traditionalist', a question which involves judgments of a conceptual nature as well as the observation of the behaviour of children and their teachers. Different emphases by different researchers in a review by William Anthony illustrate this point, regardless of his own conclusion that evidence tended to be somewhat unfavourable to progressivist theory. One interesting example in that volume is furnished by a contribution from Robin Barrow who adopts A.S. Neill's highly distinctive, not to say extreme, approach at Summerhill School as typical of progressive education:

> Neill has his spiritual heirs whom I shall refer to as 'progressives'. What marks out the progressive is this lack of concern for equipping the individual child for social survival and in such a way as to enable him to make a contribution to community life as a whole.
>
> (Barrow, 1979, p. 188)

The Plowden Report distinguished Piaget's account of the psychological development of the child from what it portrayed as a significant but less satisfactory competitor. This was the behaviourist approach pioneered by Thorndike, Skinner and others in which learning is conceived as operant conditioning: 'reinforcement in learning, habit formation and the measurement of various kinds of stimulus–response behaviour' (*ibid.*, para. 519). As the report pointed out, this was still influential in education in the United States at that time. It is arguable that the growing fusion between education and vocational training in Britain at the turn of the twenty-first century amounted to a reincarnation of behaviourism in the guise of 'competence-based' education that would provide children with the skills identified by an educational *élite* as necessary for the survival in a culture of enterprise and competition. Plowden considered the two psychological models of 'the learning process' represented by Piagetian constructivism and behaviourism respectively, favouring the former over the latter largely for what it regarded as the empirical evidence of its greater effectiveness. Others have drawn more profound, conceptual distinctions between the growth of intelligence and attempts to 'describe, in behaviourist terms, something which is essentially non-behaviouristic, namely the development of knowledge and understanding', a conception which is 'not just viciously reductionist but also utterly naive and simplistic' (Hyland, 1993, p. 61).

The vulnerability of the UK education system to such alternating and even polarising influences is a consequence of centralisation, though not a simple one. It is also an effect of the decoupling of education from the totality of the surrounding culture, itself largely determined by that all-embracing pattern of organisation and certain

other trends implicated in it. One is the habit of reconstructing relationships between education and society in disjoint, instrumental
terms: to view education as a tool for realising laudable but discrete
social aims. Another is the related propensity to elevate psychological
questions about the nature of learning above more basic, philosophical
questions about the nature of knowledge, an approach which runs the
danger of treating educational objectives as self-authenticating,
attending to the means to the neglect of the ends. I believe this distinction between psychology and epistemology is crucial and will argue
later that it was a revolution in the latter field that stimulated the
historical drive for democracy, a vision of greater human equality,
recognition of an individual right of inquiry and freedom of expression – and of the need for constitutional means of protecting them.
The place of education among these values is central but it is not one
that fits comfortably into the simple cause-and-effect mould of state-
directed instrumentalism.

Educational constants: inequality and deprivation

Despite the abrupt switches of emphasis that typified late twentieth-
century education policy, some of the problems it addresses have
remained essentially the same. So, too, have some of the proposed
solutions. The prescriptive national curriculum and didactic pedagogy
inaugurated by successive Conservative governments in the UK was
adopted with apparent enthusiasm by the incoming Labour government of 1997, though it was mitigated by an emphasis on the need for
experiment and innovation to tackle urban and rural deprivation. The
Plowden Report had considered these persistent social and cultural
problems, particularly in inner cities, recommending the establishment
of Educational Priority Areas where a policy of positive discrimination would 'make schools in the most deprived areas as good as the
best in the country' (Plowden, 1967, p. 66). By 1972, a further report,
Educational Priority, edited by Professor A.H. Halsey, was reviewing a
series of action–research projects designed precisely to achieve that
objective by eliminating inequalities of educational opportunity.
During the early months of this committee's work, however, doubts set
in about the scope and coherence of its remit:

> we began to realise that there were unsolved issues behind the
> equality debate … [This] is essentially a discussion about educa-
> tion for whom and to do what. In planning our intervention in
> schools were we forced sooner or later to consider both questions

and in doing so to question whether an EPA programme is anything more than a new formula for fair competition in the educational selection race ... Or could we assume a wide programme of social reform which would democratise local power structures and diversify local occupational opportunities?

(Halsey, 1972, p. 11)

In addition, there was the tendency of governments 'to treat education as the waste paper basket of social policy' for dealing with intransigent problems requiring more thoroughgoing social reform to achieve such aims as the 'democratisation of opportunity'. Liberal education policies, concluded Halsey, had failed on an inadequate theory of learning which focused on teachers, curricula and formal access to schools but neglected social situations, motivations and support in the family and the community: 'We have also to consider liberty and fraternity' (*ibid.*, pp. 7–8).

Within two years of achieving power in 1997, the Labour government had begun to fulfil one of its manifesto commitments through the creation of twenty-five Education Action Zones. These EAZs replicated the older EPAs in almost all respects, except for a new emphasis on the involvement of private business, consistent with the utilitarian mood of the times. They were to improve the educational performance of children and the morale of teachers; to increase involvement by parents in their children's education; and to enhance the seriously depleted sense of communal responsibility in run-down areas. Within a year and a half of the launch of the first EAZs, however, the DfEE was urging zone management teams to meet stringent targets, examination results in particular, or to face the prospect of being wound down (*TESS*, 17–03–00). Some critics regarded this abrupt change of tone as a retreat from original commitments to foster innovation and experiment in educationally deprived areas. By the spring of 2001, the Secretary of State for Education had publicly admitted that the scheme had been 'over-hyped' and that there had been a disturbing lack of innovation in EAZs (*TESS*, 09–03–01, p. 10). Something that undermined a foundational principle of the scheme was its inability to secure bids by groups of parents to take the lead in managing zoned schools. That is perhaps partly explained by the absence from the initial round of EAZ inaugurations of a requirement for local authority or commercial bidders to consult with parents or to outline their prospective roles, an oversight which is eloquent testimony of the long-standing tensions between democratic aspirations and the paternalistic realities of British education.

Liberty, fraternity and paternalism

One very obvious qualification needs to be made in any discussion of the tension between state paternalism and the ideal of an education to fit future citizens for critical, rational participation in democratic society. Teaching aimed at securing these ends is one thing; provision that respects parents' rights to have children educated according to their beliefs is another. These educational objectives can and sometimes do conflict. But what kind of conflict is it, and is it the kind that requires specific resolutions? There are different kinds of answer to these questions, outlined below and elaborated in later chapters.

For example, there is a stand-alone argument for the right of parents to have their children educated according to their beliefs. This is that it comprises one of a number of basic rights of citizenship in a free democratic society; it is not directed *instrumentally* towards particular educational outcomes such as the encouragement of critical thought or even democratic participation, desirable though these are. Respect for the educational rights of parents, however, is itself a significant dimension of democratic participation and is explicitly recognised as such by the Danish constitution as well as the European Convention and the UN's Universal Declaration of Human Rights: a defence against the arbitrariness of decision-making where authority is monopolised by one organ of the state. Having said this, there is the broad educational consideration that learning to participate in democratic society is likely to be encouraged where there is constitutional provision for the effective exercise of choice by parents – and their children. This, again, is something safeguarded by Danish law in contrast to the paternalistic approach so long characteristic of UK education policy. A neglected but important insight of some Enlightenment thinkers like Helvétius and James Mill was that the politics and cultural ethos of a society were powerful formative influences in the development of children.

A significant proportion of 'home-schoolers' in the United States teach their children away from school in order to inculcate a very specific set of religious values which they feel are threatened by the influences of school and community. Such motives might be distasteful to those who value the idea of educating children to cope in a critical and constructive manner with the multiplicity of difficulties which will confront them in a complex, pluralist society. But the problem that arises is one of establishing criteria to demonstrate that parents' choices are limiting children's potentials sufficiently to justify curtailment of their rights of educational supervision. This raises questions about the impartiality of official judgments of that kind and the contribution of formal assessment in support of them. Ironically, the evidence is that while the state attaches paramount importance to formal assessment as a measure of educational effectiveness, the performance of children educated at home on the same standardised tests seems to far outstrip that of their school-educated peers, as indeed it does on measures of 'social adjustment' – a phenomenon I examine in Chapter 8.

There is a tendency on the part of many commentators who are sceptical about parental rights to contrast them with the interests of the child, as though this particular disjunction has a paradigmatic status and is more typical than any conflict between the interests of children and the demands of a benign state and its agencies. As I will show, this is a questionable stance. There are some striking contradictions between the sentimental language of many official proclamations about the education of children and the effects of bureaucratic inertia and remoteness from the experiences of childhood. A disturbing example has been the failure of many local authorities in England to maintain records of the educational performance of 'looked-after children' – neglect that occurred despite years of government emphasis on raising standards, persistent recitation of the mantra of 'social inclusion' as well as media coverage of the desperate lives that many of these children lead before and after leaving official care (HM Inspectors of Schools and the Social Work Services Inspectorate, March 2001). Commitments, like that in Section 2(1) of the Standards in Scotland's Schools Act 2000, to secure the development of children's personalities, talents and mental and physical abilities 'to their fullest potential' should be interpreted judiciously, as laudable aspirations but perhaps dangerously ambiguous policy objectives.

There is, of course, a vital question about the wishes of the child. These are too readily conflated with the 'interests' of the child, an expression more consistent with officialdom's habit of monopolising interpretation and tacitly disregarding the legitimacy of views expressed by minors. Government attitudes towards this question have been equivocal. The devolved Scottish Parliament's first educational legislation, mentioned above, provided for regular consultation with students by their schools, though it remains to be seen how compatible such democratic aspirations are with prescriptive curricular guidelines and an intensive assessment regime. On the other hand, in 1999, Ofsted inspectors in England apparently ignored the unanimous support of children and parents for the libertarian policies in operation at A.S. Neill's Summerhill School, demanding wholesale reform in the putative interests of the children. This case and the sheer controversiality of that school raise interesting questions which will be addressed in future chapters. My present point is that where children's voices really are heard, they are inclined to differ from the official consensus concerning their true interests, and there is a rather obvious need for conscientious reflection about the means of reconciling these two things.

Ironically, much of the literature on the care of children and conditions for fulfilling their psychological needs emphasises the crucial, proximal relationship between parents and children, the intimate emotional and linguistic bonds which are woven in the home. Here, too, there is often a tendency towards high-level generalisations of a rather sentimental character: a suspicion that the ideal and the real are sometimes illicitly conflated. Nevertheless, to whatever extent the wishes of children are recognised as integral to their interests, there must be a presumption in favour of the interpretive role of the parent rather than the officially sanctioned formula. Much anecdotal experience from the home education movement suggests not only that children thrive in that educational environment, but that they have played a significant part in their parents' original decision to educate them outwith school and that they remain confirmed in that view. In other words, there is no *prima facie* case for bracketing-off education as an exception to the *general* presumption that parents are fit to rear their young. This is certainly no argument against measures to ensure that identifiable violations of children's rights and interests are a proper subject of official intervention. Nor is it an argument against possible statutory provision for assessing children's views about their education – whether at school or otherwise.

Partners?

As Plowden, Halsey and many others have shown, there is a powerful temptation to recommend close 'partnerships' between parents, children and the formal education system. On the face of things, a relationship like this provides opportunities to reconcile the convictions of parents, the views of their children and the school's experience of what constitutes a sound education. Partnership has been a continuing theme of modern education policy under different administrations and its attraction derives at least in part from recognition of the overweening influence of the home on the child. It has become commonplace to observe that only when parents and families are recruited to the educational enterprise will the vicious cycle of social inequality and deprivation be broken. The problem is that this ideal has been the subject of so much official educational cant for over a generation that there seems little reason to hope that it would be realised in a truly significant way within the prevailing state system. In addition to advocating close parent–school relationships, the Plowden Report also stressed its endorsement of Section 76 of the Education Act then in force. This paraphrased Article 2 of the First Protocol of the European Convention together with the UK government's original reservation, namely: 'so far as is compatible with the provision of efficient instruction and training and the avoidance of unreasonable public expenditure, pupils are to be educated in accordance with the wishes of their parents'. Halsey described parent–school partnerships as 'the first and essential link of school to community' which had as its ultimate aim 'mutual teaching and learning in parent child projects' (*ibid.*, pp. 190–2). Article 2 has now been incorporated into United Kingdom's Human Rights Act, together with the reservation about efficient instruction and reasonable public expenditure, of course. Partnership is, in that still rather ill-defined sense, a requirement of British law.

One of the deepest ironies about the subsequent fate of educational progressivism was that it acquired a bad name partly as a result of a notorious instance in which parent–school partnership appears to have played little or no role. The anarchic William Tyndale School was widely adopted as a symbol of the evils of progressivism and, in turn, identified with A.S. Neill's already long-established Summerhill School. Of what may be many injustices in this comparison, one that stands out is the fact that the William Tyndale scandal broke when parents themselves expressed outrage at the unstructured nature of the school's regime. Indeed, a great deal of adverse popular opinion about our schools and teachers might be fuelled by the continuing inability of the formal system to engage in genuine dialogue with individual parents.

The language of partnership has survived that massive centralisation of the education system since the 1980s, largely through the device of parental representation in the management of schools. But that democratic procedure has coexisted with a centralised system for the delivery of a minutely predetermined curriculum and, in Scotland, slightly less prescriptive curricular guidelines enforced by a rigorous inspection regime. A revealing example is a Scottish Education Department's consultation document, *Parents as Partners* (SOEID, 1998), which envisaged extensions of existing parental involvement in school management. Yet that document specifically precluded it in those matters most central to the interests of committed parents: 'the breadth, depth or content of the curriculum'. Opinion was canvassed on the quasi-contractual idea of 'home–school agreements' which, the document suggested, would impose a number of specific duties on parents while apparently recognising no further obligation on schools than the rather obvious one of ensuring that children were taught by properly qualified staff. Of course, this was a consultation paper and opportunities existed for recipients to make further suggestions. But perhaps most indicative of the paternalistic climate of UK education was the document's omission of any reference to the legal rights of parents laid down in the European Convention which was about to be adopted by the United Kingdom as the Human Rights Act that year – and this in proposed agreements which invoked the solemnity of law, if not its enforceability. As already noted, the Plowden Report had found it necessary to recommend that parents should be informed of their statutory rights to withdraw their children 'from the Act of Worship and from religious education' a full generation previously (Plowden, 1967, para. 577).

Statutory provisions for the collective representation of parents in the machinery of school management have the effect of defining limits to their involvement. The civil libertarian issue, by contrast, is about the different notion of representing the personal convictions of individual parents in their own children's education. 'Partnership' thus becomes a weasel-word which seems to imply a relationship of openness and equality but which is frequently construed as meaning a considerably more distal and subordinate role for parents in the life of their school. A preference on the part of educational professionals for an 'arm's-length' relationship with parents is understandable within the existing framework. It is inherent in the 'institutional logic' of hierarchical control, the prescriptive nature of the curriculum and an inflexible regime of assessment, inspection and 'quality control'. Essentially, parental choice is pre-empted as decisively by these recent developments as it was inhibited by the deferential attitudes of earlier generations towards schools and teachers. Governments insistently publicise their determination to raise standards. They monopolise the definition of those standards and publicly attribute responsibility for realising them to the schools irrespective of the powerful influence of local, national and global cultural milieux.

In addition, the schools are burdened rather indiscriminately with the solution of successive social problems, many of which by their nature are beyond their competence, as Halsey pointed out. All this creates a climate of parental expectation more akin to that of the consumer of end-products than that of the participant in a creative activity. Consequently, public attitudes towards failure are focused on the service-providers and their perceived shortcomings; parental discontent translates the more easily into complaint, hostility and, increasingly, litigation. Popular awareness of the existence of tightly specified standards, if not their precise nature, pervasive scrutiny of them by government and its agencies, and the production-line terminology of quality assurance and control accentuate the role of parents as consumers of finished products. Their alienation from the educational 'process' is also a by-product of that institutional logic which identifies an arm's-length welcome to intruders as the safest way of preserving the cohesion of the educational edifice.

On the other hand, it is a truism in the world of education that family background, social status and parental attitudes are key determinants of a child's educational achievement. There is nothing insincere about continuing ambitions by governments and educationalists to enlist the active support of parents, provided it is for the maintenance of whichever educational programme is in place at a given time. But there is possibly an even more fundamental and long-standing obstacle to parent partnership than that created by the comparatively recent formalisation of teaching. That is the view of the teacher as a repository of information to be communicated to the pupil, a view that is widely shared by public and professionals alike. An illuminating example is provided by Mary Simpson's account of a teacher's alarm at the prospect of introducing the topic of genetically modified foods as a component of 'Education for Citizenship': she simply did not know enough about it. Simpson comments: 'Here we have the central problem in a nutshell. The model of learning which still dominates our secondary curriculum is still that of its transmission from the expert by telling' (*TESS*, 02–02–01, p. 16). The contrast which Simpson wanted to draw was between this and the idea of a teacher who does not need to know all about such topics, but whose expertise lies in helping children to find information and to use it to form critical judgments about different arguments.

The relationship between teacher and pupil portrayed by the latter formulation is itself one that might best be described as a 'partnership'. Yet the alternative model of the teacher as 'teller' is almost all-pervading and is often reflected in the language parents use to describe education. For teachers, the consequence might be defensiveness about their insecure status as universal expert. For parents, it is likely to be a sense of irrelevance to the esoteric educational process, punctuated by occasional disillusionment or anger at hints of pedagogic fallibility, fuelled by the official castigation of failing teachers.

And, of course, there is a powerful symbolism in the very fabric of the schools: building complexes to which children are delivered by their parents and from which they are later collected at fixed times of day. The idea of partnership is also constrained by this physical context that accentuates the feeling of relinquishing authority to others, *in loco parentis*. For all these reasons, the ideal of parent–school partnerships has repeatedly transformed itself into formalised relationships at the margins of genuinely educational activity. Exceptions are rare and tend to prove the rule.

Much of the previous discussion could be construed as denigration of the well-intentioned efforts of democratically elected governments to promote a fairer and more egalitarian society – if it were not for the fact that alternative versions of the relationship between children, their parents and the state are readily available for the purposes of comparison. Some are exemplified in experimental projects by teachers and parents in the United Kingdom, others by experience in countries like the Netherlands and Denmark which have provided state-funding of a potential multiplicity of educational initiatives by citizens without exhibiting educational, social and economic differentials as gross as those evident in present-day Britain. Such comparisons, alone, do not furnish evidence of the superiority of alternative education policies and programmes. I will argue, however, that the limited recognition of civil liberties in British educational policy and practice cannot be justified on the ground that such alternatives are necessarily less effective, more costly to the public purse or more socially divisive than the existing, largely unchallenged division between state and private-sector education.

3 Why educate?

Society, the individual and education

> If we narrow the scope of education, we narrow our operative conception of civilization, and we impoverish the meaning of participation in civilized community.
>
> (Scheffler, 1973, p. 60)

In the course of its relatively brief history, universal state-maintained education has come to occupy a secure position in western democracies – in fact, such a secure position that its purposes are taken for granted by large sections of the public and the popular media. Controversy, of which there is a great deal, is usually about the effective achievement of goals which are taken as self-evidently beneficial, or which it might seem frivolous for the average citizen to dispute. Ironically, educational debate on both sides of the Atlantic seems to have focused popular attention on the idea of 'effectiveness' to the neglect of a more fundamental question: 'for what?'

Many academic authors have deplored this widespread aversion to philosophical questions about the purposes of education. In the United States, Israel Scheffler has argued for many years that a primary aim of a democratic society must be to cultivate the rational faculties of its young people rather than to treat education 'as an instrument for the implementation of designated social values, taken as ultimate' (*ibid.*, pp. 134–5). Knowledge accumulates in unpredictable ways and its practical consequences are unforeseeable. Assessment of the effectiveness of an education in 'shaping concrete results' is irrelevant to the democratic ideal of an open and dynamic society, the laws, principles and moral standards of which are constantly subject to the critical scrutiny of its citizens. More recently Harvey Siegel has condemned the widespread and 'stultifying misconception' that 'deep philosophical questions concerning values and the aims of education are somehow off-limits' (Siegel, 1988, p. ix). Yet the influence of such views on the general public and on governments, alert to electoral and media opinion, has been very limited.

In Britain, as in the USA, an increasing preoccupation with educational means rather than ends has led to the triumph of a view of education which defines the needs of children in terms of the perceived social, economic and commercial skill-requirements of society. Ironically, UK governments have extolled the economic benefits of didactic teaching practices in 'Pacific-rim' countries at precisely the moment when many oriental industrialists and educationalists called for liberalisation of their own educational regimes to promote creative and critical thinking among students. In addition, the perceived educational imperatives of global competition have been called in question by economic collapse in the east. This pragmatic western trend continues unabated, however. It accentuates an illicit notion of educational development as the acquisition of arbitrarily pre-specified intellectual and vocational 'skills' to serve putative collective ends. Obsession with measurability and its requirement for standardisation also limit rather than extend the scope for fruitful educational experiment and effectively redefine educational aims as managerial objectives – with far-reaching institutional consequences.

Alan Ryan identifies the contemporary 'vocational ideal of student competence' as the sharpest challenge to the liberal ideal of an education for future citizens which would produce 'autonomous, argumentative and tough-minded individuals' (Ryan, 1999, p. 84). Opposition between these views is more radical than it might appear on the face of things; it has ancient precedents and is rooted in very different beliefs about the significance of human understanding for the distribution of power and authority in the state.

Although educational philosophy continues to flourish, it does so in relative isolation from the concerns of the general public as well as from politicians and educational practitioners, whose conceptions of educational ends and means are constrained by a monolithic institutional framework responsible for translating universalising ideals into a system of uniform pedagogic practices. In this false atmosphere of comprehensive, pre-specified objectives, the intimate connections between democracy, personal empowerment and education *as an end in itself* are easily overlooked. As I will argue here and in later chapters, this trend threatens to disinherit a tradition that united calls for democratic representation, social and gender equality and personal liberation – one vital stimulus in the historical drive for universal, state-supported education. Thus a brief historical overview will help to identify some themes of continuing importance in educational thought.

Nowadays, few people would disagree that a certain general level of educational attainment is a necessary condition for a civilised way of life. This has not always been thought to be the case, of course. It is worth recalling that 'democracy' itself has only recently enjoyed world-wide, if sometimes insincere, approbation as the political system best suited to realise creativity and to resolve potentially violent conflicts between competing interests and systems of value and belief. Until quite recently alternative conventions have embodied sceptical, even hostile attitudes towards aspirations for social equality and democratic representation as well as deeply pessimistic views of the intellectual fitness of great majorities of people to comprehend the principles according to which their lives are organised. Some of these ancient themes have contemporary resonances in different interpretations of the function of education – as an instrument of social policy and democratic control on the one hand or as a route to personal libera-tion for democratic citizenship on the other.

Education and the citizen

It has been recognised for at least two and a half millennia that there are intimate connections between the nature of education in a society and the configurations of power, authority and subordination that define its political constitution. Plato's idealised state, his *Republic*, was to be founded on an absolutist theory of knowledge and epistemic authority profoundly at odds with the habitual disputatiousness of the citizens of classical Greek democracies including, most notably, his own Athens. The education he envisaged was consequently a rigidly prescriptive one which would equip his philosopher rulers to govern in accordance with principles of truth and justice which they alone could grasp by virtue of their superior intellectual abilities. Behind him towered the enigmatic figure of Socrates, best known as the central character of Plato's famous dialogues, including that late work, the *Republic*. But Socrates was one of the world's few great philosophers who did not write down his own ideas for posterity. A puzzle remains as a result. Socrates was executed by the Athenian democracy of 399BC for his unsettling custom of engaging fellow Athenians of all social classes and persuasions in rigorous discussion about established values and accepted truths; the specific charges against him were impiety and the corruption of youth. This undoubtedly identifies him as a critic of the direct democracy in his native *polis*, an exposer of 'incompetence and windbaggery', as Karl Popper has put it (Popper, 1969, p. 128). However, in the *Republic*, the aristocratic Plato portrayed his teacher as an apologist for a polity of strictly hierarchical social castes predicated on the idea that truth, justice and moral values are as much beyond dispute as the theorems of geometry, at least for the great majority of the population.

The integrity of Plato's political aspirations has been questioned, not least because in that work he attributes to Socrates a proposal that would deceive the population into accepting the absolute authority of a supreme clerisy. Known as the 'Golden' or 'Noble' Lie by those inclined to exonerate Plato, this was a myth based on an analogy with precious and vulgar metals: a few people are naturally fit to govern, others to support them, and the rest only to serve. Popper has described Plato's later portrait of Socrates as a betrayal – and Socrates himself as the author of a doctrine that lies at the heart of a free society. This is the idea that real understanding is achieved only by constantly testing popular myths and nostrums through debate and argument. And the political corollary of this epistemological stance is what Popper describes as 'the open society' characterised by an institutionalisation of argument, manifested in the kind of democratic institutions that provide for free inquiry and expression by individuals. Popper describes the contrast between Socrates and Plato as between two worlds: that of 'a modest, rational individualist and that of a totalitarian demi-god' (*ibid.*, p. 132).

Notwithstanding the possible distortions of Socrates' teaching by his eminent pupil, two features of it in particular have been influential in more recent educational thought. Paradoxically, neither seems congruent with the typically hierarchical ethos of schools or education systems, though close approximations have been achieved in some areas of university education. One is the Socratic 'profession of ignorance', the other an injunction to 'follow the *logos*', or to follow the logic of discourse wherever it leads. The first principle enjoins aspiring teachers to relinquish claims to authority and superior knowledge other than those that they can deploy in the egalitarian cut and thrust of inquiry about a given subject. The second commits them to the flexible investigation of a topic that is largely determined by the ideas, beliefs and prejudices of the learner, not the preferences of the teacher or the prescribed contents of a curriculum. This pupil–teacher relationship is inherently egalitarian and open-ended, guided by conceptions of truth and understanding which are to be achieved, if at all, through mutual endeavour rather than delivered as pre-specified 'learning outcomes'. The Socratic conception of learning and teaching turns on the idea that the supreme ethical virtue is the individual's search for truth through rational inquiry, and Socrates described his own role as that of a 'midwife' to the thoughts of others. Understanding emerges through reasoned discourse between people, but in individual minds according to their unique matrix of previous experience and ideas, a doctrine which I will subsequently describe as *epistemic individualism*. Scheffler has identified this kind of approach as a 'fundamental philosophical tradition of the West' and Socrates as its 'greatest teacher' (Scheffler, 1973, p. 63) but his outline of the Socratic method is in striking contrast to conceptions of educational ends and means which are so characteristic of most western education today:

> Socrates ... had, after all, no curriculum, no facts, no answers, no formulae. He had only questions, and the willingness to follow the argument wherever it might lead. He was totally uninterested in the social class, erudition, or IQ of his friends and students – interested only in engaging them in a critical quest for truth.
>
> (Scheffler, 1973, p. 63)

It is difficult to reconcile this account of Socratic method with the undoubted influence that this ancient philosopher has exercised on subsequent educational thinking, though Scheffler's interpretation is by no means idiosyncratic. And it might seem no less difficult to detect clear social and political implications in educational principles of this kind. In order to clear some ground in anticipation of later arguments, two examples are worth citing. The first is the arterial role of Socratic doctrine in the educational and political philosophy of John Stuart Mill, whose essay 'On Liberty' has itself been a seminal influence in the development of western liberal democracy. The second is the impact of egalitarian, Socratic relationships which the nineteenth-century Danish reformer Nikolai Grundtvig detected between students and tutors when he visited Trinity College, Cambridge. While this was admittedly a feature of a privileged and exclusive form of higher education in England, Grundtvig translated it into generalisable educational principles, central to the matrix of social reforms that were to make Denmark arguably the most egalitarian liberal democracy in the world. Grundtvig is still a revered figure. His ideas are explicitly acknowledged by Danish government publications as a paradigm of the proper constitutional relationship between citizens and the state in a free, democratic society. According to one official publication on the Danish education system:

Any educational approach is based on a certain view of mankind. And that view cannot be dictated by the state. No public authority can lay claim to a 'superhuman' or privileged understanding of human life. Individual lives are not neatly tied up packages that can be slotted into a theory or definition, however comprehensive or ingenious it might be.

(Carlsen and Borga, 1994, p. 17)

For the time being, I simply wish to draw attention to the intimate connections between theories about what knowledge is, how it is acquired and what the answers to such questions mean in terms of rights to exercise political authority and obligations to obey it. These questions are as crucial in determining the character of democratic societies and the place of education within them as they are in distinguishing between democracies and the kind of alternative political system envisaged by Plato, where political legitimacy derives from the alleged ability of an educated *élite* to achieve epistemic or spiritual infallibility.

Aristotle adopted a more dispassionate and external view of education for citizenship than his teacher, Plato, which might be partly explained by his greater inclination for empirical inquiry. Democracies should accept that the state is responsible for the education of future citizens to fit them for life under that particular type of constitution. Equally, though, states with oligarchic constitutions should ensure that their citizens would be well adapted to government by a ruling minority. The point of interest, here, has little to do with Aristotle's specific educational recommendations, or indeed his belief that rationality is the paramount educational end. It is the contrast between the Socratic tradition just outlined and Aristotle's tendency to identify education with training directed towards collectively predetermined outcomes. That, and the seminal conviction which he shared with Plato that education is also, fundamentally, about social control:

It is useless to have the most beneficial rules of society fully agreed upon by all who are members of the *politeia*, if individuals are not going to be trained and have their habits formed for that *politeia*, that is to live democratically if the laws of society are democratic, oligarchically if they are oligarchic; for as one individual may get out of hand for want of training, so may a whole city.

(Aristotle, 1966, p. 216)

Aristotle's latter concern has been echoed repeatedly in the modern era, particularly in the turbulent, pre-democratic period of the industrial revolution where new demands for workplace skills were sometimes precariously balanced against the perceived dangers of a more articulate workforce with enhanced organisational abilities. One further observation by that ancient philosopher has an important contemporary resonance. A problem which was typical of the most democratically inclined Greek states was a failure to define liberty: 'there are two marks by which democracy may be known – *sovereignty of the majority* and *liberty*' (*ibid.*). On one hand was the value attached to the expressed will of the majority of citizens in a state; on the other, what Aristotle described as the freedom 'to do what one wants'. These two democratic principles seemed to Aristotle to be mutually exclusive and he sought to resolve the dilemma by appealing to the doctrine that once reached, majority decisions must be obeyed: 'It ought not to be regarded as a denial of liberty to have to live according to the constitution but rather as self-preservation' (*ibid.*).

Popper has addressed a problem posed by such a 'naive' version of democracy grounded in the idea of the sovereign majority: that is, a justification in terms of the unconstrained *right* of a majority of people to make decisions and a corresponding *duty* on the part of citizens to obey. Majorities can voluntarily reject liberty in favour of despotism, and have done so on more than one occasion. By contrast, he suggests, it is healthier to view democracy as an imperfect safeguard against tyranny: a system of controls, including general elections and representative government, which are reasonably tried and tested institutional obstacles to aspiring despots (Popper, 1969, p. 123). No system of human organisation could be foolproof, but as Popper would agree, other institutional safeguards for the protection of individual freedoms can establish a dynamic inimical to despotism. I will consider these here, and in later chapters in connection with John Stuart Mill's *epistemological justification of individual liberty*. In brief, this is the insight that democracy *entails* civil liberties, an interpretation and endorsement of Dewey's view of a democracy by Hilary Putnam. And I will argue that civil and educational liberties are of a piece.

There are many facets to this question and it remains as pressing now as in the ancient world. By opposing libertarianism to majoritarianism, Aristotle evaded the central insights of the modern concept of *liberal democracy*: that the preferences and decisions of majorities are no more likely to be rationally or morally justifiable than those of minorities or individuals. In the absence of certain safeguards for individual freedoms of association, inquiry, the exchange of information and opinion (for example), there would be no basis for informed majority choices or for the legitimisation of majority decisions according to any extrinsic principle at all.

Citizens or subjects?

In the early seventeenth century, Thomas Hobbes translated Thucydides' history of the war between the militaristic oligarchy of Sparta and democratic Athens that wrought havoc throughout the Greek world for more than two decades during the lifetimes of Socrates and Plato. He undertook that translation as a warning against the dangers of democracy: anarchy, violence and a return to a brutish state of nature, disturbances that he believed were all too closely replicated by the English Civil War, through which he lived. His *Leviathan*, often regarded as the first modern example of political science, envisaged a citizenry contractually bound to submit in all things to the arbitrary will of an absolute ruler for the sake of collective security, schooled in obedience and denied access to the subversive arguments of those critically-minded Greeks. Education was most explicitly for the purpose of inculcating habits of unquestioning obedience to the sovereign power.

Hobbes had been strongly influenced by the empirical, scientific methods of Bacon, a close associate, and Galileo, whom he had met in 1636, as well as by the deductive proofs of Euclidean geometry. The deep irony is that Galileo ascribed his own revolutionary contribution to modern science largely to the influence of the speculative, critical imaginations of the ancient Greeks (Popper, 1963, p. 102). The dawn of Renaissance science marked a rediscovery of ancient traditions that had been submerged by dogma and scholasticism for nearly two thousand years. Moreover, Galileo's fame as a scientist is inextricably connected with his assertion of a right of individual inquiry as a development of, if not an alternative to, the authority of scripture. That had led to conflict with the Church and his recantation at the persuasive behest of the Inquisition.

Galileo represents an emerging predisposition to question traditional authority in a systematic manner: to justify critical inquiry in contrast to ecclesiastical emphasis on revealed truth and authoritative interpretation. That same impulse found expression in a drive for literacy that would enable ordinary people to read and interpret scripture for themselves, rather than to depend on the mediating authority of churches and clerics. These developments had deep historical roots and were to have dramatic political consequences. A fusion of religious dissent, articulating conceptions of human spiritual equality, and new belief in the accessibility of divine purposes to human reason stimulated the growth of science (Hooykaas, 1977, p. 113). It was also to become identified with the political ideal of individual empowerment through representative government. Rights and liberties became part of the reforming agenda, to be followed later by the idea of education for all. Yet the old antitheses remained: collective social and spiritual welfare versus individual mental and spiritual emancipation, social control versus the realisation of personal, critical autonomy.

The same historical events that influenced Hobbes' thought in authoritarian directions produced the first glimmerings of parliamentary democracy and a political theory that was to have far-reaching political consequences. Hobbes' contemporary, John Locke, viewed the English Civil War and its aftermath from a parliamentarian perspective. Locke's *Second Treatise on Government* contained a radical variation on the idea of a social contract that Hobbes had invoked to justify unlimited submission to political authority. Contractual obligations are mutual; they bind parties to observe strict conditions. For Locke, government was in the interests of citizens and for the preservation of their God-given rights to life, liberty and property. Although Locke was not a democrat in the modern sense, he introduced the idea of representative government according to the consent of a majority and the extremely influential doctrine of a right of rebellion against a government that broke the terms of its contract by violating those basic rights of citizenship. Locke's political theory had larger historical consequences than he could have envisaged. It inaugurated an age of revolutions inspired by the idea of human rights in Europe and America. Thomas Jefferson composed the American Declaration of Independence with Locke's 'perfect' example in mind, beginning with that famous assertion of human equality and inalienable rights to 'life, liberty and the pursuit of happiness'.

Now although that Declaration faithfully echoed Locke's tone it departed from his philosophy in at least one important respect. The 'truths' which it enunciated were described as 'self-evident', a contestable claim, not only in the light of the manifest human inequalities of the time, but one which established rights of citizenship on a purely abstract basis. Locke, by contrast, identified rights with a God-given, universal human faculty of reason. His argument could and did appeal strongly to a more secular age. 'Reason', the means of discovering truth, rather than 'Truth' itself, was the expression of divine will manifest in the law of nature which is 'something that we, being

ignorant of, may attain to the knowledge of, by the use and due application of our natural faculties'. Regardless of their origin, those
faculties committed people to mutually respectful inquiry rather than
the pre-emptive imposition of conclusions. In his major philosophical
work, *An Essay Concerning Human Understanding*, Locke emphasised
human fallibility and the provisional, untested nature of much that we
ordinarily describe as 'knowledge' – in Socratic terms which were to
inspire the idea of an education to fit citizens to lead a free and democratic way of life:

> We should do well to commiserate our mutual ignorance and
> endeavour to remove it in all the gentle and fair ways of informa-
> tion, and not instantly to treat others ill, as obstinate and perverse,
> because they will not renounce their own and receive our opinions
> … For where is the man that has incontestable evidence of the
> truth of all that he holds, or of the falsehood of all he condemns,
> or can say that he has examined to the bottom all his own or other
> men's opinions?
>
> (Locke, 1991, p. 360)

Locke is, of course, only one representative of that Enlightenment
tradition which challenged traditional authority with the alternative of
independent, critical thought. It included such influential thinkers as
Rousseau and Kant. But Locke's name, together with that of his friend
Isaac Newton, became 'proverbially associated both in England and
the Continent' with the dawn of a new era of invention and industry
as well as religious, moral and intellectual emancipation (Halévy, 1952,
p. 6). It was also to become the era of 'philosophical radicalism', a
configuration of democratic, egalitarian and feminist ideals expressed
by thinkers and activists like Godwin, Wollstonecraft, Owen,
Bentham, James Mill and his more famous son, John Stuart. One of
the central tenets of this broad movement probably derived from
Locke's decisive emphasis on nurture, experience, rather than nature as
the key determinant of human achievements and inequalities. It had
been developed by Helvétius into an influential thesis that provided a
linchpin between politics and education; individuals learn not only as a
result of explicit teaching, but from their social and cultural milieux
and, importantly, from the type of political constitution under which
they live (Halévy, 1952, p. 20). And this latter point, I will argue,
deserves greater emphasis than it has received in much European
education policy, particularly in the United Kingdom where 'education
for citizenship' is now an item on that agenda. As the previously cited

example of Denmark suggests, constitutional history bears heavily on contemporary practice by establishing an ethos and a pattern of broad expectations on the part of citizens and their leaders that changes incrementally from generation to generation.

Like all traditions, philosophical radicalism lacked neat boundaries but was intimately associated with the nineteenth-century process of electoral reform and the drive for universal, state-supported education. However, that Enlightenment tradition was largely eclipsed by older, more authoritarian conventions against which John Stuart Mill, its most illustrious heir, was to campaign throughout his life. Perhaps the least frequently noted but most consistent theme in his many works was the need for radical educational reform that would reinstate the Socratic ideal that inspired the plan of his own extraordinary education by his father, James, and Jeremy Bentham. That experiment which began in the second decade of the nineteenth century is well known, of course, and has often attracted criticism for the remorseless demands that it placed on the young Mill's critical, analytical abilities (Mill, 1965b). On the other hand, it is less widely recognised as an implementation of Helvétius' educational theories and an intended paradigm for 'philanthropists, religious or irreligious, who at this time were obsessed with the idea of reforming humanity by pedagogy' (*ibid.*, p. 285).

Mill senior was concurrently active in the Lancastrian movement's campaign for universal access to education. However, the ideals that inspired that drive – representative government, the elimination of social and gender inequalities and the prospect of an informed and critical electorate – were to be only partially realised; indeed, they were postponed for more than a century. The established Church of England convened the British National Society and a period of bitter competition ensued between its church-sponsored schools and the more secular institutions favoured by Mill. As a result, while 'a majority of the population was receiving no education, the establishment of a Lancastrian school in a locality was likely to produce a second school to serve the same district under the auspices of the church' (Burston, 1973, p. 67). Mill's educational initiatives finally collapsed under the weight of both internal and external conflicts between religious and secular conceptions of educational purpose. His principal educational legacy was the foundation of University College, London, though there is, too, the very significant contribution to educational thought by his son, John, which I will consider more fully in Chapter 6.

John Mill's much-debated reservations concerning the democracy which was emerging in Britain and America during his lifetime are largely understandable as alienation from a system of schooling for the privileged classes in which the ideals of individual critical rationality and autonomy were not only lacking, but quite explicitly disavowed. In 1832 he had compared the intellectual achievements of a millennium in England and France unfavourably with those of a century and a half in classical Greece; '[a]t school, what is the child taught except to repeat by rote, or at most to apply technical rules, which are lodged, not in his reason, but in his memory?' (Mill, 1946, p. 38).

Liberty and the paternalistic state

Eight years later, Church and state stood side by side as though in fearful response to the secular radicalism represented by Mill's critique of the education system of his day. The Committee of Council on Education instructed Her Majesty's Inspectors of Schools that 'No plan of education ought to be encouraged in which intellectual instruction is not subordinated to the regulation of the thoughts and habits of the children by the doctrines and precepts of revealed religion' (Morris, 1972, p. 283).

Public education was thus to be directed, quite explicitly, at mind-control! Yet it would be wrong to suggest that religious motivations, alone, were inimical to the emancipatory ideals of philosophical radicalism and the ideological movements associated with it. An equally powerful countervailing force was to have long-term implications for the organisation and practice of education. That was an ingrained belief in the radical inequality of social classes and a determination to protect the status quo against a potentially insurgent working class. That, and the demands of a burgeoning industrial sector for a disciplined workforce. Writing as Secretary to the Privy Council for Education the previous year, 1839, J. Kay-Shuttleworth had justified increased state aid for education on the ground that it would help to defray some of the costs of maintaining social order incurred by the need to employ large numbers of troops, police and prison warders (Foster, 1974, p. 190). Even before it became a compulsory, state-maintained institution in 1870, English education had fallen hostage to a determined state-paternalism that was to survive periods of *laissez-faire* and the de-regulation of industry and commerce. In the 1830s, government had offered modest grant aid to factory schools of the kind pioneered by Robert Owen. However, much education in the early and middle years of the nineteenth century took place in Sunday schools, though this is not to say that it was invariably of a religious character or even particularly compatible with religious aspirations.

Many of these schools were funded by factory owners to train the growing child labour force, and the intervention of the clergy was not always welcome (*ibid.*, p. 28). Either way, the accent was firmly on disciplining children to accept their humble station in life and the limited skills appropriate to it, provoking occasional outbursts of indignation by members of the emerging trade union movement alert to some of the more ambitious educational ideals of the age: 'instead of teaching the poor, or endeavouring to excite a free and independent spirit among them, the conductors of these schools might be considered as preparing children for slavery and degradation' (*ibid.*, p. 191).

Democratic reform, and the rights of citizenship which were thereby defined, took place hesitantly against a background of deep ideological divisions. They were sometimes reflected starkly in public utterances concerning the educability of the masses. The Parliamentary Reform Act of 1867 increased the electorate to just under one in ten of the adult male population. John Mill, by that time a Member of Parliament, succeeded in winning the support of more than eighty parliamentary colleagues for an amendment which sought to enfranchise women on the same terms as their menfolk: an impressive but insufficient number. Elected as Rector of St Andrews University in Scotland in that year, Mill spoke pessimistically about the social and political implications of what he saw as a narrowly instrumental system of education, a 'strangely limited conception of what it is possible for human beings to learn' which 'not only vitiates our idea of education, but ... darkens our anticipations as to the future progress of mankind' (Mill, 1984, p. 222).

And in that same year of parliamentary reform, Walter Bagehot published his classic work, *The English Constitution*. It offered a penetrating insight into the realities of political power in the United Kingdom. The celebrated Lockian principle of the separation of the legislative and executive powers of government that was firmly enshrined in the American Constitution was frequently but incorrectly ascribed to the British system of government. In fact, a fusion of the powers of Parliament and the Cabinet was the 'efficient secret' of the Constitution rather than debilitating separation, claimed Bagehot triumphantly. It was the engine that drove the system, hidden behind the ceremonial facade of monarchy that maintained the ignorant but potentially troublesome masses in conveniently deferential postures. Bagehot's analysis of the embryonic British democracy echoes the cynicism of Plato's 'Noble Lie' and his lack of faith in the possibilities of education to enable ordinary people to participate effectively in determining the rules and principles that would govern their way of life:

> The lower orders, the middle orders, are still, when tried by what is the standard of the educated 'ten thousand', narrow minded, unintelligent, incurious ... And a philosophy which does not ceaselessly remember, which does not continually obtrude, the palpable differences of the various [social classes] will be a theory radically false.
>
> (Bagehot, 1963, p. 63)

The concentration of power at the centre which Bagehot detected has remained a feature of British government. It has been accentuated in the post-1870 age of compulsory state-maintained education by increasing prime-ministerial patronage and party discipline. Accompanied by gradual extensions of the franchise, it has resulted in a series of contrapuntal relationships between different traditions in educational thinking. Matthew Arnold's highly influential vision of a *common* culture reflecting 'the best that has been thought and said in the world' was predicated on his belief in the state as the agent of a general perfection which would encompass all sections of society (Arnold, 1966, pp. 6 and 204). He shared John Stuart Mill's admiration for classical culture and his revulsion at the narrow, mechanistic ethos of industrialising British society. Like Mill, he viewed the growing assertiveness of the 'raw and uncultivated masses' with apprehension. But where Mill clung to a Socratic example and the vision of a society in which citizens would be free to follow their own ideals and conduct their own 'experiments in living', Arnold identified more with the Aristotelian vision of a monolithic democracy and neglected the problem that 'the best that has been thought and said in the world' has always been a matter of fierce controversy.

There is an apparent tension between the collectivist principle of majoritarianism and what Aristotle described as the libertarian preference for 'doing as one likes'. In a chapter of that title which reflected that philosopher's influence in his own education, Arnold argued for the state as the repository of what is best in society and culture: 'our *best* self'. This transcendental idea of the state would be a defence against the anarchy threatened by contemporary preoccupations with liberty, particularly on the part of the politically ambitious working class (*ibid.*, chapter II). In English law, he said, there was no clear idea about 'the citizen's claim and the State's duty'; a situation which could be resolved only by entrusting education to the state rather than to the various social factions which were then asserting rights of educational supervision. Arnold's dilemma was that he fully recognised the essential factionalism of the state itself and, as a result, his conception of a cultural order that transcended the limitations of real human societies remained abstract and recondite (Williams, 1963, pp. 135–6). His educational philosophy was nonetheless deeply influential.

Mill's reservations about the incipient democracy of his time focused on the converse danger that popular opinion and outright prejudice would express themselves through a monolithic state hostile to individual liberties. And these liberties, for Mill, were the principal source of social and cultural progress. Reviewing de Tocqueville's analysis of democracy in America, and particularly the common tendency for a centralisation of political power, he foresaw the need for protection against a form of despotism which could emerge out of a democratic world: 'the absolute rule of the head of the executive over a congregation of isolated individuals, all equal, but all slaves' (Mill, 1965a, p. 116). The educational implications of Mill's position involved a universal right of children to education and financial support by the state to secure that right, but a determined avoidance of direct state control of education on the ground that it would become a 'contrivance for moulding people to be exactly like one another' according to the preferences of dominant social factions.

That sentence of Mill's succinctly described a powerful incentive shaping the organisation and ethos of the English education system in the infancy of British democracy. Despite his *laissez-faire* credentials in economic matters, Sir Robert Lowe responded to the inevitability of an extension of the franchise in 1867 with the ironical remark: 'we must educate our masters' (Ryan, 1999, p. 50). He refused government financial support for educational initiatives 'by any person whatsoever' and insisted on safeguards to 'ensure that children were not merely intellectually instructed but were subject to a total atmosphere conducive to right moral and social discipline' (Morris, 1972, p. 284). The 1870 Education Act established a tradition of state-paternalism in British education. It not only survived periodic resurgences of educational liberalism, but subsumed them effortlessly. Then it reasserted itself in the rejection of liberal educational values in favour of vocationalism by governments of different persuasions in the final years of the twentieth century.

Education or training?

Many early educational initiatives in Britain had been unashamedly directed towards the creation of a competent workforce. Nineteenth-century Sunday schools frequently served the interests of local industrialists and received support from them. Government had provided modest financial aid for factory schools on the understanding that their business was to provide basic skills relevant to industrial requirements (Inglis, 1972, p. 447). Industrialisation in the context of such a stratified society lent itself readily to a distinction between the training of the masses for a predetermined station in life and the education of a social élite. The distinction, moreover, had origins in the Socratic opposition of 'art' to 'technique': the difference between the search for an understanding of underlying principles in human activity and the mere application by rote of conventional rules. It was a duality congenial to a society in which the role of the few was to lead, and of the rest to follow. Mill, of course, disputed the relevance of this distinction. The impoverished education of English social élites was also a matter of unreflective memorisation and the application of mere technical rules.

In the United States, on the other hand, Dewey sought to reconcile vocational and liberal conceptions of education by including practical activities like crop-cultivation and baking as the basis for developing children's scientific curiosity and critical awareness. This might have been a realistic ambition in small rural communities in America. As with so many other educational endeavours, much would depend on how these activities were related to their objectives in practice: whether a narrower idea of relevance to the needs of particular communities would eventually prevail. But the egalitarian, democratic traditions of that country also seem to have encouraged Dewey to adopt a communitarian view of the relationship of education to citizenship which was innocent of the usual liberal suspicions of the state. He was as fiercely opposed to rote-learning and the inculcation of dogma as Mill had been. But where Mill feared subordination of the individual quest for meaning and truth to the arbitrary imposition of collective democratic purpose, Dewey's interpretation of democratic education was an altogether more holistic one. As a result, he tended to equivocate between individual, rational autonomy on the one hand and social consensus on the other as immediate educational ends. For Mill, genuine social consensus would be the desirable outcome of a civilised contest between the conflicting ideas and ideals of citizens, an outcome which could only be the harder to realise if the discipline of rational criticism was pre-empted by conceptions of moral consensus, however ostensibly worthy. Different rational considerations will indicate different points of convergence: different kinds of consensus which cannot be anticipated in advance of the conflict of ideas and values. This contrast between the two philosophers is symbolised by their respective formulations of the function of education:

> Though one man cannot *teach* another, one man may *suggest* to another. I may be indebted to my predecessor for setting my own faculties to work; for hinting to me what questions to ask myself; but it is not given to one man to answer those questions for another ... Knowledge comes only from within: all that comes from without is but *questioning*, or else it is mere *authority*.
>
> (Mill, 1946, p. 32, original emphasis)

Dewey's 'pedagogic creed' is in stark contrast to Mill's account of the Socratic dialectic:

> Our task is on one hand to select and adjust the studies with reference to the nature of the individual thus discovered; and on the other hand to order and to group them so that they shall most definitely and systematically represent the chief lines of social endeavour and social achievement.
>
> (Dewey, 1974, p. 421)

Both men shared a faith in rational inquiry as a unifying activity. But from his broader political perspective, Mill anticipated a time when a premature sense of common purpose would transform a democracy into a thoroughly servile society. One route is likely to be through a multitude of good intentions, of which the prioritisation of moral consensus in the classroom will be a significant microcosm. Another is the prioritisation of vocational and other 'skills' which are considered relevant to the practical life of the community. These are distinct aims. But as I will argue, contemporary educational policies have optimistically included both in the remit of the typical classroom, often through a bizarre combination of the idea of skills and moral virtues. The readily identifiable, finite qualities of the former are harnessed to the indefinitely debatable qualities of the latter to create the impression that virtually all aspects of good citizenship can be delivered by means of a carefully programmed curriculum. For the present, one example will convey the vaulting ambition of some modern governments to reform society by specifying educational aims at remorselessly high levels of abstraction and encapsulating them as something discrete and communicable – in this case the putative skill of 'working with others':

> By working cooperatively, young people experience at first hand the importance of respect, caring, justice, democracy and equity while at the same time developing their capacity for empathy, resilience, and optimism through participation, leadership, negotiation and respect for others.
>
> (LTS, 2001, p. 8)

There is no hint here of the tough-mindedness and independent judgment in Ryan's notion of the democratic citizen. A crucial equivocation between education and training is obscured by this litany of virtues which is itself riddled with equivocation between what is desirable, what is possible and what actually is achieved by schools or students. Scheffler's words of warning from a previous generation in America seem particularly appropriate:

> the notion that education is an instrument for the realization of social ends, no matter how worthy they are thought to be, harbors the greatest conceivable danger to the ideal of a free and rational society. For if these goals are presumed to be fixed in advance, the instrumental doctrine of schooling exempts them from the critical scrutiny that schooling itself may foster.
>
> (Scheffler, 1973, p. 134)

As it turned out, Dewey's aspirations for a community of common purpose and 'a growing unity of sympathetic feeling' were to be supplanted by a ruthlessly pragmatic consensus against which he struggled unsuccessfully. That was the industrial ideal of social and economic efficiency which overwhelmed American public education in the early twentieth century and created the momentum for a bureaucratic concept of education that has become pervasive both there and in the United Kingdom.

Critical citizen or educational product?

It is, perhaps, appropriate to emphasise again that there is no necessary contradiction between the idea of developing the critical and creative faculties of individuals and certain conceptions of collective well-being as proper ends of education. Nor can unambiguous categorical distinctions be drawn between them, though all too often individual and collective ends are described superficially as different aspects of a seamless whole. In fact they are intimately connected and the very concept of education implies degrees of individual integration within the social nexus, but the particular nature of that connection is of vital importance. A cardinal feature of the liberal tradition has been alertness to the fallibility of authority and a corresponding recognition of the rights of citizens to dissent effectively from commonly accepted norms. However, that principle has proved to be extremely vulnerable to the alternative convention in educational policy and practice.

Two quotations and a brief discussion of their significance should help to illustrate this contrast as well as the issue of democratic vulnerability. The first, cited by Callahan, from the *American School Board Journal* of 1917, represents the economic pragmatism which invaded the early twentieth-century American state school sector: an influence which is by no means exhausted in the United States and, as just mentioned, has asserted itself in Britain:

> The school is a factory. The child is the raw material. The finished product is the child who graduates. We have not yet learned how to manufacture this product economically. No industrial corporation could succeed if managed according to the wasteful methods which prevail in the ordinary school system.
>
> (Callahan, 1962, p. 176)

These words represent a common view in unusually blunt terms. The social functions of education are manifest. The educational task is a managerial one: precise identification of the most appropriate means of achieving predetermined objectives which are taken to be uncontroversial or self-authenticating. One professor of educational administration, writing in 1931, maintained that 'the success of a corporation is dependent nine parts on management and one part on all other factors ... a maxim equally applicable to a public school system' (*ibid.*, pp. 248–50). In this and similar ways, public attention in America was diverted from questions about the education of young people for life in a free democratic society to the means by which schools could manufacture a workforce to serve the dominant industrial–commercial culture.

Such vulnerability to dogma in a nation founded on Lockian principles of personal liberty might be attributable to the conformist tendencies in American democracy detected by de Tocqueville and Mill in the previous century. It also registers the fragile hold of that human rights tradition on popular consciousness in the absence of very specific constitutional provisions. Inalienable rights to challenge epistemic and political authority which had played so crucial a part in establishing the American nation were displaced in the state school system by tacit endorsement of a utilitarian ideology. Dissenters, including Dewey, were too few, and their arguments probably too arcane to withstand public opinion and a popular press eager to see the fashionable idea of scientific management applied to the 'process' of education.

The justification of educational aims

Although the question of justifying educational aims and methods is a large one which I will address in the following two chapters, it seems appropriate to relate it briefly to the current discussion and to the historical perspective which I have adopted. Scheffler's idea of critical rationality connects educational aims with what Putnam describes as 'the epistemological justification of democracy'. No social end, popular though it might be, should be regarded as immune from criticism and challenge: 'there can be no final answer to the question of how we should live, and therefore we should always leave it open to further discussion and experimentation. That is precisely why we need democracy' (Putnam, 1992, pp. 180–200). And as Mill said in his justification of the related principle of individual liberty, social utility is no exception; it is as open to question as other human aspirations (Mill, 1965a, p. 274). Central to this tradition is an acceptance of fallibility which unites the rights of individuals with those of democratic majorities and governments. Realisation of each category of rights is conditional on recognition of the others. What is at stake is not the prioritisation of 'freedom' over 'democracy' because, as Putnam interprets Dewey, 'civil liberty is necessary *for* democracy' (Putnam, 1992, p. 200).

Scheffler has argued that education in a democratic society should not fit people to the requirements of a predetermined division of labour. The alternative is a 'counter-revolutionary return to formalism … related to the urgency of national needs' which:

> tends to foster the view of the teacher as a minor technician within an industrial process. The overall goals are set in advance in terms of national needs, the curricular materials prepackaged by the disciplinary experts, the methods developed by educational engineers – and the teacher's job is just to supervise the last

operational stage, the methodical insertion of ordered facts into the student's mind.

(Scheffler, 1973, p. 61)

Many British teachers would regard this as a prescient description of the system of education that has now decisively replaced the 'progressivism' of an earlier generation. Scheffler proposed the alternative, 'fundamental philosophical tradition of the West', which originated in Socrates' injunction to 'follow the logic of argument' and included Kant's prioritisation of reasoned discourse as the guiding principle for social conduct. Others, including Mill, have held that the same principle has an institutional significance that encompasses the organisation and practice of education. But it should also be recalled that this tradition of thought is rooted in an anti-authoritarian theory of knowledge associated with the rise of modern science, philosophy and, eventually, democratic forms of government. The relationship is symbolised by Newton's uncharacteristically enduring friendship with Locke (White, 1997, pp. 234–5) and by the Enlightenment motto of the Royal Society of which they were both members: 'Not by authority'. Locke's insistence that teachers should acknowledge and build upon children's intellectual curiosity by treating them as 'rational creatures', and his injunction that 'children's enquiries are not to be slighted' (Locke, 1913, p. 104), foreshadowed the epistemic individualism of Mill and his lifelong campaign against didactic and programmatic educational method.[1] Contemporary writers, for example Tyrell Burgess (1998), have drawn similar conclusions from Popper's theory of knowledge.

The vulnerability of the liberal–Enlightenment tradition

Despite its impressive credentials and irrespective of evidence for its effectiveness, the liberal–Enlightenment tradition in education has succumbed repeatedly to an urgent sense of social priorities of one kind or another. Many of the Dissenting Academies of the eighteenth and early nineteenth centuries are a cogent demonstration that education through a critical, discursive search for truth does not represent a flight from social and economic imperatives. Founded in reaction to the Act of Uniformity 1662, these schools promulgated the new empirical, scientific methodologies. Their contribution to the growth of science and technology was quite disproportionate to their size and number, confirming the close links between religious nonconformity and industrial innovation which Merton and Hagen have described

(Merton, 1979; Hagen, 1962). Yet their educational influence proved ephemeral and, as I have already pointed out, by 1840 the British government was instructing HM Inspectors to discourage education which did not ensure regulation of the thoughts and habits of the children by the doctrines of revealed religion. That preoccupation with control has hardly diminished, though the manner in which it has been expressed has varied from generation to generation.

Thirty years ago the Plowden Report envisaged an education which would be concerned with 'the whole man'. Now the focus has narrowed perceptibly to an emphasis on the transmission of basic skills. According to a recent report, 'education for work' enjoys a position of 'central importance' in UK curricula and the drive is on to accord work-related activities a prominent, if not pre-eminent, place in formal assessment (HM Inspectors of Schools, 2000). Education and enterprise share a vocabulary of numerical targets, quality assurance, performance indicators and audits, though some all-embracing ideals of global citizenship have been grafted on, audaciously, to the ancient and narrow aim of producing a competent but compliant workforce. The pedagogic role is construed as a lowly one in a management hierarchy under unprecedentedly centralised direction. My point is certainly not that these developments are unpopular, though the appropriateness of the means, even to the specified ends, is largely untested. It is that they are nearly all-encompassing and encroach on respectable alternatives.

The 'cult of efficiency' described by Callahan might or might not have contributed directly to the present sense of crisis in American education and the decisions of huge numbers of parents to withdraw their children from formal state education. Nevertheless, preoccupation with an industrial–commercial model reasserted itself with the publication in 1983 of the Presidential Report, *A Nation at Risk* (Molnar, 1996). From the title, one might have inferred that this document addressed the palpable 'civic deficit' in the United States and that its principal concern was with the future of American democracy. But in Alex Molnar's words, it was the signal for corporate America to mobilise, and he catalogues numerous commercial ventures which received public funding in efforts to improve the effectiveness of state education during the Reagan and Bush administrations of the 1980s and 1990s. Many of these initiatives proved to be commercial failures, though one of the most enduring, the Whittle Communications Corporation's Edison Project, now runs seventy-nine American schools and aspires to manage fifty British schools if and when it achieves profitability (*Times Educational Supplement*, 28–01–00, p. 27).

The policy of an earlier, legally separate venture by Whittle Communications, Channel One, had a particularly intimate bearing on the issue of civil liberties. In the early 1990s that company concluded legal agreements involving 9,000 American schools for the provision of educational videos. What distinguished this initiative from a plethora of others which introduced commercial advertising into schools was a contractual undertaking by school boards to ensure that 90 per cent of pupils did in fact watch these advertisements. As Molnar puts it, 'Channel One ... used the coercive power of the state to *force* children to watch its commercials' although historically, 'denying a person his or her liberty has only been justified by a legitimate appeal to the highest and most compelling public interest' (Molnar, 1996, pp. 53, 76).

It certainly does not follow that the centralised UK education system would permit such blatant commercialism in schools as a result of private–public ventures. On the other hand, experiments in private sector involvement may join nationally prescribed curricula, obligatory testing and Ofsted's rigorous inspection regime as further instruments of educational control rather than of liberation. In this environment of relentless innovation there is the need for a more robust defence than yet exists of the individual rights of citizens and their children to pursue alternative educational ideals by different methods. The crucial question concerns balances to be struck between the respective rights of parents, their children and the state, and on these the UK appears to differ significantly from some close European neighbours.

4 Ours to reason why?

The human rights issue

> The respect of parents' freedom to educate their children according to
> their vision of what education should be has been part of international
> human rights standards since their very emergence.
>
> (Katerina Tomasevski, Special Rapporteur,
> UN Commission on Human Rights, 08–04–99)

Human rights are now firmly on educational agendas: a welcome
development, from the standpoint of this book. Yet there is a danger
that the abundance of declarations, conventions and laws will
encourage selective interpretation reflecting the domestic priorities of
those very authorities who promote the notion of human rights in a
global context. Temptation to heighten, lower or omit emphases
according to institutional priorities is probably encouraged by differences in the legal status of various authoritative instruments like the
United Nations Universal Declaration, the European Convention and
the Convention on the Rights of the Child. There are also philosophical questions about the justification of human rights theories which
cannot simply be taken for granted; some Asian countries, notably
China, refute the concept of universal human rights as a western
construct which is alien to their cultural traditions. The philosophical
issues are profound and controversial. At the end of this chapter and
in later ones, I hope at least to indicate the pivotal importance of
educational freedoms and the concept of the critically autonomous
learner in the universalising tradition of human rights that ultimately
generated those international agreements.

In a wider context than that of education, the UK government has
insisted upon the *universality* and the *indivisibility* of human rights in
the following unambiguous terms: 'we fail to honour the Universal
Declaration and cannot claim to be upholders of human rights unless
we commit ourselves to securing *all* rights for *all* people' (Foreign

Office, 1999, p. 19, my emphasis). In 1993 the Vienna Conference on Human Rights achieved international agreement of a rhetorical nature on the universality of human rights. The problem might therefore seem to be less about general principle than about practical interpretation. Sharp contrasts remain, however, about the extent to which different parties to such agreements have interpreted educational rights in law and policy as expressions of a constitutional relationship between individual citizens, their children and the state. The inevitability of at least some variation in interpretations by different states is formally recognised by the doctrine of 'a margin of appreciation' invoked by the Court of Human Rights in cases brought under the European Convention, though this is a concession to international *realpolitik* rather than a matter of principle, and it is controversial (Harris *et al.*, 1995, pp. 12–15).

Questions about the citizen's right of individual self-determination in democratic states assumed practical urgency with the demise of totalitarian regimes in Europe, some of which originally emerged under the auspices of democratic constitutions. Education naturally featured in deliberations as the all-important vehicle for the formal transmission of a cultural and political heritage. In 1948 the United Nations Universal Declaration of Human Rights concluded Section 26 on the right to free, compulsory, elementary education with an assertion of the 'prior' right of parents to choose the kind of education their children receive. This was widely accepted as a necessary defence against the indoctrination of young people by the state. The European Convention, now incorporated into British law, represents a move beyond the UN Declaration. It translates the aspirations of the latter into more precise terminology that would facilitate legal enforcement. A basic educational obligation in Protocol 1, Article 2, is expressed in the negative form, 'no person shall be denied the right to education', to allay the original fears of some signatories that the UN Declaration's more positive assertion of a general right might prove unduly burdensome (*ibid.*, p. 541). That 'prior' right of parents to choose their children's education in the UN Declaration is translated as the right of parents to ensure that their children are 'educated and taught' in conformity with their religious and philosophical convictions.

The fact that Article 2 had to be included, at a late stage, in the First Protocol and that it attracted an unusually large number of national reservations is indicative of the discord among signatories about the role of education in a democratic society. Where the state and its education authorities adopt strongly interventionist policies, the difficulty of reconciling them with the ostensibly liberal provisions of those international agreements can be acute. In practice, legal enforceability has meant relatively little where parental rights are concerned. The 'stormy genesis' of the right to education in the Convention appears to have produced decisions by the Court of Human Rights that protect the state against the wider implications of parental rights as they were eventually formulated. '[T]he convictions which are to be taken into account are to be interpreted narrowly and ... the burden on the parent to demonstrate their relevance to his stand is heavy' (*ibid.*, p. 544).

Where the state cannot respond to parents' convictions it must permit them to establish schools that do so, or to educate their children themselves. Legal opinion seems to be that the state has the right to ensure that alternative forms of education meet certain criteria of adequacy though it has no obligation to support them financially or in any other way (*ibid.*, p. 546). As I will argue later in this chapter, official enthusiasm for control and standardisation in Britain have raised questions about the compatibility of the state's power of educational supervision with the spirit, if not the letter, of the Convention. For the moment, however, I am concerned with official predispositions of a more general kind towards the interpretation of educational rights as they are articulated in different international agreements.

For instance, the devolved Scottish Parliament's Standards in Scotland's Schools Act 2000 is concerned, as its title implies, with the right of the child to a 'school education'. It refers only indirectly to the right of parents to educate children other than in a school that was laid down in earlier legislation (the Education (Scotland) Act 1980, 35(1)) but not to the educational liberties protected by the European Convention and the Human Rights Act 1998. On the other hand, this Act *does* closely paraphrase some of the more ambitious aspirations in Sections 28 and 29 of the UN Convention on the Rights of the Child (Standards in Scotland's Schools Act ss 2(1), 2(2)). In both documents these are expressed in terms which are philosophically ambiguous and potentially very controversial and consequently of uncertain legal effect. Thus the new law requires local authorities to direct education 'to the development of the personality, talents and mental and physical abilities of the child or young person to their fullest potential'. But there must be considerable doubt about the legitimacy of any role the state assumes in order to 'develop' the personalities of young people as distinct from their academic, technical or artistic abilities. Then there is also the extraordinary ambiguity of the concept of a 'fullest potential' in relation to the all-embracing terminology of the clause in question.

Who, if anyone, ever has achieved a sufficiently transcendent understanding to determine what a person's fullest potential might be in any of an indefinite number of situations? And on this point, it should be recognised that small but significant numbers of people achieve academic and other distinctions long after completing extremely mediocre school careers. In addition, there are continuing disputes between parents and local education authorities concerning the adequacy of the most basic provisions for children with 'special needs'.

It is true, of course, that Scottish and UK statutes must be interpreted in conformity with the provisions of the European Convention, narrow though judicial interpretations of it have tended to be. Yet the use of domestic legislation to promote very general ideals can establish a momentum for idiosyncratic interpretation. And where these ideals are expressed at high levels of generality, practice is likely to deviate significantly from the less prominently advertised but nonetheless crucial principles on which the original international agreement was founded. Besides, different rights may be in mutual conflict.

The French constitution provides that education in state schools must be strictly secular, a principle of neutrality to protect children against religious proselytising which seems to be endorsed by the overwhelming majority of French teachers. This is, of course, also consistent with the fundamental concern of the European Convention to ensure that education should not become indoctrination, a consideration relevant to the historical purpose of the Convention. The principle was challenged in 1998 by two female students who were excluded from a lower secondary school in La Grand-Combe in southern France for insisting on wearing Muslim headwear, the hijab. They were later re-admitted to their school after their parents initiated proceedings against the education authority for infringing their right to education (*TESS*, 14–01–00). Conversely, parents in Almeria, Spain, were sued by their education authority for educating their son at home because they had principled objections to the authoritarian, competitive ethos of Spanish education. A court had previously rejected the official case against the parents for lack of evidence of neglect (*TESS*, 01–10–99). Each of these examples illustrates the potential for conflict between the child's right to education, the supervisory rights of parents and the rights and responsibilities of education authorities.

There have been undoubtedly sincere efforts by British governments to encourage greater parental interest and involvement in the education of their children. However, I have already referred to the deliberate preclusion of parental involvement in matters relating to the curriculum by one central government discussion paper (SOEID, 1998) even though curricular matters are likely to relate directly to the religious and philosophical convictions of a significant minority of parents. The idea of nationally prescribed, assessment-driven curricula, tightly defined learning outcomes, a 'skills' conception of education and its conflation with vocational training, are the kind of issues about which parents may have principled objections in terms of the purposes and quality of schooling. Moreover, government measures to raise educational standards by establishing national criteria and publishing 'league tables' can prove to be a double-edged sword. In certain cases, parents have set up their own, alternative classes in reaction to standards in local state schools that are well below national norms. And in some cases they have encountered determined local authority opposition (*TESS*, 29–10–99).

There are other important questions concerning the representation of parents and other sections of society in the formulation of education policies. Inevitably, a highly centralised mass education system will address a plurality of concerns and it will do so in collective terms, though by no means invariably through representatives who have been elected to protect those interests. The Anglican and Roman Catholic Churches have resisted the possible loss of their voting rights on local education authorities in the event that those bodies were to be abolished by central government (*TESS*, 27–11–98). Nevertheless, records of low and declining church membership and attendance must cast doubt on the extent to which the churches represent the views of significant proportions of parents. Despite this sort of uncertainty about the nature and extent of its constituency, the Church of Scotland in one administrative area of that country called for the 'naming and shaming' of schools which failed to hold acts of religious observance at least once a week (*TESS*, 15–01–99).

Parents are, of course, collectively represented at national levels through parent–teacher associations and associations of school governing bodies. In addition, governments in the United Kingdom address them collectively by publishing large, if not overwhelming, amounts of information about school performances, policy objectives and initiatives to improve pupil attainment. Yet one of the few pieces of research into parents' reactions to this avalanche of documentation suggests that they typically find it 'vague, boring, irrelevant and worthless' (*TESS*, 10–03–00). Most of them valued close relationships with teachers, prioritised their own children's interests and attached more importance to the local reputation of schools than to their standing in national 'league tables'. The blunt truth is that, no matter how well intentioned government efforts to involve parents in this collective sense, such measures cannot adequately address the diversity of individual concerns. And, most importantly, the collective representation of parental views cannot be a substitute for respecting those conscientiously held individual beliefs about education and teaching which are supposed to be safeguarded by the human rights legislation currently in force.

There is a need to factor the protection of civil rights and liberties into mass educational systems coherently, as I believe examples I will consider in this and future chapters demonstrate. One result of the long-standing interventionism of central governments in British education is that there appears to be little public consensus about whether lines are to be drawn between the rights and responsibilities of citizens and those of the state and, if so, where. An example was the proposal in 1999 by the UK and devolved Scottish Parliaments to repeal legislation prohibiting local authorities from promoting homosexuality 'as a pretended family relationship' (Local Government Act 1988, s. 28). Overwhelming popular opposition led to a protracted search by both governments for an acceptable alternative: official guidance concerning the forms of words with which teachers could convey values associated with different kinds of conjugal relationship to their pupils. Agreement was finally reached in 2001 that appeared to satisfy demands both for the inclusion of 'marriage' and for non-discriminatory references to other kinds of 'stable relationship'. The state, it seems, has become the guardian of popular morality even on those comparatively rare occasions when it would prefer not to be.

Education for citizenship

In Chapter 3 I reviewed contrasting emphases on the relationships between education and citizenship. They may be summarised briefly as an historical interplay between two dominant ideas: education to achieve collective ends, and education directed towards individual autonomy. It might be objected that educational philosophies and policies have rarely embraced either extreme or that these opposites can be reconciled unproblematically. Although the first objection is undoubtedly correct, the second is more suspect because it evades the difficult but necessary task of explicitly prioritising one educational end over the other. And where this is not done, the institutional interests and pressures of a centralised education system tend all too easily to lay greatest emphasis on arbitrarily identified collective values and objectives.

Certain rights and liberties established by law or convention may be compatible with official policy objectives and receive specific affirmation as a result. Alternatively, they may be treated as tacitly understood and passed over in silence or referred to with dismissive brevity. Proposals for citizenship education differed significantly between England and Scotland in this respect. The Crick Report recommended that this new subject should be specified as a separate item in the national educational framework to ensure explicit understanding of political institutions and processes (QCA, 1998). A corresponding consultation document proposing citizenship education for the devolved Scottish system concluded 'that it is neither appropriate nor adequate to create a new subject' of this kind and that citizenship education should be infused throughout the curriculum (Learning and Teaching Scotland, 2000, p. iii). More significantly, the Crick Report recommended that learning outcomes should include substantial references to political, economic and legal-constitutional topics, including the European Convention that contains the most succinct and explicit legal definitions of citizenship yet formulated in Britain. The much less specific proposals in the Scottish consultation document contained no reference to this foundational statutory instrument and no substantive recommendations for the teaching of specifically political, legal and constitutional subjects. Indeed, that paper went so far as to quote the Scottish Council on the Curriculum's view that 'an understanding of the political structures and processes, of rights, obligations, law, justice and democracy will not be sufficient' (*ibid.*, p. 4). Yet it would not have been reasonable to infer from this that existing teaching on such complex topics was adequate, given the already overcrowded curriculum and the evidence of widespread youthful disengagement from democratic processes and ignorance about them which inspired the initiative in the first place. However, a general and idealistic extract from Article 29 of the Convention on the Rights of the Child was included in the introduction to the Scottish document. Education, this extract maintained, should prepare the child 'for responsible life in a free society, in the spirit of understanding, peace, tolerance, equality of sexes and friendship among all peoples, ethnic, national and religious groups' (*ibid.*, p. 1).

In a manner typical of many officially inspired documents on education, the content of *Education for Citizenship in Scotland* was festooned with aspirations for mutual respect, peaceful co-operation and a sense of responsibility between people and towards the environment, but it did not dwell exclusively on these laudable but vague generalities. 'Political literacy' was included, with what seems to be symbolic significance, in a footnote as 'knowledge of political systems and processes, rights and responsibilities and appreciation of how decisions are made and change effected in a democratic society' (*ibid.*, p. 4).

Thus the hard currency of politics was certainly mentioned. Indeed, most aspects of domestic and global affairs were at least summarised against bullet-points in an annex, if not included in the main body of the text. But this pinpoints a disconcerting feature of that consultation document and many other official UK publications on education. The task of interpretation, in the absence of secure conceptual anchorages, becomes a matter of identifying dominant emphases within the ever-expanding remit of schools. And, of course, what is taught will ultimately be determined by a variety of internal and external institutional pressures. Not least among these is the very real fear that many teachers have of the schools inspectorates, their capacity for criticism beyond hope of any truly effective appeal and the policy of disseminating their judgments to the public via the media. Aversion to authoritative legal and constitutional definitions of democratic politics and citizenship and a preference for broadly indicative but commonly unrealised ideals suggests a disquieting possibility: that is, an alternative conception of citizenship adapted to the priorities of the educational hierarchy, spelled out in an endless succession of guidelines, promoted by educational managers and enforced by a rigorous inspection regime. This kind of monopolisation could easily result in a myopic focus on conformity and subordination to centrally prescribed standards, even in those cases of alternative educational enterprises that are predicated explicitly on the idea of a democratic education. As I will argue later in the present chapter, the intervention of the Office for Standards in Education in the affairs of A.S. Neill's Summerhill School has provided a disturbing example of this authoritarian tendency.

It might seem uncharitable to take issue with the benign intentions of those who recommend the teaching of universal tolerance, friendship and equality. However, these ideals are only rarely and incompletely achieved, and then usually when translated into substantive legal and constitutional principles. Nor are they even characteristic of the ethos of the powerful bureaucracies which oversee the educational process, an ethos which has led to unprecedented levels of stress and professional disillusionment among teachers. Yet another is that the idealising emphasis radically distorts the history of democratic institutions. It fails to acknowledge the conflict and sacrifice which produced them and which may be required for their preservation in future. Understanding of the protracted efforts of the international community to reach a consensus on core principles of citizenship in a free society and a grasp of the historical motivation for those efforts are important qualifications for mature citizenship. They provide the only assurance that the ideals of universal friendship and tolerance represent more than unfocused sentiment, a recognition that they are located in a real world of tensions and conflicts which always have required formal resolution through social, legal and constitutional reform.

Educational rights and reservations

The Convention on Human Rights and Fundamental Freedoms (the European Convention) includes legal protection for specific individual educational rights and liberties. The already binding provisions of the Convention took effect in the UK from October 2000 when it was incorporated into UK law by the Human Rights Act 1998. Despite the apparent legal specificity of the Convention's educational provisions, it is striking that two nations as similar as Britain and the Netherlands responded quite differently to them. Indeed, the two education systems seem to be based on quite different civil libertarian premises.

As previously mentioned, controversy over educational rights among signatories to the Convention meant that they were included in a protocol which was ratified at a later date after draft statements had been referred to the Consultative Assembly's Legal Committee. That committee expressed disquiet at the lack of effective guarantees concerning the right of parents in respect of their children's education. Eventually, in March 1952, these were included as Article 2 of the First Protocol, though with the addition of reservations by certain governments, Britain's included (Weil, 1963, pp. 35–6). The Human Rights Act 1998 incorporates the Protocol in question together with the original reservation of the UK government. Article 2 reads:

> No person shall be denied the right to education. In the exercise of any function which it assumes in relation to education and to teaching, the State shall respect the right of parents to ensure such education and teaching in conformity with their own religious and philosophical convictions.

Reservations by some of the signatories to this Article are worth quoting because they reflect controversies that arose during the formulation of the European Convention. The British government accepted the second sentence of Article 2:

> only so far as is compatible with the provision of efficient instruction and training, and the avoidance of unreasonable public expenditure.
>
> (Human Rights Act 1998, chapter 42, schedule 3, part II)

By contrast, a qualification by the Netherlands government, echoed in its policy of publicly funding educational initiatives by parents, was that:

> The state should not only respect the rights of parents in the matter of education but, if need be, ensure the possibility of exercising those rights by appropriate financial measures.
>
> (Convention for Human Rights 1952, Other Declarations Made by States, n. 11)

while Ireland argued that Article 2:

> is not sufficiently explicit in ensuring to parents the right to provide education for their children in their homes or in schools of the parents' own choice, whether or not such schools are private schools or are schools recognised or established by the state.
>
> (*ibid.*, n. 8)

Clearly, the legal implications of Article 2 and the British government's reservations concerning it will continue to be clarified by test cases under the new Human Rights Act. Case law from elsewhere in Europe suggests that the general predisposition of the Court of Human Rights has been to interpret the European Convention as providing the right to education laid down in the first sentence of Article 2, but that particular interpretations of parental rights are considered largely a matter for individual states. And, it seems, the idea of 'socialisation' in a school context has weighed heavily in the Court's decisions. Parental convictions are also required to be reasonably substantial and to meet at least minimal standards of coherence.[1]

A number of uncertainties arise about the likely interpretation of Article 2, quite apart from the educational significance of other provisions of the Human Rights Act concerning freedom of thought, conscience and religion (Article 9), freedom of expression and the exchange of information and ideas (Article 10) and freedom of association (Article 11), for example. There is clearly potential for conflict between the child's right to education and the supervisory rights of parents laid down in Article 2. For instance, one limitation on parental rights is the prohibition in Article 14 of discrimination on such grounds as gender, race and religion that might be invoked against attempts to differentiate between the education of male and female children.

Another question concerns the extent to which denial of the right to education might be interpreted in ways which oblige parents to ensure teaching of a kind precisely specified by government and its agencies, a possibility raised by the intervention of the UK Secretary of State for Education in the case of Summerhill School which I discuss below. On this issue of interpretation, it should be borne in mind that an important function of instruments like the European Convention is to anticipate future violations of human rights as a result of social change. They provide insurance against incremental extensions of state power which might eventually be used for less enlightened purposes than those originally conceived. Moreover, formally constituted rights and freedoms do not emerge from a vacuum. They are expressions of antecedent traditions of thought and it is to those that we should return for a fuller awareness of their institutional implications.

Britain's well-developed doctrine of the state as *parens patriae*, responsible for the interests of minors, might also predispose government and the courts in that country to interpret parental rights narrowly. Attention could be directed more to the need to protect children from strongly deviant parental beliefs than to the principle that seems to have inspired the educational provisions of the European Convention. That is the requirement for a system of checks and balances to prevent excessive government domination of the induction of young people into their culture: legal protection of a right to differ within a broad framework of obligations associated with democratic citizenship. Hamilton defends the rights of children against narrowly sectarian education in a context of growing religious freedom in England and America. But she also points out that judges in both countries had appeared 'largely unaware of relevant international instruments' (Hamilton, 1995, p. 340).

Questions arise about the adequacy of existing machinery for arbitrating between the respective rights and interests of parents and children and the accountability of those who exercise formal powers in this respect. Official prescriptions concerning the best educational interests of children may prove difficult to justify. Some examples I will consider in subsequent chapters underline the need for a new system of sensitive checks and balances to redress the consequences of official fallibility and to subject official claims and powers to critical public scrutiny. On the other hand, the possibility of conflict between the constituted rights of children and those of their parents remains. But so, too, do various opportunities for resolving them within the spirit of the European Convention and the Convention on the Rights of the Child. A genuinely independent, well-resourced children's rights commission is one possible example. However, the UK government rejected a proposal for such a body in 1999 on the ground that existing public authorities adequately protected children's rights and interests, ensuring that 'their voices are heard' (Newell, 2000). A series of scandals involving long-term physical and sexual abuse of children in the care of British local authorities undermined the plausibility of that claim and perhaps encouraged subsequent moves towards the establishment of regional UK commissioners for children's rights.

However, my present point is a minimalistic one: there is insufficient evidence to justify restrictive interpretations of the rights laid down by Article 2 on the kind of state-paternalistic grounds rejected by countries like the Netherlands and Denmark. Indeed, the first major research study of the prospects for 'lifelong learning' in developed countries by the Organisation for Economic Co-operation and Development confirmed the findings of earlier studies of literacy, that most basic index of educational attainment. Britain ranked thirteenth out of eighteen countries on literacy scores designed to register the routine competence of 16- to 25-year-old people, well below the Netherlands and even further below Denmark, whose average scores were exceeded only by Finland (OECD, 2001, pp. 49–50). Another interesting finding of this OECD report was that America, which ranked below Britain on measurements of literacy, had the highest upper secondary completion rates of all the states in the study. Of course, it would be dangerous to infer a negative correlation between formal schooling and educational attainment on the basis of such limited data alone. And it would be equally premature to identify the liberal education regime of Denmark as the key factor in that country's high ranking in the study. On the other hand, evidence of this kind must reinforce doubts about the justification of restrictions of parental rights according to the mantra of educational effectiveness, as does research data on the achievements of home educated American and British children.

Religious conviction comprises much of the educational case law in Britain and America, involving issues that might seem obscure or extremely marginal to most people (Hamilton, 1995, p. 341). Nevertheless, they do raise further questions in the context of Article 2. How substantial or articulate must a belief be to entitle parents to insist that the education and teaching of their children should be in conformity with it? And how far might deeply held and articulate philosophical beliefs concerning the proper ends and methods of education conflict with increasingly uniformist government prescriptions to which there is already considerable hostility in the academic community and among parents?

One possibility is clearly that there will be differences between the state and the independent sector though, once again, the recent Summerhill dispute calls in question the willingness of government to recognise that distinction in terms of such matters as curriculum and assessment. A number of small independent schools sought partial state funding for alternative methods of education and curricula under the umbrella of the Third Sector Schools Alliance, but have faced continuing indifference from government ministers who appear strongly attached to the idea of the national curriculum (Third Sector Schools Alliance, July 1998).

In any event, justice demands that any system of monitoring alternative educational provision should be fair and not unduly onerous. It does not follow that because an agency is charged with responsibility for ensuring educational standards that it will do so fairly, competently or with due regard to the legitimate variety of educational purposes and methods in a free society. And the case of Summerhill School in Suffolk provides a reason for such concern.

The Summerhill controversy

In 1949, British government inspectors visited Summerhill School, which had been founded in 1921 in Leiston, Suffolk, by A.S. Neill as an experiment in free and democratic education. They remarked on the atmosphere of toleration and contentment in the school, which did not require attendance at classes and which operated according to rules determined by a school 'parliament' with unlimited powers of discussion by the children. One pupil, who later became a skilled maker of precision instruments, did not attend a single class in his thirteen years at Summerhill, though most children did eventually attend classes quite regularly. The inspectors were charmed by the 'delightful' manners of the children, their lack of inhibition and self-consciousness. Although they expressed some reservations about the levels of academic education, the inspectors had seen no evidence to suggest that former Summerhill pupils had experienced particular difficulties in meeting the demands of society at large or those of institutions of higher education. They recommended the school as a valuable example of educational research (Neill, 1975, pp. 77–86).

Half a century later, in 1999, Summerhill School upheld the same principles as those which originally inspired Neill. The difference was that it was operating within an environment of deep official hostility towards any deviation from standardised educational prescriptions. A 'Notice of Complaint' was served on the privately financed school by the Secretary of State for Education and Employment following a highly critical report by inspectors from the Office for Standards in Schools (Ofsted). That notice was subsequently withdrawn and the Secretary of State agreed to pay a proportion of the costs of an appeal by the school against the Notice. His abrupt change of heart removed what might have become an early test of the legal significance of the new Human Rights Act. The case did, however, highlight implicit tensions between exponents of alternative educational philosophies and a government committed to central control of virtually all aspects of education – as well as a consequent potential for litigation. In addition, it accentuated concerns about the accountability of Ofsted and the competence of that powerful agency to report objectively on any form of education that deviated, no matter how conscientiously, from standard prescriptions.

The issue of parental consent should be mentioned. Summerhill achieved popular notoriety through media coverage of its libertarian concept of education. Emulation of that approach by at least one local authority inner-city school, the William Tyndale School, was said to have encouraged near-anarchy and under-achievement among pupils. But the salient contrast is that Summerhill is financed by fee-paying parents who subscribe to its philosophy and who elect to enrol their children there. Unpopular – even extreme – though its approach might be, there is no evidence that it has ever been imposed regardless of the convictions of parents or the wishes of their children, a conclusion reinforced by their indignant responses to the Ofsted inspection and the Secretary of State's subsequent action. In other words, the situation is not comparable with one in which unconventional educational methods had been adopted by a school irrespective of parental convictions.

The Notice of Complaint followed the most recent of several reports on Summerhill by Ofsted.[2] It appeared to have wide implications for all educational initiatives, requiring as it did *timetabled lessons, prescribed study programmes, systematic assessment and attainment* '*in line with national expectations*'.[3] Many parents and educators who do not subscribe to Summerhill's extremely libertarian educational philosophy might nevertheless object in principle to such programmatic schooling and to the inspectorate's apparent enthusiasm for educational uniformity. It is, after all, arguable that the kind of criteria italicised above are relevant at best to mass schooling and that they conflate two distinct requirements: the conditions for effective learning by individuals and those customary for the management of large-scale organisations.[4] Bearing in mind the conclusions of that 1949 inspectors' report, a worrying aspect of official insistence on standardisation is that it might drastically reduce the scope for research on the effectiveness of alternative modes of learning by implicitly accepting such variables as classrooms and age-matched student cohorts as parameters within which most or all investigation occurs.

The Ofsted report had required Summerhill to 'ensure that all pupils are fully engaged in study across a broad and balanced curriculum throughout their time in school', a demand fundamentally in conflict with the school's philosophy. Yet the future implications of the Secretary of State's acknowledgement of A.S. Neill's philosophy and of the principle that 'learning is not confined to lessons' remained uncertain. Nor did the case resolve a particularly ominous feature of Ofsted's policing of schools. Despite a government undertaking to review Summerhill's TBW ('to be watched') status on that agency's list and the peculiarly intensive regime of inspections which it had involved, the agreement reached between the Secretary of State and the school left Ofsted's role unchanged in relation to schools in general.[5]

An independent report on Summerhill by several prominent academics, educationalists and business people[6] highlighted several issues which appear to be directly relevant to the rights laid down by Article 2 of the European Convention and the British government's reservation concerning it. So far as 'efficient instruction and training' are concerned, this report argued that Summerhill children achieved better than average results in public examinations (GCSEs) for non-selective schools. It also maintained that the school had been achieving faster-than-average rates of improvement, a significant accomplishment as forty of the school's fifty-nine children had come from overseas and some had little knowledge of English when they first arrived. Anticipating the objection that higher levels of achievement might have been expected, given the social and economic backgrounds of the children, the report pointed out that a significant proportion of young people had been transferred to Summerhill because they had failed to thrive in more conventional schools. More apparent was the overwhelming support of children and parents for the school's philosophy and practice. Nor was Summerhill in receipt of local education authority or central government funding, a point consistent with the requirement for avoidance of unreasonable public expenditure as a result of an exercise of parental rights. A further aspect of the Summerhill case intimately connected with the issue of children's and parents' rights was the school's strong commitment to democratic procedures which, the independent report insisted, had been seriously undervalued by the Ofsted inspectors.

This discussion is not, in itself, intended to favour particular alternatives to contemporary school education. My aim has been to raise questions about the justifiability of state intervention in pursuit of what are deemed collectively desirable social ends. One principle embedded in the liberal–democratic tradition to which I have referred is formalised to some extent by the European Convention and the Human Rights Act 1998. It is a presumption in favour of the liberties of individual citizens in the absence of clear evidence that this would infringe the rights and interests of others or cause identifiable harm, a theme developed notably by J.S. Mill in *On Liberty*. Mill also asserted a universal right of children to education and financial support by the state to secure that right. On the other hand, he rejected the idea of direct state control of education on the ground that it would become 'a mere contrivance for moulding people to be exactly like one another' to suit the preferences of 'a monarch, a priesthood, an aristocracy, or the majority of the existing generation' (Mill, 1965a, p. 352). A system that arbitrarily excludes or limits diversity sacrifices the intellectual, moral and emotional development of young people for a mirage of social consensus. It is an interesting but neglected aspect of Mill's work that, of the major philosophers, he was most steadfast in proclaiming the fundamental intellectual equality of all people, regardless of social class, race or gender. Educational freedom and diversity were the routes to social equality, creativity and adaptability; they were also basic conditions for realising a mature democracy. It is at least worth considering the hypothesis that a uniform system of mass education consolidates rather than mitigates social inequalities, that it provides fertile breeding grounds for prejudice and for the adoption of perverse cultural norms, actively discouraging individual creativity and initiative.

I have been concerned with educational rights that are, in theory, universal. However, in the last analysis it is extremely unlikely that many UK citizens would insist upon them, or indeed be aware of them. It seems that most parents, if not teachers, are reasonably satisfied with the current education system.[7] Educational alternatives are probably destined to remain a minority concern, and for that reason pose little threat to established interests. But for that reason, too, there is a danger that official enthusiasm for conformity and standardisation will trespass on the rights and freedoms of parents and their children.

The universality of human rights

A number of the cases mentioned above raise questions about the real significance of proclamations concerning the universality and interdependence of human rights. As mentioned, the United Kingdom government is insistent about this in the global context and forthright about its commitment to 'secure all rights for all people' (Foreign Office, 1999, p. 19). However, that resolve must be balanced against an international background of restrictive judicial interpretations of educational and other rights and a marked tendency in the UK for government and its agencies to invoke international agreements on the basis of what sometimes appear to be *ad hoc* judgments about their relevance to established or preferred domestic policies.

One difficulty is that interpretations, particularly by courts, appeal to the fact of an historical agreement and the sparse form of words in which it was couched. Such agreements are of vital importance to the human rights tradition, of course, because they help to translate broad aspirations into enforceable rules. This answers one sceptical claim by Bentham, that rights are meaningless abstractions, one member of a 'tribe of fictitious entities', unless they are the direct result of legislation: a legal positivist view that law alone creates rights (Bentham, 1948, p. 224). But that position rules out any appeal for clarification to human rights traditions antecedent to the enactment of laws that, nevertheless, owe their existence, meaning and purpose to those traditions. On the other hand, specific agreements between countries with varied cultural traditions are likely to be achieved only if their terms are broad enough to permit variable interpretation and the incorporation of reservations by the parties to them. This has been the case with the European Convention, as I have already remarked, and the political expedient of making concessions to entrenched cultural traditions is formally recognised under the Convention by the device of a 'margin of appreciation':

The margin of appreciation doctrine ... is none the less a controversial one. When it is applied widely, so as to appear to give a state a blank cheque or to tolerate questionable national practices or decisions, it may be argued that the Convention authorities have abdicated their responsibilities ... The difficulty with the doctrine lies not so much in allowing it as in deciding precisely when and how widely to apply it on the facts of particular cases.

(Harris *et al.*, 1995, p. 2)

Application of such a doctrine to particular cases inevitably involves justification in terms of the ordinary meaning of the words that describe any right in question. And this cannot be accomplished without a consideration of their traditional contexts of usage (Brown, 1998, pp. 83–108). Indeed, this principle is enshrined in the basic rule governing the interpretation of the Convention, that it 'shall be interpreted in good faith in accordance with the ordinary meaning to be given to the terms of the treaty in their context and in the light of its object and purpose' (Vienna Convention on the Law of Treaties, 1969, Article 31). Bentham's position on rights, as Mill observed of his general inclination in social and political analysis, was to reconstruct the world *de novo*, and in doing so to dismiss the 'whole unanalysed experience of the human race', imputing a metaphysical perfection to linguistic meaning (Mill, 1963, p. 92). That consideration embraces the moral standards that are prior to and embodied in laws for the protection of rights according to traditional notions of fairness. But the problem remains for the exponent of universal human rights that the traditions that provide the necessary interpretative background are themselves variable and often culturally specific. This, in turn, is the source of another form of human rights scepticism: 'the notion of a right presupposes a system of social rules and since these are historically and culturally specific, there can be no legitimate talk of universal human rights' (Ingram, 1994, p. 12).

According to this thesis, individuals cannot be distinguished as prior to or independent of their social and cultural roles in the fundamental sense required by the notion of access to universal rights. Social roles, tribal affiliations, religious convictions all constrain the choices available to individuals, and sometimes they do so stringently by limiting the ability even to conceive of exercising the putative rights and liberties in question. According to this criticism, universalising claims make no sense; it is a fallacious, metaphysical enterprise to abstract individuals from the particular communities that determine their sense of social reality and constrain their aspirations.

However, it is one thing to acknowledge the powerful cultural constraints on the individual as anthropologists like Boas, Sapir and Benedict have, but quite another to subscribe to a determinism in which individual identities and choices are submerged their cultural and linguistic milieux. This is a theoretical stance associated with Sapir, whose notion of 'the tyrannical hold that linguistic form has upon our orientation to the world' (Kluckhohn and Leighton, 1960, pp. 207–8) was exaggerated by Whorf's thesis that '[T]he individual is utterly unaware of this organisation and is constrained completely within its unbreakable bonds' (Whorf, 1959, p. 256). Cultural relativism, carried to such extremes, is clearly inimical to the idea that diverse human languages and cultures have sufficient in common on which to base a theory of universal human rights because the contrasting values they embody lack common denominators. But thoroughgoing relativism, as distinct from an appreciation of human diversity, is simply incorrect. For one thing it is self-refuting because its central claim deprives it of a logically privileged position among the plethora of internally consistent or equally valid world views which it postulates. It cannot account for social and historical change. Nor can it explain the universal human ability to transcend what are sometimes profound linguistic differences to achieve mutual understandings, however imperfect: that 'common behaviour of mankind' which Wittgenstein identified as 'the system of reference by means of which we interpret an unknown language' (Wittgenstein, 1968, PI 65).

One value is universal, however, and it is a necessary and sufficient condition for the idea of universal human rights. That is the concept of truth which, I maintain, is entailed by the possibility of language, the necessary condition of its intelligibility. Popper has described this human faculty as one which confers on humans the unique advantage of 'vicarious experience': the ability to learn from the mistakes of others, to accumulate a repertoire of knowledge and understanding which is independent of our own immediate experiences and which transcends generations. Of course it is perfectly possible to misuse language, to use it manipulatively or dishonestly, but such perverse uses are parasitic on the normal expectation that words have dependable meanings and identifiable referents. Truth, in this sense, is a universal norm in all human societies and truth-telling entails the notion of rational justifiability. Meaningful propositions are capable of being supported or refuted by reasons and these may, or may not, be judged to be adequate to particular circumstances. This argument, I believe, has a particular relevance to ideas about moral agency and moral obligation. For, once habitual, unquestioning acceptance gives way to a sceptical appraisal of claims to moral authority or demands for political obedience, there arises an implicit requirement for rational justification. This is not to ignore the reality that moral standards are frequently enforced, but simply to point out that enforcement is no more than that: it is simple coercion for those who remain unconvinced of the justifiability of the standards imposed on them.

It is nevertheless important to draw attention to the powerful constraints that language and culture do sometimes impose on the cognitive and moral potentials of individual people in certain traditional societies, past and present. Appreciation of the immense stability over time, the homeostatic functions of custom and ritual in aboriginal communities, for example, provides valuable clues to the conditions which have enabled historical individuals to disengage themselves from the 'tyrannical hold' of languages, myths and cultural milieux. I have argued this case in detail elsewhere (Brown, 1998) and simply indicate it in broad outline here. The point is not that such manifestations of individual autonomy ever do, or could, amount to a complete divorce between a 'metaphysical' person and the totality of their culture; the process is invariably incremental. But patterns of assimilation and contact between alien cultures can stimulate critical appraisal of conflicting traditional beliefs and values. Demands for the justification of tradition on the basis of evidence may be associated with developments of this kind – and also the urge to hypothesise and test the plausibility of alternative states of affairs. Popper has identified this kind of break with tradition as the genesis of the 'open society' in the cases of Classical Greece and, subsequently, the European Renaissance. Jack Goody and Ian Watt have described the revolutionary cognitive impact of the 'democratic' tool of alphabetic literacy on traditional communities as a means of storing and exchanging information and, eventually, of institutionalising the criticism of prevailing myths and values (Goody and Watt, 1963).

Discovery of the fallibility of traditional wisdom and the emergence of various philosophical and scientific modes of sceptical inquiry were linked historically to doctrines of human rights which invoked the universal faculty of reason. Locke developed the Thomist conception of divinely ordained natural laws, but his contemporaries were quick to identify the secular implications of his view that revelation should be judged by reason (Nuovo, 1997, pp. ix–xxvi). His emphasis on the tenuous nature of human understanding and the consequent importance of mutual toleration pointed towards a fallibilist rationale for human rights that was to be powerfully developed by Mill into a doctrine of individual liberty. Rawls has summarised Mill's central argument in these terms:

> the institutions of liberty and the opportunity for experience which they allow are necessary, at least to some degree, if men's preferences among different activities are to be rational and informed. Human beings have no other way of knowing what things they can do and which of them are most rewarding. Thus, if the pursuit of value, estimated in terms of the progressive interests of mankind, is to be rational, that is, guided by a knowledge of human capacities and well-formed preferences, certain freedoms are indispensable ... the suppression of liberty is always likely to be irrational.
>
> (Rawls, 1973, p. 210)

Rawls does qualify his endorsement of Mill's argument by pointing out an apparent limitation imposed by his conception of 'the progressive interests of mankind'. Where any such end of social endeavour is proposed, it might assume priority over other ends, including liberty. 'The liberties of equal citizenship are insecure when founded upon teleological principles. The argument for them relies on precarious calculations as well as controversial and uncertain premises' (*ibid.*, p. 211). Mill, however, recognised that any idea of social well-being is as open to question as all other human aspirations. In an extended passage of *On Liberty* he attacked the assumption of infallibility involved in any attempt to justify restraints on individual freedoms on the ground of utility (Mill, 1965a, p. 274). Truth is what will define the interests of progressive beings; it is a regulative ideal of fundamental significance in their affairs and the teleology on which the liberties of equal citizenship are founded.

The role Mill ascribes to normative concepts of truth and rationality accounts for the appearance of inconsistency detected by some critics between his espousal of both utilitarian and libertarian ethics. Utility is not some finite, specifiable state but rather an ideal opposed to transcendental or intuitive conceptions of value. It is relevant to my present argument to note his renunciation of a justification for the message of *On Liberty* in terms of 'abstract right'. Rights derive from the perennial counterpoint between human authority and the fallibility of human knowledge. His principal task is that of translating the insight that all assertions of epistemic or moral authority entail rational justification according to standards which are constantly subject to change and which are often opposed to one another. But that onus of rational justification is rigorous and continuous; rigorous because it must be intelligible to each and all who are held to be subject to moral authority; continuous because standards of rationality are themselves subject to historical change and controversy and are thus fallible. Hence, for Mill, all restraint, *qua* restraint, is an evil because it violates that universal requirement for a rational justification that could command moral assent.

Skorupski maintains that Mill's case for individual autonomy could have been strengthened by explicit acknowledgement that it is itself 'a categorical human end' (Skorupski, 1991, p. 37) but he underestimates the significance of Mill's renunciation of abstract right in favour of an epistemological justification of the liberty-principle. We live as social beings but we learn and understand as individual minds grappling with a heritage of diverse ideas, beliefs and theories. Mill's position is that to justify any human end entails an open invitation to rational appraisal, the transparent exercise of authority, the institutionalisation of personal liberties and, crucially, the education of reason rather than the dogmatic inculcation of conventional knowledge and virtues. In this sense, the reciprocal obligations of citizens and governments at least resemble a 'social contract' and are implied by the nature of human rationality, the primary source of inalienable human rights. Mill does not propose anything resembling a blueprint for a tolerant, free society, but introduces a dynamic for social change and a principle on which to judge both the authority and effectiveness of social institutions in that process of change. As Nuovo says of Locke, that inquiry is ongoing, open-ended and non-dogmatic: 'Its aim is truth that is beyond perfect definition' (Nuovo, 1997, p. xxvi).

Thus the idea of universal human rights is, I believe, inextricably and uniquely connected with human language and rationality. Far from being a narrow principle, the inherent requirement for rational justification has wide-ranging institutional implications as the criterion of political and moral legitimacy. The cultivation of reason and habits of critical appraisal are central to the conception of a moral community. As I will argue in the following chapters, this places educational rights and freedoms at the very heart of human rights.

5 What price freedom?

Economy and effectiveness in education

Without a grown-up idea of education but still confidently setting out
to set it to rights, we are like men wanting to set the church to rights
without knowing what religion is.

(Maskell, 1999, p. 57)

Some democratic societies, notably Denmark, have formulated education policies according to a basic constitutional principle of individual
liberty. Alternatively, the freedom of British citizens to take educational initiatives is subject to the limitation mentioned in the previous
chapter, that they should provide 'efficient instruction and training'
and avoid 'unreasonable public expenditure'. In the last chapter I
suggested the need for vigilance about the interpretation of those
reservations by governments and their agencies. Nevertheless, it will
seem reasonable to most people that individual freedoms have their
price, that the choices parents make should be required to meet certain
standards consistent with the fundamental right of the child to education. The arguments presented in this book do not challenge that view.
In fact they support the interconnected principles that educational
rights require a robust defence but that those rights must be demonstrably about the child's *education* and, moreover, that they should
accommodate the child's developing responses to it. However, I believe
that the previous chapter identifies the need for a tolerant, impartial
means of balancing these different requirements. Concepts like 'efficiency' are not value-neutral; they are related internally to
philosophical judgments concerning the aims of education, whether
these are acknowledged explicitly or not. The present chapter is
concerned with this concept of 'efficiency' as it has been applied in
education and examines the cogency of some definitions that have
been elevated to the status of articles of faith by successive governments.

Duke Maskell's words, above, resonate with indignation about eighteen years of remorseless innovation in British education which have had the effect of 'multiplying cures that aggravate the disease' (Maskell, 1999, p. 158). The motive that has inspired these illusory cures was the abrupt disappearance in the UK of the distinction between education and training, which, according to Maskell, had been recognised since the days of Socrates. His claim involves a degree of literary licence because, as I argued in Chapter 3, that ancient distinction has been clear and consistent only in connection with the education of social élites. For great majorities of people, the aim of such schooling as was available tended to be the achievement of social conformity and the production of a competent workforce. What *did* occur in the last two decades of the twentieth century was a deliberate conflation of the ideas of education and training throughout nearly all levels of the British education system with a minimum of public debate. The policy decision was symbolised by adoption of the titles 'Department for Education and Employment' and, even more explicitly, the 'Scottish Office Education and Industry Department'. However, the change was considerably more than terminological and it affected all levels of the British system.

The American cult of managerialism had achieved unprecedented popularity in the public education system and dominated it for much of the twentieth century, though critics like Callahan have described its consequences as tragic (Callahan, 1962, pp. 248–50). Nevertheless, as if inspired by that American example, UK governments inaugurated an era of pervasive educational managerialism. Although the trend has been an international one, it has been undoubtedly more comprehensive in Britain than in countries other than the United States as a result of the high degree of bureaucratic centralisation in this country's education systems. These changes have been a quite deliberate invocation of the management practices of industry and commerce as models of efficiency. Transformation in management systems has been accompanied by a burgeoning vocationalism in education policies and the profundity of the ideological revolution which has taken place is most evident in the ubiquitous vocabulary of 'skills' and 'competencies' and 'learning outcomes' that has replaced not only more traditional descriptions, but also *conceptions* of student achievement. Qualitative aspects of education are perceived increasingly in quantitative and behaviouristic terms, a development that Hyland traces back to that early twentieth-century 'social efficiency' theory which had such an impact in the United States (Hyland, 1993).

Industrial efficiency is almost invariably a quantitative concept, and British education has succumbed to obsessions with measurement, development planning and generic level descriptors which have increasingly burdened teachers with responsibilities for form-filling and record-keeping, some of the most frequently cited reasons for an exodus of experienced teachers from the profession and difficulties in the recruitment of younger ones. The trend has also penetrated further and higher education. Professor Alison Wolf of London's Institute of Education voiced the common complaint that:

> The NVQ (National Vocational Qualifications) movement was influential in arguing for a competence-approach to assessment. Government, industry and quangos all put money into the idea. Yet the research shows that it is wrong. It is too top-down, too bureaucratic, too much work and becomes an endless process of rubber-stamping rather than learning.
>
> (*Times Higher Education Supplement* (*THES*), 31–3–00, p. 39)

Quantification is also an international trend, justified to some extent by growing economic and political integration within Europe and beyond, but hampered by problems of comparability between diverse systems of assessment. The Organisation for Economic Co-operation and Development has proposed 'mean literacy scores' and 'under-achievement rates' as broad but useful indicators of educational quality between member states. I referred briefly to the OECD's findings under these headings in the last chapter. They merit some repetition in a discussion of the ideas of educational efficiency and effectiveness which have been dominant themes of those two decades in which Britain has so decisively emulated American preoccupations with an industrial–commercial model. Ironically, the broad picture is one of disastrous under-achievement by both American and British young people who completed their secondary education between the years 1994 and 1998, by which time educational managerialism had become firmly entrenched in the United Kingdom.

Americans between the ages of 16 and 25 achieved mean literacy scores lower than those of their peers in all but one of eighteen countries studied, with the exception of Poland, despite the fact that the United States had one of the highest completion rates for upper secondary education. American rates of under-achievement, defined as performance below the minimum level of competence to cope with the demands of everyday life, were worse than in any other country in the study and more than five times those of the countries registering the highest mean literacy scores, Finland and Denmark. British young people registered only a slight improvement on these scores, ranking thirteenth out of eighteen on measures of literacy, below Portugal, which has relatively low upper-secondary completion rates. Measures of under-achievement by British young people were three times those for Finland and Denmark (OECD, 2001, p. 49).

Now it is of course true that gross statistics of this kind are always arguable and there are undoubtedly many cultural and economic facets to the problems of literacy and under-achievement, many of which I would not wish to describe as measurables. Perhaps, though, one fairly firm conclusion can be drawn from a broad brush-stroke picture of this kind: it offers very little support for the insistent justifications which have been offered for the introduction of industrial and commercial values and techniques into state education, or for the particularly intrusive role adopted by British governments. Measures of literacy must be reliable indices of the quality of education in a very basic sense, at least. But the absence of a positive correlation between such measures and American upper-secondary completion rates, in particular, suggests that many of the presuppositions about the advantages of conventional schooling require more sceptical appraisal than they usually receive. This is even more obviously true when account is taken of the abundant evidence of superior average performances by the growing legions of home educated children in that country. The British myth of progressive education to which I referred in Chapter 2 and that inspired such radical changes in policy and practice has now been joined by the chimera of industrial efficiency.

Quite apart from the contestable idea that industrial production bears a plausible analogy to the proper aims of schooling, it is not even true that it represents, *per se*, any obvious standard of efficiency. The greatest technological revolution of the late twentieth century, which itself has had a huge impact on education, was the development of the personal computer by a small network of amateur enthusiasts in the United States. This handful of so-called 'nerds' famously outperformed the combined resources of a giant multinational corporation like IBM, substituting for the inflexibility of its elaborate management systems and hierarchies their own vision, creativity and problem-solving talents. Efficiency, far from being an absolute, is relative to the nature of the tasks in hand. Economic efficiency itself cannot be epitomised adequately by general features of industrial management and the greatest contribution to educational efficiency might be achieved by eliminating the ever more convoluted bureaucratic systems which are invented in the hope of achieving it. If schools are factories, as the previously quoted American educational administrator so bluntly put it, one of the intriguing possibilities raised by the successes of the home education movement is that the buildings, the management hierarchies, the ever proliferating burdens of paperwork and regimented production lines are irrelevant to the manufacture of a quality product.

Of course, it is true that there are important connections between the quality of the education young people receive and their subsequent employment prospects. Few would dispute the proposition that one vitally important function of education is to fit future citizens for productive roles in their society. That is not the issue; the salient point is that a sound education, as traditionally conceived, is a perfectly adequate basis for subsequent specialised vocational training and, when achieved, an education of this kind provides the best prospects of worthwhile employment for the individual. In *some* respects, the trend towards vocationalism in British schools has amounted to very little more than an insistent restatement of long-standing educational aims. The novel language, however, articulates a widespread prejudice that teaching resembles training and that learning is a matter of acquiring predetermined routines. Thus, those most basic educational aims, literacy and numeracy, are now described as 'core skills' and it appears to be shortcomings in these traditional, *general* areas of learning which concern most employers, rather than a lack of specifically vocational or technical abilities. But terminological manipulations like this are dangerous because they appear to offer vocational justifications for programmatic educational regimes directed towards narrowly defined minimum standards. As Alan Ryan has said:

> the present insistence on raising standards by regimentation ... runs too high a risk of reintroducing the idea that children from humble backgrounds need a narrowly vocational set of skills, and in an inegalitarian society what that will infallibly mean is that it is all they will acquire.
>
> (Ryan, 1999, p. 119)

Now these criticisms might be deflected by the claim that contemporary education policies have very much wider, more liberal aims, including the encouragement of effective and responsible citizenship and the full development of the child's personality, talents and mental and physical abilities.[1] As I have noted several times, broad ideals of this kind are repeated endlessly in official educational circulars. What they lack is not sincerity but cogency. An appropriate response is that if they can be squeezed into the crowded curriculum at all, it will be by forcing them into the Procrustean bed of a 'skills' conception of learning that is actually inimical to the realisation of those very ideals.

Educational newspeak: skills and competencies

This new international vocabulary of 'skills' and 'competencies' is diagnostic of the extent to which a general ideological commitment to a global market economy has penetrated the intimacies of the classroom. Workplace techniques have supplied the model to which the achievements of young intellects must now conform. This development has been more than nominal; it is one that dominates pedagogic practice, largely by virtue of some of the popular connotations of the term 'skills'. They can be precisely specified in advance; they can be communicated by successive, determinate routines; and individuals can be assessed reliably according to the level of competence with which they exercise them. All this seems to be true of the traditional idea of a skill, at least. Perhaps because it is so compatible with the characteristic input–output processes of industrial production the terminology now embraces aspects of intellectual and emotional development for which it would once have been regarded as quite inappropriate. In fact it still is so regarded by many, though their criticisms fail to impede the juggernaut of industrialised education no matter how incisive they may be.

Another reason for the hegemony of skills-talk is that it corresponds to certain conceptions of the psychology of learning and long-established traditions of research in that field. Hence the idea of 'generic skills' has achieved a degree of acceptability in official educational literature which it lacks in philosophy, where there is continuing scholarly controversy and, among other things, concern about a paucity of empirical evidence for skill-transfer between 'cognitive domains'. McPeck (McPeck *et al.*, 1990, p. 97) has argued that much contemporary skills-language 'semantically masquerades as a description of general abilities' and Smith (Smith, 1992) endorses this criticism of the confusion between semantics and psychology by wondering, rhetorically, how long it will be before children are taught 'doubting skills' and 'trusting skills'. I will consider that debate more fully in the following chapter, and now simply raise the consideration that critical understanding is invariably grounded in familiarity with a subject-matter and cannot be conveniently abstracted from it for pedagogic reasons.

Managerial jargon reflects preoccupations with measurables like age-related attainment targets and what are presumed to be objectively observable manifestations of the ethos of learning environments. Despite the very questionable identification of education and enterprise, 'education for work' now enjoys a position of 'central importance' in the curriculum and the drive is on to accord work-related activities a prominent if not pre-eminent place in formal assessment (HM Inspectors of Schools, 2000). Increasing use of modular courses means that young people's experience of learning is that of continuous assessment against tightly pre-specified learning outcomes which, as I will argue below, involve dangerously arbitrary judgments about what constitutes acceptable performance and appropriate knowledge. According to research conducted by one professor of education, British children have become 'by far the most heavily assessed in the world' (Richards, 27–04–01, p. 14) a situation that is itself morally contentious, particularly as many experienced educationalists question the reliability of the new testing regime as an index of educational achievement. Modularisation is consistent with the flawed skills-conception of learning and lends itself to a rote system of continuous and internal assessment by educational institutions under the supervision of educational bureaucracies. These developments have already produced a major educational catastrophe in Scotland, which I discuss below, and their political implications for the liberties of citizens and their children are worrying. The public examination system which is so crucial to the future of children and young people becomes ever more dependent on government and its agencies; a dynamic is established which shackles the learner ever more closely to educational institutions and the bureaucracies which dominate prescribed programmes of study. Anxieties about low standards of educational attainment in the public sector schools of the United States prompted moves in 1994 for legislation on state-mandated standardised tests and assessments by schools to define 'what all students should know and be able to do' in preparation for 'productive employment in our Nation's modern economy' (Educate America Act 1994). As American opponents pointed out, 'we will have surrendered an enormous amount of our freedom of education, which is a foundation for freedom of thought ... It is hard to grasp the enormity of what we stand to lose' (Kaseman and Kaseman, 1995).

In Britain policy has been increasingly dictated from the centre for nearly a generation. Adoption of the new business ethic has been a function of the hierarchical organisation of the system and the potential of central and local government education departments to disseminate ideas rapidly throughout it. Career expectations at all levels of administration as well as at 'the chalk face' are harnessed to plausible usage of a novel vocabulary which cascades downwards and outwards from these centres of policy – sometimes irrespective of users' understandings of what particular words, phrases and 'key concepts' were intended to mean by those who coined them. As already mentioned, the trend now embraces higher education as well as the primary and secondary sectors and here, according to Alison Wolf, '[m]ore time is being spent sitting in rooms arguing about phrases and specifications and less time is spent on seeing whether people understand them' (*THES*, 30–03–00, p. 39).

An illustration of this trend is relevant here because it has a clear bearing on issues concerning the legitimisation of public policy and the determination of educational objectives. A case in point is the widely adopted term 'core skills'. That report to the Scottish Executive by HM Inspectors of Schools, which I have just cited, attributes a pivotal role to these skills in the educational enterprise. One indication of this is that the phrase appears on virtually every page of their 54-page document, sometimes several times over. Nevertheless, the report indicates that its inspection of provision for education for work by twenty-eight Scottish schools revealed 'wide variations in awareness and understanding of core skills':

> Although it was generally the case that staff in some secondary and special schools were familiar with the idea of core skills, few had yet interpreted them fully in the context of their subject curriculum. Fewer still had … associated them with a coherent programme in education for work.
>
> (HM Inspectors, 2000, p. 40)

One probable reason for such incomplete understanding is suggested by the absence from the report of a cogent account of what 'core skills' are supposed to be even though they are accorded such prominence in it. The nearest thing to a definition, repeated in several brief paragraphs, identifies 'skills in numeracy, communication, problem-solving, ICT and working with others'. But such generalities must leave many readers wondering what teachers have been trying to do for the past century and more. (Information and communications technology is clearly the exception here, both because it is new and because it is the one item in the list that is defensible as a 'skill', though one that is now well established in school curricula.) The suspicion must be that the incomprehension of many teachers was due not to the novelty of the concepts involved but to the unexplained decision to group traditional educational aims within an arbitrary nomenclature. But this is a mere surface manifestation of something more problematic about the idea of 'core skills'. That is the mystique imposed on some reasonably intelligible educational objectives, albeit expressed at high levels of generality and abstraction, investing them with a spurious technical precision and specificity.

This last point is more obvious in the case of such indefinitely broad categories as 'communication', 'numeracy' and 'working with others' than it is with 'problem solving'. For the latter, together with the related concept of 'critical thinking', has been the subject of protracted and unresolved philosophical controversy which goes to the heart of epistemology and theories about the acquisition and growth of knowledge (Brown, 1998). Of course, philosophical disagreements may be seen as esoteric, with little direct application to the practical concerns of day-to-day education. But they nevertheless have immediate relevance to the intelligibility of the concepts with which they deal and cannot be abstracted from them for some practical purpose without becoming vacuous and susceptible to arbitrary interpretation. One researcher's conclusion following a very extensive review of problem solving and the secondary curriculum was that the subject is lamentably ill-defined, lacking coherent theoretical underpinnings and so broad that it is equivalent to 'advice on teaching people how to live and how to think'. He commented apologetically:

> I have great sympathy with anyone who has read this review … thus far and exclaims in impatience, 'This is all very well – but what should I be doing about it? Spell out the messages for classroom practice and for curriculum policy.' It may be that the only proper 'academic' response is: 'I can do nothing to help, go and work out your own salvation.'
>
> (Holroyd, 1989, s. 7.1.3)

These considerations irrespective, 'core' or 'key skills' now have official sanction as key elements in a fusion of the formerly distinct activities of education and training, and government funding of training places in the further education sector depends partly on the ability of colleges to deliver them. Ironically, a combination of low student motivation and uncertainty about the enthusiasm of employers and universities for these putative skills has led to calls by national training organisations for them to be de-coupled from other funding requirements (*TES*, 20–04–01, p. 25). Even more disconcerting is the equivocal conclusion about skills and competencies reached by a report of the Organisation for Economic Co-operation and Development, *Education Policy Analysis 2001*, which was the product of research into international labour-market skill requirements for the twenty-first century and the implications for 'lifelong learning'. Referring to what it described as such 'workplace competencies' as team-work, communication skills and problem-solving skills, the authors admitted uncertainty about whether they should be developed in on- or off-job training or in more traditional educational contexts because 'more research is needed to justify and guide substantial changes in the context, contents and methods of teaching and learning aimed at developing new competencies and skills' (OECD, 2001, pp. 112–13).

An explanation of the continuing seductiveness of the skills-conception is no doubt what Wolf (above) describes as the 'chimera of standardisation' which makes politicians feel safe, despite unsettling many in the academic community. Adoption of an industrial vocabulary also resonates with deeply rooted popular prejudices that the whole purpose of education is to get a job, although official reinforcement of this servile and impoverished view might well be a significant reason for continuing under-achievement. Moreover, the idea of helping to enlighten individual children's minds, treating them as ends-in-themselves, has little grasp on the popular imagination and has had a bad press compared to the down-to-earth objective of drilling them to fulfil preordained, collectively sanctioned social and economic ends. Now, of course, the official literature emphasises the rapidity of global social and economic change and the need for an adaptable workforce for the future. Ironically, the response has been for education policies to assume rigid and prescriptive forms. The transformation has been astonishingly complete, threatening a decisive break with the philosophical tradition with which this book is concerned through the enforcement of educational uniformity on the basis of a myth sanctioned by the mantra of 'raising standards'.

Moving educational goalposts: a 'national calamity'

Until August 2000, secondary education in Scotland enjoyed a solid international reputation. Then it became embroiled in what one prominent Scottish educationalist has described as 'a truly national calamity' affecting hundreds of thousands of examination candidates, prospective candidates and their families (Paterson, 2000). However, that calamity was of much more than national significance; it was the outcome of policies that were one expression of an international drift towards vocationalism and a 'competence-based' approach to teaching and assessment. The first evidence of trouble emerged when children failed to receive the results of their Scottish 'Higher Still' examinations, the entry qualifications for university, on the appointed date. Delays in the publication of these redesigned examination results were compounded by thousands of incorrect gradings. Students who had exceptionally good records of achievement were told they had failed; others were awarded passes in subjects that they had not studied and in which they had not been examined. The crisis became more profound, inevitably casting doubt on the reliability of all the results issued by the recently established Scottish Qualifications Authority and on its competence to repair its defective operation in time for the following academic year. Although Scottish universities took immediate steps to mitigate the consequences for applicants to undergraduate courses, lasting damage was done to the reputation of the Scottish secondary education examination system and to the international standing of qualifications earned by young people in that country.

Disturbing though administrative failures on this scale were, they fail to convey the scope of the calamity that had overtaken Scottish education, its political and educational origins and its deeper implications. The government minister responsible for education to the newly devolved Scottish Executive refused to resign on the ground that he did not have direct supervisory responsibilities for the SQA, an independent executive agency of government. Although his decision was justifiable in terms of the principle of maintaining a separation of powers and avoiding excessive political interference in education, it simply relocated the problem as one about the democratic role and accountability of official, semi-autonomous bodies with immense power over the futures of young people.

That question resolves itself ultimately into one about the purposes of education and the respective rights and responsibilities of citizens and the apparatus of the state, as Professor Lindsay Paterson made clear in his commentary on this debacle (*ibid.*, pp. 181–6). Beneath the welter of technical problems that beset the new examining body were other, more fundamental and philosophical issues. The new Higher Still had been inspired by a desire to achieve 'parity of esteem' between academic and vocational courses and qualifications and greater breadth in the curriculum. But as Paterson recounts, that goal was established with minimal public debate by the expedient of simply imposing a uniform system of modularised courses as well as a greatly increased burden of internal assessment and record-keeping on teachers and schools. In effect, an approach which had been common in vocational training was imposed on the academic curriculum without due consideration of the redefinition of knowledge and understanding implied by that arbitrary decision. 'Parity of esteem' does not entail a uniformity of approach between education and training. An earlier report on the reform of Scottish school-leaving examinations had rejected modularisation, despite recognising that short, 'bite-sized' courses and assessments might improve access to qualifications by a wider range of students. The reasons for rejection were identified as a fragmentation and trivialisation of otherwise coherent educational courses, a gravitation towards over-assessment and assessment-driven learning, and unavoidable commitments to internal assessment by teachers because the process of fragmentation would create serious obstacles to external marking.

In the event, these reservations counted for very little. The vocationalism championed by the Scottish schools inspectorate triumphed at the expense of what Paterson describes as 'concern with the cultural purpose of education' that had been a feature of previous Scottish educational reforms. The idea of curricular breadth was adopted uncritically:

> Nowhere ... was there a discussion of what breadth might be, philosophically or educationally. It was equated quite simply with students doing lots of types of courses, which can at best be described as a principle of management. Breadth could then quite readily be associated with modularization.
>
> (Paterson, 2000, pp. 73–4)

These reforms were accompanied by a shift of emphasis away from the traditional 'norm-referenced' evaluation of student performance to 'criterion-referencing'. Instead of assessing individual student performance in relation to the standards achieved by all other students, individual performances were judged according to prescriptions concerning what they should know or be able to do. This distinction is not absolute but it does register a clear move in the direction of pre-emptive definitions of what knowledge is valuable and appropriate to particular stages of educational development, and this has always been a matter of deep philosophical controversy. At the same time, the modular approach involves a systematic decomposition of subjects into self-contained units which limit the scope for able students to adapt, cross-reference and relate knowledge gained in one area of study to another in a creative and critical manner. The new emphasis is less on analysis and evaluation than on demonstrating conformity to tightly pre-specified and epistemologically arbitrary definitions of various subject matters.

The concrete example of literacy testing in the UK provides a useful preliminary illustration of this trend. In its review of the second year of the National Literacy Strategy, the Office for Standards in Education reported that attainment in writing had remained almost static and failed to reflect improved attainment in reading. One expert commentator observed that a genuine and sustained improvement in reading would generate a sustained improvement in writing and that the latter is a more reliable thermometer of literacy than the mere ability to retrieve information from a text (Gibbons, 27–04–01, p. 23). This clash of definitions is about much more than the technicalities of pupil assessment. At stake is the concept of literacy itself, its depth, purpose and the coherence of its component elements because the public system of assessment inevitably drives the pedagogy, influencing and sanctioning certain popular and professional interpretations of the abilities in question. To maintain that some pupils are good readers but poor writers might be compared profitably to the claim that others are able to talk fluently but with little understanding of what they are saying.

Now philosophical and educational issues of the kind in question have a clear bearing on the concept of educational efficiency with which this chapter is concerned. That is especially the case where there may be substantial differences in conceptions of the purposes of education, or, for that matter, the purposes of teaching traditional subject matters. And the difficulties arising from the imposition of official definitions of educational efficiency or effectiveness are clearly illustrated by controversies about the teaching and assessment of English (though not only English) that surrounded the Scottish examinations fiasco. For one of the accusations levelled by many teachers of this subject against the Higher Still reforms was that they had redefined and degraded it. After many years of consensus about the importance of studying literature for its own sake and to encourage the criticism and appreciation of a variety of uses of language, the new curriculum changed the goalposts. Learning English became a utilitarian matter of achieving linguistic 'competence' for everyday or vocational purposes rather than that of communicating a broad cultural and linguistic heritage within which such instrumentalism was only a contingent element. Despite a petition by nearly half the English teachers in Scotland, the Higher Still Development Unit proceeded with the reforms as though the only relevant issues were administrative or technical in character:

> the inspectorate and ultimately the government were implicitly saying that the purposes of the entire reform were not officially open for debate. The aims and philosophy of Higher Still having been settled by the inspectors and the politicians, any objections that teachers raised could be about no more than the details of implementation.
>
> (Paterson, 2000, pp. 90–3)

The political response to widespread accusations that the inspectorate had arrogantly disregarded the extent of teachers' disagreement was prompt removal by the Education Minister of its role in determining curricular change – a peremptory decision which might have satisfied many critics but which did little to address an important question about how such a concentration of power in so few hands, affecting a whole generation of young people, had come about in the first place.

Politicians and administrators offered repeated assurances about management reforms and adjustments to the new system but doubts remained about its ability to deliver examination results accurately and on time by the following year. Much concern focused on the 'robustness' of the SQA's information technology systems to process the data generated by student assessments.[2] It might have been more appropriate to question the presuppositions on which the new regime was founded and its ability to provide a coherent account of the true educational significance of that avalanche of data. For as Paterson noted, the shift towards modularisation seemed to express a belief that established fields of knowledge can be subdivided into discrete units of competence for the purposes of assessment (*ibid.*, pp. 161–2). And that is true only of very circumscribed aspects of any of the intellectual traditions that comprise human knowledge.

Undeterred by philosophical controversy and the ominous precedent in Scotland the previous year, the Qualifications and Curriculum Authority proceeded with radical modifications to the traditional GCE Advanced Level examination regime in England. That system, which had enjoyed a global reputation as the 'gold standard' for school-leaving qualifications, now featured essentially the same convergence between educational and vocational objectives and strategies as had its Scottish precursor, notable among which were the putative 'key' skills of communication, numeracy and information technology.[3]

The newly introduced vocational A level began what promised to be an undistinguished career with disturbingly high failure rates among students who attempted the first module early in 2001.

Why philosophy?

Claims that questions of a philosophical nature are prior to and definitive of any coherent account of educational effectiveness or efficiency are unlikely to satisfy many of those whose main preoccupation is the urgent need to raise educational standards for practical social and economic purposes. A hint of this attitude was contained in the Scottish Higher Still Development Unit's response to the objections by many English teachers that the reforms tended to degrade their subject to one of mere 'communicational competence'. According to Paterson, the Unit cited an alleged opinion in the further education sector that English was an academic, literary subject unrelated to 'real world' communication needs (Paterson, 2000, p. 93). But the identification of skills and competencies appropriate to 'real world' needs in opposition to traditional educational objectives inevitably involves arbitrary, stipulative judgments about the nature of that 'real world'. In addition to poets, playwrights and novelists, the real world includes journalists, lawyers, scientists, public servants and any number of other professionals whose linguistic abilities and literary experiences are crucial to the practice of their callings. But ordinary citizens in democratic society can only participate effectively if they share the rich and varied languages of these professions to whatever extent is sufficient for them to make informed, critical judgments about their social and political roles and influences. To adopt definitions of need in a context of specialised vocational training and then import them into education is to violate a fundamental liberty of democratic citizenship by preemptively defining the world that the citizen occupies.

More than a decade before the crisis in the Scottish qualifications system, Harvey Siegel had condemned the habitual aversion of educational policy-makers and practitioners to philosophical questions about the aims of education. In a contribution to an American debate on the subject of 'minimum competency testing' involving principles of a kind which were later to assume such practical immediacy in Scotland he observed that:

> Any philosophically defensible view of the aims of education –
> and especially the view that critical thinking is an important
> educational aim – will preclude conceiving of education along the

occupational training lines that the needs assessment approach assumes.

(Siegel, 1988, p. 122)

The concept of 'needs assessment' had been invoked against previous accusations[4] that criterion-referencing falsely implied the existence of absolute standards of value against which student performance could be assessed. One counter-claim sought to mitigate the charge of arbitrariness by proposing empirical research to determine the 'real world' requirements of specific clienteles for various kinds and levels of skill. But how, asked Siegel (Siegel, 1988, p. 124), do we decide what skills a student will need in the future, when that future is undetermined, and if we are committed to the educational ideal of enabling students to *create* their own futures, rather than to have to submit to them? Even if we could know what skills might be most in demand at a future time when present-day students reach their maturity, we could not be justified in manipulating an entire education system to secure proficiency in them on that empirical basis; there are prior, philosophical questions concerning the character and justification of the social order.

Siegel's objection goes to the heart of the educational issue. Vocational training has its perfectly justifiable, socially necessary place, as a moment's reflection on the importance of nurses, electricians, surgeons or carpenters will confirm. But to fudge the distinction between that and education, such a dominant trend in contemporary policies, is to envisage a thoroughly servile society. The idea of assessing particular social or economic needs, of appealing to the apparent requirements of the 'real' world, as a criterion of educational practice and assessment is a huge step beyond anything that could be described as an education policy. It amounts to a redefinition of social rights and obligations and the values associated with them. And foremost among the new values which are proposed is the inviolability of the socio-economic *status quo* as the measure of what is, and what is not, worth knowing and doing. In this down-to-earth, businesslike spirit, a spokesperson for the Scottish Confederation of British Industry complained that vocationalism in schools had not gone far enough; the 'core skills' defined in educational policy documents had been given undue prominence over 'work-related values and attitudes' and 'customer service skills' (Farrow, 05–05–00). On *that* needs assessment, the efficiency of education would be measured by the profitability of the supermarket and the burger-bar.

Moreover, the contemporary official preoccupation, 'generic core

skills', seems to be intended to register practical educational commitment to fundamentals. It is, however, a deeply equivocal notion that
exploits different connotations of words like 'generic' and 'core', to
facilitate the arbitrary selection of substantive features of these putative skills by whatever authority happens to be in control of a regime
of continuous assessment. Thus 'literacy', to take the previously cited
example, is typically broken down into sub-components like listening,
speaking, reading and writing. Taken in conjunction with the trend
towards continuous, modular assessment, the terminology encourages reductive, stipulative definitions of knowledge and skills,
drastically limiting the scope for creative and critical thought. As
long ago as 1988 one professional body commented on proposals for
the statutory UK national curriculum in English:

> The move to operationalise [these proposals] with respect to
> English immediately reveals the difficulties involved in the
> construction of levels of attainment for the subject. We are aware
> ... that these hierarchies are crude and arbitrary ... The danger is
> that the lists will be self-justifying, establishing and creating the
> products they describe. Once defined within the Act, these hierar-
> chies will set a supposed order of development to which teachers
> will teach and against which children will be tested.
>
> (Kimberley *et al.*, 1992, p. 3)[5]

Literacy, whether redefined as communicative competence or not, is
'generic' in the all too obvious sense that it is a necessary qualification
not only for most occupations in a modern technological society but
also for participation in a literate culture and for effective citizenship.
The new appellation adds nothing to this unless, perhaps, the words
'core' and 'skill' convey a subliminal message that the 'skill' in question
is henceforth to be interpreted in a more basic, functional sense for the
purposes of teaching and assessing individual children. These
purposes are different, however, from the more provisional use made
of the concept of 'functional literacy' by the OECD, for example, as a
broad and preliminary indication of comparative levels of basic educational attainment in different countries.

No matter how indefinite the true scope of literacy, it does rest on
what might be described as tangible 'core' skills: the ability to decode
written symbols and to understand and apply the basic rules of syntax.
This fact in no way mitigates the charge of arbitrariness, however,
because basic though they may be, these psychological functions are
profoundly complex, poorly understood and a subject of continuing

scholarly debate, as I discuss in my next chapter. A principal ground for concern is that political pressure for nationally standardised measures of achievement at the different stages of education promotes confusion between these core elements of literacy and the idea of literacy as itself a core skill; that the latter notion sanctions a too-exclusive concentration on presumed 'basics' and inappropriately mechanistic forms of teaching and assessment.

On the other hand, the notion of assessable generic core skills now also encompasses such nebulous qualities as 'personal effectiveness', sometimes described as 'working with others', in addition to 'problem solving' which I have already mentioned. A serious difficulty about the assessment of individual children on the lines of the first of these putative skills is that they are relational in character and are likely to vary unpredictably according to social context. Not only do patterns of co-operation between age-matched peers in classrooms offer extremely limited and socially untypical opportunities to judge abilities of this kind, but the assessment itself is laden with value judgments about how they correlate with relationships in the wider world. How, for example, could personal assertiveness be weighed reliably against respectful attention to the views of others without some assessment of the cogency of those views? What estimation of personal effectiveness, other than a morally judgmental one, is possible in the case of the able student who shuns the co-operation of less able peers in a private pursuit of excellence? Does a predisposition for proximal, face-to-face co-operation bear any logical or psychological comparison with the equally co-operative but more distal activity of scientists involved in an acrimonious exchange of scholarly papers about a disputed issue? The point is that by identifying broadly indicative descriptions of behaviour as 'skills' we falsely impute a specific character to them. By attaching the appellation 'generic' to those skills, we create the illusion of identifiable, underlying psychological mechanisms that can be called into operation irrespective of subject-matter. In fact what we do is to create a semantic vacuum that can be filled, if at all, by the arbitrary preferences of those who wield greatest power in the determination of educational policy and practice. And, in the context of assessment-driven curricula, this arbitrariness involves the danger that children are judged *as people* rather than on what they know and on what they can do with that knowledge. The definition of educational efficiency is not the prerogative of politicians or officialdom. Lindsay Paterson concluded his review of the collapse of the new Scottish examinations regime[6] with an appeal for a sustained public debate about the philosophy and purposes of education that has a compelling logic:

> Education affects us all. It is simply too valuable to be left to any single social group. It is certainly too important to be left to educational experts.
>
> (Paterson, 2000, p. 96)

6 Learning, teaching and learning to learn

Some epistemological perspectives

> Whatever does not spring from a man's free choice, or is only the result of instruction and guidance, does not enter into his very being, but still remains alien to his true nature; he does not perform it with truly human energies, but merely with mechanical exactness.
>
> (von Humboldt, 1969, p. 76)

My main aim in this chapter is to register a point that is seriously neglected in the highly politicised atmosphere of contemporary educational policy-making. This is that many of the educational questions that have been resolved by *fiat* in recent years have been features of a perennial debate concerning the nature of knowledge, how we acquire it and the appropriate institutional means of communicating it. The enduring character of this debate has little to do with scholarly fastidiousness or disconnectedness from what some complacently identify as the 'real world'. It reflects the deep complexity of the issues involved and the fact that disagreements about them are, in a real sense, also disagreements about the nature of society and how we should live. A free, democratic society is not only one which *tolerates* disagreements about questions of this kind; it is itself an institutionalised expression of the conflict of ideas and values which arises when critical inquiry and a quest for truth replace passive assimilation of officially authorised myths and nostrums.

Recent controversy in British education has not been confined to questions about practical aspects of teaching and assessment. It encompasses the conduct of research in education and, by implication, conceptions of the nature, scope and social purposes of education. Chapter 1 opened with a few remarks about the contrasting paradigms to which apparent allies in this debate actually have appealed. James Tooley's critique of the quality of some contemporary educational research was welcomed by the former Chief Inspector of Schools,

Chris Woodhead, as a stimulus for improving standards 'in the class-room' (Tooley, 1998). According to Woodhead, part of the rationale for commissioning Tooley's report had been similar reservations about educational research expressed by David Hargreaves. However, as I pointed out, Woodhead's introductory remarks ignored Hargreaves' well-publicised belief in a need to dismantle traditional educational systems in favour of 'an infinite variety of multiple forms of teaching and learning' (Hargreaves, 1997a). That vision transcends the limits of the contemporary classroom and the kind of educational research which might be conducted within them, though government policy has nevertheless tended to reflect a myopic preoccupation with learning and teaching in that now traditional setting.

In the spring of 2001 *The Times Higher Education Supplement* reported a hostile response by a number of educational specialists to initial proposals for 'an apparently common-sense solution to the problem of making academic research relevant to the real world' (*THES*, 13–04–01, p. 8). These proposals by the National Education Research Forum, which included David Hargreaves as Chief Executive of the Qualifications and Curriculum Authority, were for a national educational research strategy (NERF website, 01–05–01). NERF's general aim of stimulating high-quality, evidence-based research included more specific objectives. There was felt to be a need for advice and guidance on priorities for research that would involve the estab-lishment, in advance, of criteria for determining relevance and quality. In addition, a strategy for achieving endorsement of these criteria by the funders and publishers of research was recommended. The draft was immediately attacked for expressing 'a philosophically bankrupt view of education' which, while ostensibly recognising the need for public debate about its nature and purposes, threatened to 'foreclose on that debate by defining the nature and purpose of education'.[1] Other criticisms concerned the threat to academic freedom posed by the centralising aspirations of the NERF proposals in the context of a highly politicised education agenda. As another critic put it: 'In a democracy, it is important that a significant part of education research is free to investigate issues that lie outside, or even directly counter to, those political priorities'.[2] The response to these criticisms by NERF was that rather than attempting to predetermine the direction of educational research, it was indeed opening up a well-informed debate about 'the nature and purposes of education'.

The aim of this chapter is to reflect on the awesome scope of this question and its historical controversiality. Despite the confident rhetoric of governments about 'the learning society', 'lifelong learning' and 'the knowledge economy', the ways in which we learn and the status of the knowledge and understanding that we acquire always have been subjects of controversy. These questions are too profound and many-sided to admit of anything like final answers and the consequences of pretending that they do may be dangerous.

What is education? The question of parameters

Stipulative definitions of education, popular in contemporary politics, tend to be formulated within the narrow parameters established by the comparatively recent institution of universal state-maintained schooling. Broadly conceived, education is a process of cultural transmission. This truism is more significant than it might first seem if we take account of the diversity of the ways in which that transmission takes place and of the patterns of culture with which they are associated.

All human societies bequeath cultural repertoires to rising generations. These may be extremely idiosyncratic and stable over vast periods of time, like the ancient 'songlines' of Australian tribal society, or subject to gradual evolution. In rare cases they may develop explosively to confront us with an enigma. This was famously the case with some diminutive Greek communities of the first pre-Christian millennium. They generated the first examples of systematic critical inquiry and an abundant, formidable scholarship – despite their political instability and the comparative simplicity of their predominantly agricultural economies.

Whichever of these patterns of cultural transmission is dominant in any given society, all represent differential relationships between 'culture' and 'cognition'. We understand these relationships imperfectly: in terms of broad generalisations and often controversial theories about the social consequences of environmental change, cultural assimilation and conflict – or technological developments which may have exponential cultural implications.[3] And, of course, differing patterns of teaching and learning are implicated in these variable relationships between culture and cognition. Much of the contemporary interest in the posthumous works of the Soviet psychologist Lev Vygotsky reflects growing awareness of the complex, poorly understood ways in which the particularities of a culture are symbolised and internalised by individuals in the dialogue between teachers and learners in the broadest sense of these latter terms.[4]

Those who demand an education relevant to the needs of the 'real world' are inclined to forget that it was once authoritatively defined as the earth-centred product of a single act of creation. That view was rigidly enforced even when Galileo, inspired by the Greeks of two thousand years earlier, revived their tradition of critical debate about the nature of reality and asserted an individual right of inquiry into that.[5] The origins of that cognitive transformation in ancient Greece are of more than antiquarian significance, however. They mark the exfoliation of a human ability to view mythological explanation dispassionately or critically and to entertain alternative hypotheses. The radicalism of this emancipation from universal forms of mythopoeic explanation is easily underestimated by modern minds accustomed to the explicit use of metaphor, symbolism and represen-tation. As Frankfort has pointed out, 'it is this tacit or outspoken appeal to reason, no less than the independence from "the prescriptive sanctities of religion", which places early Greek philosophy in the sharpest contrast with the thought of the ancient Near East' (Frankfort *et al.*, 1968, p. 262).

Quite apart from the direct influence of Socratic, Platonic and Aristotelian ideas in the development of educational thought, the unprecedented achievement of the tiny Greek city states of antiquity commands attention as a phenomenon which cries out for explanation. The fact that they *were* unprecedented raises numerous questions about possible relationships between different physical and social envi-ronments and modes of human cognition. It prompts questions about the interplay between formal and informal modes of learning and teaching. Apart from the intellectual influence of the Sophists, the pattern of schooling for the privileged youth in the Greek *polis* appears to have been a rather unremarkable one involving rote memo-risation of the Homeric epics, floggings and gymnastics. And, of course, the Greek spirit of critical inquiry flourished for only a brief period before more or less disappearing for nearly two millennia until it was revived in the seventeenth century. This must contribute a sense of urgency to questions about the sustainability of the institutions that encourage and disseminate critical and scientific thought, as Popper warned.[6]

For Mill, the Greeks were also of more than antiquarian interest; they afforded a basis of comparison with the educational methods that prevailed in nineteenth-century society:

> Modern education is all *cram* ... The world already knows every-thing, and has only to tell it to its children, who, on their part, have only to hear, and lay it to rote (not to *heart*) ... Is it any wonder that, thus educated, we should decline in genius? That the

ten centuries of England or France cannot produce as many illustrious names as the hundred and fifty years of little Greece?

(Mill, 1946, pp. 28–40)

It is symptomatic of the tunnel vision that afflicts modern perspectives on education that Mill is rarely counted among its leading theorists, despite the fact that he returned to the subject repeatedly in his otherwise influential essays on society and politics, not least in *On Liberty* and in his *Autobiography*. The explicit purpose of the latter work was to leave a record of his own education that he described as unusual and remarkable, as indeed it was by any standard. He maintained that the outcome of that experiment had given him the educational advantage of a quarter of a century over his contemporaries despite what he described as his modest natural intellectual endowments (Mill, 1965b, p. 11).

Reasons for the neglect of Mill as an educational thinker of the first rank are perhaps obvious. His own education had been intense and rigorous, not to say severe. It was conducted at home by his father within a paradigm which is now unfamiliar, as an experiment to demonstrate the indefinite intellectual potential of all individuals and the unlimited social and political benefits which might accrue from an education that prioritised critical, discursive inquiry (*ibid.*, pp. 68–9). And it was a quite deliberate preparation for the unrealised ideal of democratic citizenship. However, his enthusiasm for the ideal was to be dampened by intimations of popular authoritarianism that he read in the continuing failure of public education to encourage individual critical autonomy and even to discourage and repudiate it (Brown, 1998, pp. 159–80).

Mill's ideas on learning and teaching occupied different parameters from those in which modern debates on the subject are conducted. His focus of attention was not the institutional setting that has since become almost synonymous with the idea of education. He was not only indifferent to any kind of programmatic pedagogy, but hostile to the imposition of any method other than that of 'free inquiry', an uncompromising Socratic search for truth. One person cannot *teach* another but may *suggest* to another by questioning, he insisted. That 'slavish, mechanical thing which the moderns call education' was inimical to intellectual power and love of truth because 'the reasoner is shown his conclusions, and informed beforehand that he is expected to arrive at them'. Opinions were received into the mind where they lay 'as forms of words, lifeless and devoid of meaning'. By contrast, pupils should be encouraged to interrogate their own consciousnesses, to observe and experiment upon themselves for no other process could lead to genuine understanding (Mill, 1963, pp. 74–5).

Despite Mill's reputation as a pioneering theorist of liberal democracy, it is all too easy to dismiss his view of the relationship between education and politics as anachronistic. After all, one of his aspirations, universal state-supported education, has been realised on a huge international scale. The paradigm appears to have changed. It is instructive, therefore, to consider some aspects of education that have remained disconcertingly constant. For instance, Richard Paul has deplored the 'critical thinking' deficit among American students in the 1990s and the responsibility of the public schools system for it in language that resonates strikingly with Mill's:

> Most educational commentators and most of the general public seem to agree on at least one thing: the schools are in deep trouble. Many graduates, at all levels, are characterized as lacking the abilities to read, write and think with a minimum level of clarity, coherence and a critical/analytical exactitude. Most commentators agree as well that a significant part of the problem is a pedagogical diet excessively rich in memorization and superficial rote performance and insufficiently rich in, if not devoid of, autonomous critical thought.
>
> (Paul, 1990, p. 102)

The international 'critical thinking' debate in the philosophy of education has gathered momentum in recent years and has generated a substantial literature reflecting a variety of contrasting and contradictory views. Ironically, the mantra of 'critical thinking' has found its way into the catalogue of 'key skills' in official educational curricula without acknowledgement of that controversy. This forecloses on discussion of at least one crucial issue. Is 'critical thinking' a term that denotes the proper educational approach to subject matters in general or is it a generalisable repertoire of mental abilities, irrespective of subject matters, which can be applied to them successfully? That has been a kernel of philosophical debate and it is fundamental to the concept of education itself and the methods appropriate to it. It is also closely connected with an ancient epistemological concern that is now pivotal to the new discipline of cognitive science; what can we know and how do we know it?

Yet uncertainty and disagreement are rarely reflected in the confident pronouncements of politicians and their officials on the subject of sound educational method. Much of the debate about how best to teach children is barely, if at all, distinguishable from questions about the most effective ways of managing our institutions. Indeed, the managerial role of educators is not only more openly acknowledged now than previously; as I have argued in previous chapters, it has become all-pervading.

The problem is that schooling is now ubiquitous and has been nearly uniform for well over a century in its most concrete essentials: teachers, classrooms and cohorts of age-matched pupils supported by labyrinthine administrations. Education policies and practices betray a systematic confusion between the requirements for order and account-ability in large-scale organisations and the idiosyncratic needs and potentials of individual learners. I think this point is well illustrated by the previously cited case of Summerhill School and the UK govern-ment's demand for *timetabled lessons, prescribed study programmes, systematic assessment and attainment 'in line with national expectations'*. It is as though these requirements describe the necessary conditions for effective learning. They do not; they describe a hier-archy of organisational needs: for educators and students in mass institutions to be in the same place at the same time; for all levels of management to know who is supposed to be learning what, and when; for easily digestible evidence of student and school performances for the public domain; for governments to demonstrate firm commitment to improve educational standards to a discontented media and public.

There is another measure of the extent to which we confound these distinct aspects of education that should, incidentally, meet demands for 'evidence-based' research. Most people are likely to find it deeply counter-intuitive that large numbers of children, from varied back-grounds, educated entirely outside the formal school system, significantly outperform their school-educated peers. Yet, as I will demonstrate in Chapter 8, the evidence is that they do so according to exactly the same criteria as those used for student assessment in schools. One puzzling aspect of this phenomenon is that successful learning, as officially defined and measured, does not seem to depend on the availability of trained teachers. Now it is one thing to dispense with the physical and organisational apparatus of education. To be able to dispose of the specialist expertise of professional educators raises even more basic questions about the necessary conditions for the transmission of knowledge. For it seems preposterous to suggest that untutored or inexpertly tutored children should be able to acquire even the most basic elements of a cultural repertoire that has been accumu-lated laboriously in the course of human history and then only by certain societies. Children cannot be expected to make the transition from the Palaeolithic to modernity by their own unaided efforts.

Part of the answer must lie in the obstacles to the effective transmission of specialised knowledge erected by the institutions of mass-teaching, including the limited and declining professional autonomy of teachers. As Mill argued, the ideals of educational excellence and critical autonomy may be achieved only where expertise is recognised as the ability to know how to pose appropriate questions and engage in discursive inquiry with the learner rather than to act as a conduit for the prescriptions of others. The ability to parrot a form of words or to perform an algorithm might meet certain standards of achievement, but it does not necessarily amount to understanding. Once again, the fundamental problem is about the nature of knowledge, how it is acquired and how it is integrated within the unique matrix of an individual's consciousness. These are complex questions. Nevertheless, there is a value in reflecting, even briefly, on certain attempts to answer them which have a direct bearing on the current vogue in educational policy-making for providing authoritative solutions before the problems have been properly considered.

Some problems about the nature of learning

The abrupt imposition across formal school curricula of the concept of generic 'core' or 'key' skills is symptomatic of modern impatience with philosophical justifications. In notable respects it is a variation on a theme explored by Plato in his accounts of intellectual confrontations between Socrates and those individual teachers and rhetoricians known as the Sophists. The issue then, as now, was whether intellectual skills could be imparted by explicit instruction, through the inculcation of technique. Socrates disputed this on the ground that instruction obstructs the development of knowledge by usurping the learner's task of grappling with the implications of concepts and integrating them coherently with others in their intellectual repertoire.

The argument of dialogues like the *Gorgias* was that what often passes for understanding is a parody of the knowledge acquired through that critical process; that what are often accepted as skills and abilities owe their plausibility to their parasitic relationship to genuine inquiry but are themselves intrinsically vacuous. Anderson pointed out a contemporary implication of Socrates' criticism of Sophistic skills-training: that it 'was cutting at the root of the modern psychological theory of abilities' because those abilities, 'taken by themselves instead of as part of the general activity of the individual, are falsified and misdirected' (Anderson, 1963, p. 208). That modern version of the tendency in question is so widely accepted that it has become a tacit presupposition of much teaching and research. Typical of this has been a conviction that studies of artistic creativity, for example, may safely disregard aesthetic criteria in the search for 'underlying' psychological abilities (Vernon, 1970, pp. 9–10), an assumption which begs the question about the reliability with which manifestations of creativity could be identified. The task requires immersion in a subject-matter or a tradition because instances of creativity are intelligible only against that background.

Anderson's observation concerning that psychological theory of ability has been echoed by Chomsky. Psychology, he maintains, has been diverted into side channels through failure to recognise the logical priority of the structure of systems of knowledge and belief in the explanation of human behaviour (Chomsky, 1972a, p. 44). He indicates the undesirable consequences of educational approaches that violate this logical requirement by redesigning curricula to exploit techniques for 'rapid and efficient inculcation of skilled behaviour'. The problem is not that it is difficult to construct objective tests to demonstrate the effectiveness of a given method in achieving particular outcomes in the terms defined:

> But success of this sort will not demonstrate that an important educational goal has been achieved ... What little we know about human intelligence would at least suggest something quite different: that by diminishing the range and complexity of materials presented to the inquiring mind, by setting behaviour in fixed patterns, these methods may harm and distort the normal development of creative abilities.
>
> (Chomsky, 1992, p. 101)

Originality does not exist exclusively at the frontiers of the sciences and other disciplines. Innovatory thought, as Mill pointed out, is not the prerogative of the 'future discoverer' who must first learn all that is already known in a particular field and only then to commence 'an entirely new series of intellectual operations' to enlarge human knowledge. In Chomsky's account of linguistic creativity, understanding at any level, from the most elementary to the most sophisticated, involves recursive and recombinatorial operations. According to his anti-behaviourist thesis, children routinely utter intelligible sentences that they cannot have heard previously in their limited experience, indeed sentences that may never have been uttered by anyone before. There is at least an analogy here with the indeterminate but rule-governed matrix that comprises human knowledge. The theorems of mathematics, the methodologies of historians and social scientists as well as the art of the poet or the musician, are not closed systems. They are fields that are explored continuously from different starting points within that unique matrix of each individual's cognitive repertoire and personal history. Just as intelligibility in language depends on the observance of syntactic and semantic rules but is capable of indefinite development, so the products of human thought are rule-governed but open-ended.

The temptation to stipulate methodology in advance is probably greatest in subjects which are the most manifestly rule-governed. But even in the rigorous, deductive field of mathematics it poses the danger of foreclosing on originality by over-identifying algorithmic procedures with the mental processes involved in calculation. In an era obsessed with the assessment of children from the earliest ages, it is worth recalling that identical observable performances by two children on a simple arithmetical calculation do not register identical cognitive operations. One child might correctly deduce that $3+3+3=9$ without sharing the other's awareness of its equivalence to the multiplication function, $3\times3=9$. The rather obvious point of this example is that there are limits to the informative content of formal assessments. But, by the same token, the formal notations and modes of expression characteristic of fields of knowledge cannot summarise understanding with any finality because they are not identical with it; they are not *isomorphic* with understanding, though there is often a temptation to treat them as if they were. And this is more likely to happen in the case of continuous unit assessment than in more traditional terminal assessment because of the heavier onus on the designer to compartmentalise and thus formalise test content as a putative measure of understanding.

The physicist Richard Feynman indicted the confusion between algorithmic method and the nature of conceptualisation in the 'new math' scheme introduced in California grade schools in the 1960s that he had been invited to evaluate. In his judgment it was unjustifiably rigid: 'We must leave freedom for the mind to wander about in trying to solve the problems ... The successful user of mathematics is practically an inventor of new ways of obtaining answers in given situations' (Gleick, 1994, p. 401). One famous long-term series of studies, in particular, illustrates the pitfalls in describing the development of understanding in formal and general terms.

Cognitive stage theory

Piaget and his Genevan school have conducted some of the most systematic research into the intellectual development of children through a putatively universal succession of age-related cognitive stages. As I mentioned in Chapter 2, the Plowden Report commended this theory partly because it was based on empirical investigation; to borrow a more recent phrase, it was 'evidence-based' research. Yet it has become increasingly controversial, not only because educational practitioners drew arguably incorrect inferences from it, but because predictions central to the theory have often been confounded by further empirical research (e.g. Donaldson, 1990). Other critics have indicted the entire Piagetian attempt to found a theory of knowledge on biology and psychology as conceptually flawed.

Slight modifications of Piagetian tests of children's abilities to 'conserve volume' or to understand logical class-inclusion statements have produced results at variance with Piaget's conclusions, even though they were said to involve 'the same' underlying logical procedures. Some experiments have demonstrated that children can be taught to perform logical tasks that they had been unable to do previously without help. Objections that this amounts to 'cheating' on a test designed to investigate the stage at which children develop particular mental faculties raise a more profound question originally addressed by Plato: *if* a task of a particular logical form can be learned *at all*, does this not entail the pre-existence of a corresponding logical structure in the learner's mind?[7] Another variation on Piagetian themes has tested his thesis concerning the reputedly animistic nature of young children's thought. Although they may be inclined to talk as though inanimate objects are alive, it turns out that they are less likely to agree that they share certain characteristics with living creatures like the ability to grow or feel pain. The concept of animism breaks down into alternative possibilities that include lack of experience of uses of the term 'alive' and a tenuous grasp of the distinctions adults draw between object functions and animate behaviour. In other words, word-meaning accumulates and is gradually integrated within the various *social* institutions of language. Words do not have unique meanings and there is, as a result, no possibility that they can be comprehended at a single moment. Nor can they have the same semantic import for children and adults in everyday situations or in the experimenter's laboratory (Vygotsky, 1989, p. 61). Consequently, as Vygotsky pointed out against Piaget, we cannot arrive at uncontaminated 'forms of thinking inherent in the child's intelligence'; they are enveloped in a veil of language that we cannot penetrate and they evolve through discourse.

One kind of response to the disconfirming instances I have just mentioned is that removal of the ambiguities in the original, sparse experimental settings by the use of more familiar objects changes the logical character of the problem for the young experimental subject.[8] A counter-response has been that these differing performances are the result only of different *operational definitions* of the problem in question, that children must use the same 'logical abilities' to succeed on the new tests as those investigated by the original ones. Tests of a pure and invariant logical ability are contaminated by other factors like 'social context, language, perception, attention and memory' (Siegel and Hodkin, 1982, p. 65).

There is, however, yet another explanation, as I have contended at greater length elsewhere (Brown, 1998, pp. 22–30). This is that the 'contamination' in question is inherent in all such experimental situations. There is no way of distinguishing in the fundamental sense required by the Piagetian enterprise between the language and social context of a test-situation and the experimental subject's apprehensions of the logical structure of a problem. Experimental apparatus is intrinsically devoid of significance. It is only by invoking the semantic meaning of the linguistic exchanges, the language-dependent symbols and the social relationships in the test situation that a logical task can be specified. Language remains the common denominator of intelligibility, even in those situations where we try to eliminate it for experimental purposes. It is reciprocal and dynamic. For this reason the modelling of generalised mental abilities, no matter how useful as an heuristic strategy, cannot achieve the necessary purchase to offer a 'bottom-up' account of human learning. That, if it is to be found at all, lies in the reciprocities of dialogue and the mutual exploration of ideas. Dennis Phillips warns against Piaget's attempt to attribute the characteristics of abstract, formal systems to the mental operations of his subjects: 'we may be led to conclude that the formalism of the theoretical system must be directly represented by an isomorphic formalism in the mind of the child' (Phillips, 1982, p. 23). Or, as Wittgenstein said of our tendency to assert a preconceived idea as something to which reality must correspond, '[w]e predicate of the thing what lies in the method of representing it' (Wittgenstein, 1968, PI 104).

The forms of knowledge

Another critic of the habit of treating logical principles as though they were laws governing mental processes was Paul Hirst. Hirst also attacked the idea that general descriptions like 'effective thinking' can be specified independently of the criteria established in a public domain comprising traditional categories of understanding. These public criteria of intelligibility and validity are the necessary basis of judgments about such generic descriptions as 'effective thinking' in, say, mathematics, literary appreciation or biology. However, he attempted to move beyond this cogent general criticism of educational aims couched in terms of psychological and affective states to identify the categories, or forms of knowledge, in which these criteria have become established. This proved to be a move too far because, as I will argue, the accumulation of traditional modes of understanding has been the result of long-standing critical discourse during which even the logical and methodological foundations of disciplines have been subject to constant, sometimes revolutionary, change.

Perhaps ironically, Hirst was one of a group of philosophers of education, including R.S. Peters and R.F. Dearden, who proved influential in the reaction against Plowden's emphasis on child-centred education. Their particular contribution had been to weaken resistance to emerging political and populist pressures for state intervention and the specification of educational objectives which eventually took the form of a national curriculum and curricular guidelines (Darling, 1994).[9] Hirst attacked generic definitions of educational ends 'in terms of mental abilities and independently of fully specifying the forms of knowledge involved'. His broad thesis was that 'understanding the nature of curriculum objectives is first and foremost a matter of understanding what is involved in the acquisition of knowledge' (Hirst, 1974, p. 27). More specifically, Hirst defended a long-standing epistemological tradition that originated with the Greeks and included Matthew Arnold, R.G. Collingwood and, notably, Michael Oakeshott. His particular interpretation of that tradition was that:

> the development of mind has been marked by the progressive differentiation in human consciousness of some seven or eight distinguishable cognitive structures ... This is to say that all knowledge and understanding is logically locatable within a number of domains, within, I suggest, mathematics, the physical sciences, knowledge of persons, literature and the fine arts, morals, religion and philosophy.
>
> (*ibid.*, p. 25)

Hirst did not deny that there were overlaps between these different forms of knowledge, though he did describe them as logically distinct from one another, involving elements that are irreducible to any of the others. He spelled out the curricular implications of his thesis in a series of conditionals. If the development of rational minds is the ultimate educational aim, and rationality depends on the acquisition of knowledge, it follows from the logically segregated nature of knowledge that all children should pursue a liberal curriculum that consists, at least, of these seven characterising forms. Now the irony that I mentioned above is that to whatever extent Hirst might have contributed, knowingly or otherwise, to demands for an officially prescribed curriculum, he also assisted the consolidation of political control over education. And that has increasingly encouraged the definition of curricula in terms of the kind of objectives which he repudiated: generalisable skills, affective states and vocational competences.

A factor compounding the irony about Hirst's original position is that his repudiation of these popular objectives was a powerful restatement of the classical argument whereas his case for logically distinct forms of knowledge proved untenable. What he had sought was a characterisation in terms of the internal logical characteristics of cognitive domains, rather than in terms of the traditional metaphysical account of a correlation between the structure of mind and the structure of reality. That, he evidently believed, would help to answer demands for 'an education whose definition and justification are based on the nature and significance of knowledge itself, and not on the predilections of pupils, the demands of society, or the whims of politicians' (*ibid.*, p. 32). But in a later essay he acknowledged that his concept of a liberal education had been explicitly stipulative; the logical relationships between the different forms of knowledge were 'manifestly many and complex' and he was unclear to what extent those relationships could be mapped (*ibid.*, pp. 30–53 and 90–1).

Despite the epistemological problems of defining the forms of knowledge, others were prepared to map out the school curriculum in great detail. Apparently in response to the demands of society and, no doubt, to the whims of politicians, a national curriculum was given statutory force in England and Wales in 1988, though the fallibility of human judgments revealed itself in a succession of almost annual amendments to that canonical definition of worthwhile knowledge. This transition from abstract theory to concrete policy, I suggest, is a reminder of a very real if elusive aspect of human knowledge; it has social, institutional dimensions which are crucial to an understanding of its nature and growth. This point is well illustrated by the weaknesses of an earlier and more architectonic form of 'domain-theory' to which Hirst's thesis bears affinities: Michael Oakeshott's conception of the modes of human experience.

Writing in the early 1930s, Oakeshott was insistent on the mutually exclusive characters of domains of knowledge, describing confusion between disciplines like science, history and philosophy as 'the most fatal of all errors' (Oakeshott, 1933, p. 5). There is, of course, always the possibility of a 'category error' but Oakeshott was not concerned with a case-by-case refutation of category errors; he insisted on a once-for-all criterion to distinguish between the internal logics of the categories of experience that he identified.

Oakeshott presented his thesis in its most elaborate form in *Experience and its Modes*. Three decades later he continued to maintain that 'the languages of history, of philosophy, of science and mathematics – are all of them *explanatory* languages; each of them represents a specific mode of explanation' (Oakeshott, 1967, pp. 327–8, original emphasis). Elsewhere he described these 'languages' as 'logically distinct universes of discourse'. He was unwilling to concede the possibility even of meaningful communication between them other than a 'conversation' in which there is no truth to be discovered, no proposition to be proved and no conclusion to be found. Participants in this discourse simply talk past one another. They do not persuade, inform or refute one another because the criteria of intelligibility are internal to each discrete disciplinary language (Oakeshott, 1967, p. 198).

A philosophical stance of this kind has pedagogic implications. For one thing, the segregation of knowledge involved is inconsistent with the idea of teaching generic skills. There simply are no significant methodological commonalities between Oakeshott's domains. By the same token, the highly specialised character of disciplinary 'languages' seems to imply protracted periods of induction for learners and authoritative interpretation by their teachers. Nor does the idea of a child-centred education, beginning with the needs and interests of the child, meet the stringent requirement for the learner to submit to the epistemic authority of the teacher. Indeed, for Oakeshott school education is 'learning to speak before one has anything significant to say', where 'what is taught must have the qualities of being able to be learned without necessarily being understood' (*ibid.*, p. 306).

Oakeshott's thesis courts the relativistic conclusion that there are no external standards by which to judge the meaning and truth of any proposition within a particular discipline or 'mode of experience'.

They are self-authenticating because there is no general standpoint from which to conduct such an appraisal, though Oakeshott's philosophical analysis seems to be an attempt to do precisely that. The very possibility that novices can learn these disciplines demonstrates that they are rooted in the commonalities of human experience and criteria of intelligibility instantiated in them, no matter how arcane they may become at more sophisticated levels of articulation. Moreover, by portraying diverse modes of experience as seamlessly self-consistent, he overlooks the extent to which unresolved inconsistencies within disciplines have driven critical inquiry, a feature of the growth of knowledge that led Kuhn (below) to characterise it as a succession of 'paradigm shifts'. But there is another serious objection to the invocation of 'unique disciplinary logics' that is such a notable feature of the domain theory expounded by Oakeshott and others.[10] How is such exclusive internal consistency ever achieved? These assertions cry out for explanation in evolutionary terms.

The tendentious nature of this appeal to the rigour of logic reveals itself in Oakeshott's description of history as a 'homogenous, self contained mode of experience' which attempts to 'explain the historical *past* by means of the historical *past* and for the sake of the historical *past*' (Oakeshott, 1967, pp. 145 and 156). I have emphasised the word 'past' because a subsequent stage in Oakeshott's argument was to deny any possible connection between the study of history, the practical concerns of everyday life or the 'plots' and 'themes' of social change which concern the social scientist. This he did by introducing the sceptical claim that history is part of the world of present experience; it is nothing more than present evidence and 'what lies beyond the evidence is actually unknowable'. But this invites logical objections. Can evidence refer only to itself? Could any two or more pieces of evidence be justified as relating to the same thing, if that thing is beyond present knowledge? Are we never justified in believing that an historical document had an author, a context or a point beyond whatever is contained in the words on the page? Historical inquiry inevitably reaches beyond any available present evidence; it involves the presumption that the human motivations and linguistic meanings of former periods approximated sufficiently to those of the present to make it possible to interpret evidence of the past coherently. The definition of a discrete realm of experience that emerges in Oakeshott's account is stipulative, tautological and unsustainable.

Although continuing to insist on the distinctiveness of the modes of experience, Oakeshott did revert occasionally to the imagery of a 'miscellany of utterances' that *only gradually* acquire specific characters (*ibid.*, pp. 151–2). This was a more significant concession than it might at first appear. It was a recognition of the need to describe how specialised inquiry emerged from common forms of understanding, that there is a continuum between the two and therefore standards of mutual intelligibility. And that requires understanding of the social environments and controversies that have fostered developments of this kind. In other words, the specification of a form of knowledge is a sociological and historical task, not simply a logical one. But at this point, the narrow conception of disciplinary-specific logics gives way to the more diffuse notion of evolving, controversial *traditions* of thought. And Oakeshott did indeed use the terminology of tradition effectively as a weapon against his principal intellectual foe. This was the rationalist whose preoccupation with techniques of inquiry and communication reveal an exaggerated faith in the efficacy of abstract rules and principles that can be taught and learned by heart and applied mechanically.

Oakeshott's attack on the vacuity of generic learning strategies was powerful enough for Popper to comment that 'there was not much in the rationalist literature that could be considered an adequate answer to his arguments' (Popper, 1963, p. 121). But Popper's own portrayal of disciplinary understanding is that of traditions of inquiry subject to continuing critical appraisal and development. The acquisition and growth of knowledge are the results of attempting to solve a body of problems identified by preceding investigation in an institutional environment of debate and criticism. The knowledge represented by the great critical traditions is dialogic, conjectural and unfinished.

'Paradigms' and the problem of 'paradigm-shifts'

Physical science, and physics in particular, probably corresponds most closely to popular conceptions of a clearly defined, rigorous discipline susceptible to unambiguous characterisation in terms of logical structure and methodological principles. Yet the difficulties in defining a form of knowledge in terms of internal logical characteristics are perhaps most cogently illustrated by the work of one frequently cited physicist-turned-historian of science. Thomas Kuhn famously proclaimed 'the insufficiency of methodological directives, by themselves, to dictate a unique, substantive conclusion to many sorts of scientific question' (Kuhn, 1970, pp. 3–4). Neither the form nor the occasion of revolutionising scientific developments is predictable from within established conceptual schemata and procedures. The best-known example was the sudden emergence of relativity theory that explained all the phenomena previously explained by classical physics but according to fundamentally different principles, though Kuhn paraded many more examples to illustrate his thesis. According to Kuhn, scientific evolution has consisted of the replacement of one 'paradigm' of normal science by another when an accumulation of internal logical inconsistencies render the original paradigm untenable. But successive paradigms are mutually 'incommensurable' and there is no strictly *logical* reason to prefer one rather than another. Thus, argued Kuhn, no comprehensive definition of a scientific paradigm is possible. Instead, he opts for a sociological characterisation of a science rather than a logical or methodological definition. There is, he claimed, 'no standard higher than the assent of the relevant community' (*ibid.*).

But this retreat to a relativistic criterion, in Kuhn's case the definition of a form of knowledge and a mode of inquiry by its practitioners, is hardly a solution. Science is what the relevant community of scientists say it is. We are entitled to ask what constitutes the 'relevance' of a particular community, especially in the historically familiar context of opposed schools of thought. Clearly, criteria of relevance cannot be deduced by the circular procedure of analysing the Kuhnian paradigm, for it is the absence of such an unambiguous standard that prompted the appeal to communal assent in the first place. Once again, we seem to be confronted with an arbitrary, stipulative definition of a form of knowledge, this time as the result of an attempt to ground rational inquiry on the irrational basis of collective belief. But is scepticism about the nature of knowledge and truth inevitable? Siegel has stated the problem as follows:

> There appears to be a significant tension between the fact that principles evolve and change, on the one hand, and the requirement that they purport to be and are taken to be impartial and universal in order to fulfil their function of governing the definition and assessment of reasons within a rational tradition, on the other. If they evolve and change, how can they be impartial and universal? If impartial and universal, how can they change?
>
> (Siegel, 1988, p. 134)

Criticism, rationality and morality

The tension between changing standards of rationality and the urge to ground human knowledge in absolute certainty was a fundamental concern of Popper's philosophy. He denied that such metaphysical certainty was attainable, associating a craving for it with authoritarian theories of knowledge and with tribal or totalitarian social systems. In *The Logic of Scientific Discovery* he described the central problem of epistemology as that of the growth of knowledge that he considered could best be studied by examining the progress of scientific knowledge (Popper, 1977, p. 15). And the central feature of scientific progress, he maintained, is critical theory testing. No theory can ever be proved beyond all doubt because, as Hume had pointed out, we cannot legislate against the logical possibility that future evidence will render it untenable. And, indeed, both Kuhn and Popper emphasise from different standpoints how frequently scientific thought has been revolutionised by the exposure of errors and inconsistencies in dominant theories. Popper's fallibilistic theory of knowledge, however, had very wide social and political implications. These were aptly summarised by Mill: our best guarantee of the certainty of the beliefs on which we base our actions is 'a standing invitation to the whole world to prove them unfounded' (Mill, 1965a, p. 273). Popper characterised the attitude informing this unconditional willingness to subject our beliefs to testing by others as 'critical rationality'. In other words, both he and Mill reject the seductive idea of a superordinate, constant standard of rationality that is itself at some point beyond rational appraisal.[11]

Throughout his philosophical career Popper upheld the principle that human reason is internally connected to institutions of free inquiry and debate and the critical evaluation of traditional understandings: that the preservation of those institutions required democratic forms of government which safeguarded personal liberties, a condition he immortalised in the phrase 'the open society'. However, the spirit of critical rationality at the heart of this open society was one that Popper recommended on moral rather than epistemological grounds. This was a position he felt compelled to adopt despite its inherent weakness as a mere *assertion* of moral will rather than as a rational conclusion. Rational justifications must come to an end somewhere; '[s]ince all argument must proceed from assumptions, it is plainly impossible to demand that all assumptions should be based on argument'. This ultimate stance he described as 'an irrational *faith in reason*' and also a faith in other human beings (Popper, 1969, pp. 230–1, original emphasis). Now the weakness of Popper's ultimate justification of rationality is not so much that it *is* a moral one, but that it places the critical rationalist on a logical footing with the avowed irrationalist – particularly, as Popper points out, because it is typical of the totalitarian ideologist to claim humanitarian motivations.

The critical rationalist's dilemma consists of an apparent inability to justify reason by reasoned argument, at least in an ultimate sense.

There are, however, some considerations that contribute towards a solution of this dilemma. Siegel, for instance, has underlined the inescapability of demands for rational justification with a parody of the irrationalist's demand: 'why be rational?' In other words, rationality is self-justifying because 'to entertain the question seriously is to acknowledge the force of reasons in ascertaining the answer' (Siegel, 1988, p. 132). Bailey, too, has argued that thoroughgoing critical rationalism, being itself open to the possibility of refutation, places the onus on the would-be critic to construe an effective counter-argument (Bailey, 1998). This latter solution, however, seems to re-assert the paradigm of rational criticism as an ultimate justification of Popper's position. Being open in principle to refutation, his epistemological stance evades the necessity of providing its own justification, but on his own critical rationalist terms. What seems to be required is an examination, however brief, of that notion of *ultimacy* or *finality* that might help to rescue the idea of justification by rational argument from the realms of abstraction to something on a more human scale. I believe this is possible, even if only in outline here, and that the argument should help to relate the foregoing epistemological issues to the question of justifying human rights, and especially educational rights, which I discussed in the final section of Chapter 4. It also helps to bridge the gap between a faith in rationality of the kind Popper expressed and the continuing demand for its justification according to non-arbitrary principles.

My argument in that chapter appealed to the relationship between universal rationality and universal rights. It hinged on the idea of the normative force of truth-telling in all human society and human relationships by virtue of the distinctive human faculty of language. Language (as distinct from the vocal expression of affective states and brute force) regulates social relationships. It defines those relationships in terms that crucially include those of authority and obligation. Yet language is inconceivable in the absence of commitments to truth-telling as a fundamental obligation.[12] The logical point is that mutual intelligibility is definitive of language and it depends on that universal human commitment to the idea of truth. As Popper maintains, 'with the descriptive function of human language, the regulative idea of *truth* emerges, that is, of a description which fits the facts' (Popper, 1972, p. 120).

Deceit and manipulation are, of course, real phenomena. But they are possible only because utterances have commonly agreed meanings, because there are common standards for determining what is and what is not the case. Words have at least a core of dependable meaning, even if their denotations and connotations sometimes cause us philosophical bewilderment. In other words, statements and descriptions can be clarified according to public criteria of intelligibility as meaningful, or as corresponding to some shared notion of reality. Language entails the principle of justifiability according to shared notions of meaning and rational discourse. Authority-claims embody at least a tacit appeal to rational justifiability. The enforcement of 'moral' standards against those who do not agree with them or who do not understand them, in the absence of an ongoing commitment to reasoned dialogue, amounts to brute force. This, as I suggested, is the basis of Mill's claim in *On Liberty* that 'all restraint *qua* restraint is an evil'.

These commitments to truth and reasoned justification indicate at least one sense in which naturalistic description is of a piece with normative prescription: one solution to the long-standing philosophical problem of deriving values from facts. Popper's idea of critical rationality *is* a moral one; it is also a teleological principle immanent in the human condition. And as both he and Mill maintained, there are social and political conclusions to be deduced from it; respect for personal and civil liberties; institutional guarantees against arbitrary power, prejudice and discrimination; transparency in the exercise of authority; and maximisation of opportunities for individuals of all ages and conditions to develop their critical potentials. These rights and freedoms, as well as the social conditions on which they depend, are more than just options; they are the ultimate measures of morally justifiable relationships between people.

Critical dialogue: learning to learn

Popper's theory of knowledge has inspired a number of educationalists to trace its implications for educational theory and practice. Tyrrell Burgess has mounted a fierce criticism of contemporary educational systems, particularly the centralised and authoritarian British system, in terms of a comprehensive failure to educate according to 'Popper's account of the logic of learning and his insistence that all learning begins with problems' (Burgess, 1998). Burgess claims that the traditional organisation of formal education is inimical to learning, involving as it does prescriptive, assessment-driven curricula, age-bound grouping and the remorseless provision of answers to unasked questions. But the significance of this idea of a 'logic of learning' is not what might be all too easily inferred from the use of this kind of phrase: namely, that it is possible to systematise educational content and method according to firmly established psychological principles.

Popper's *non-authoritarian epistemology*[13] is an account of the growth of knowledge in the sciences and other fields that is, simultaneously, an account of the way in which individuals learn from their mistakes. Its starting point is the anti-inductivist insight that all observation is theory-impregnated, that we learn as a result, first, of having our preconceptions falsified and, second, by the attempt to solve that problem. From the start, we carry with us the baggage of our individual experiences: an idiosyncratic, personal repertoire of language, ideas, beliefs and expectations which we accumulate, nevertheless, in a social context. The extent of possible variations in this largely tacit background, or world view, can be illustrated by the degree of alienation between contrasting cultures. Thus, a western anthropologist and a member of a totemic, aboriginal community might be described plausibly as walking side by side through different landscapes. What for the one is a featureless desert is, for the other, a perceptual field laden with various totemic significances and utilitarian possibilities. It is when aspects of these varying cognitive repertoires encounter challenges, sometimes from one another, that learning takes place. New concepts develop which will, in turn, encounter new challenges. Popper is insistent that this is the underlying dynamic of all learning, including those very important, unconscious forms of learning that are also part of every person's individuality. We learn, as Burgess points out, as individuals, and 'this holds even for army columns and chorus lines' (*ibid.*).

Burgess maintains that the notion of a dynamic 'logic of learning' is not a behavioural, a psychological or a sociological one. However, this disjunction is probably too radical because it tends to de-emphasise the fields from which Popper adduced powerful evidence for his thesis. For instance, he disputed the possibility of certain and objective knowledge in individual minds, replacing it with the idea of 'conjectural knowledge' that attains a degree of objectivity only through a process of social interaction. Scientific objectivity, he maintained, is not a product of the individual scientist's impartiality but of the 'socially or institutionally organized objectivity of science' through the 'intersubjective' activity of theory-testing and mutual criticism (Popper, 1969, pp. 220–1). Knowledge is acquired by individuals but only ever as a facet of continuing dialogue between people, even in the symbolic forms of writing, mathematical or scientific notations. In an important sense, understanding emerges through an argumentative engagement with the idiosyncratic expression of the ideas of others in order to find areas of common agreement or clear disagreement. The growth of knowledge in society and effective learning by individuals are symmetrical in this sense; both relate directly to the prevalence of critical discourse. This conception provides insight into the social and historical processes that have alternately accelerated and retarded the growth and individuation of knowledge. They do so according to the degree to which particular social institutions encourage or suppress the articulation of problems immanent in the experience of a community.[14]

Popper's thesis closely resembles Mill's earlier account of the cultural origins of critical thinking. Both philosophers, of course, subscribed to the example of the Socratic dialectic but, in addition, both located the origins of disciplined inquiry more generally in Greek disputatiousness, a condition that Mill once described as 'intellectual culture left to its own guidance' (Mill, 1965c, p. 189). Learning to learn is not so much a matter of acquiring a repertoire of predetermined analytical and organisational techniques as of beginning to experience the world as a complex of challenging problems for which traditional explanations are only ever partially satisfactory. It might seem paradoxical to those most impressed by the systematising nature of the major intellectual traditions that their foundations were laid so comprehensively in those small, politically ill-disciplined ancient communities. The 'critical disposition' so evident in them, as well as the emergence of democratic institutions, was the expression of a new, sceptical attitude towards traditional epistemic and, thus, political authority. But scepticism, alone, is nothing like a sufficient explanation for the spontaneous emergence of that ability to 'learn how to learn'. That must include the extraordinary enhancement of dialogue stimulated by the perception of problems in traditional wisdom that converted these polities into what Matthew Lipman has called 'communities of enquiry' (Lipman, 1991, p. 73). Lipman echoes Popper on the interpersonal dynamics of learning, from the different but compatible perspective of Vygotsky's philosophical psychology.

Popper and Vygotsky shared the idea of language as a tool that enables us, in Popper's words, to 'lift ourselves by our bootstraps' and achieve full self-consciousness and the capacity for rational thought (*ibid.*). Vygotsky's special contribution to this imagery was his account of the internal relationship between the mental processes of the individual and the variety of cultural meanings mediated by the use of language. With the onset of language, children enter a specific cultural nexus of historically negotiated word-meanings that accumulate and

gradually mould their apprehensions of reality. Individual psychological functions cease to be even a legitimate object of research because
the appropriate methodology becomes that of interpreting the meanings contained in linguistic exchange and its derivative symbols. This is
the principle that invalidates the Piagetian enterprise; the commonly
drawn distinction between individual minds and their environments is
not operationally valid. At the very point at which meaningful communication with the developing mind of the child becomes possible, it has
become integrated with the social and physical environment through
immersion in the matrix of language. And, incidentally, that means, in
Popper's terminology, that our first conscious observations are already
theory-impregnated:

> The word is a thing in our consciousness ... that is absolutely
> impossible for one person, but that becomes a reality for two. The
> word is a direct expression of the historical nature of human
> consciousness.
>
> (Vygotsky, 1989, p. 256)

Where much traditional psychology has attempted to measure what
are notionally the intrinsic abilities of the child, Vygotsky posed the
alternative conception of 'a zone of proximal development': the level
beyond those conventional measures of ability which a learner can
attain with the assistance of an adult or more capable peer. Learning is
defined as a function of interaction between people and the characteristics and qualities of that interaction are crucial in determining what
is actually achieved. Much as Burgess follows Popper in recommending educational methods that enhance dialogue between learners
and teachers and which prioritise the epistemic perspective of the
learner, Lipman anticipates the benefits of a Vygotskian curriculum
'dedicated to unsettling the mind and forcing it to come to grips with
what it might normally take for granted' (Lipman, 1991, p. 73). The
outcome of his vision was the introduction in some American and
British schools of his programme of 'philosophy for children'.

It might seem something of a luxury to arrive via a theoretical
excursion at a conclusion favouring educational approaches that value
dialogue and the critical analysis of ideas. After all, this is the kind of
thing that is earnestly professed as an aim in practically every item of a
superabundant official educational literature. But the Socratic principle involved is not so easily accommodated by a system that decides
in advance what is to be learned and how, in contemporary parlance, it
is to be 'delivered' to the learner. For this very terminology betrays

deep misconceptions about the nature of knowledge and the way in which it is acquired. There are some radical institutional implications in the idea of an education that will generate a self-sustaining passion for learning and honour the legacy of the critical traditions.

7   How others do it

Some international alternatives

[In Denmark] the schools' educational freedom does not just rest on an idée fixe. The entire structure rests on a very special view of human beings and a very special view of the relationship between the individual and the state.

(Carlsen and Borga, 1994, p. 17)

A long and respectable tradition upholds the importance of freedom in education although the concept may be interpreted in different ways. John Locke might be described as the first major exponent of 'child-centred' education in opposition to the prevailing authoritarianism of the schools of the late seventeenth century. Children's capacities for reasoning emerge as soon as they begin to acquire language and adults should respect their rational status by engaging in discourse with them rather than 'magisterially dictating' to them what they should learn. They should be allowed the liberties and freedoms suitable to their ages, and not be held under unnecessary restraints (Locke, 1913, p. 83). To the extent that he appealed to the 'psychology' of the child, however, it was very much in terms of the respect for human rationality that underpinned his philosophical case for political rights and liberties. That tradition was continued by Rousseau, Helvétius and the Mills. Central to it was a conception of the reciprocal relationship between the nature of individual human beings and the character of their society: a doctrine with radical educational and political implications. As Rousseau put it, '[m]an is too noble a being to ... serve simply as an instrument for others ... for men are not made for their stations, but their stations for men' (Lawrence, 1970, p. 157).

A more recent perspective in theories informing educational alternatives is primarily concerned with the nature and developmental needs of the individual child, a tradition of educational thinking exemplified by the influential ideas of Montessori, Isaacs and followers of Piaget. This emphasis was undoubtedly encouraged by the merger of two distinct twentieth-century developments: the consolidation of universal, compulsory schooling and the growth of the discipline of psychology which heightened sensitivities to the impact of early childhood experience in the maturation of personality.

This is not to say that a theoretical focus on individual psychology precludes concern with its social and political manifestations. Nevertheless, the issue of prioritisation remains a subject of debate in the social sciences and philosophy.[1] My point is that a fusion between those two trends, the spread of compulsory schooling and the growth of research into individual psychology, has fostered a distal view of the relationship between education, on the one hand, and society and politics on the other. The stable, institutional context of the school in democratic societies has facilitated a decoupling of educational desiderata from broader questions of constitutional politics and a subsequent recombination in predominantly instrumental terms between the two. The educational needs of children were psychologised and considered in relative isolation from the conditions of democratic politics. Correspondingly, social problems and needs tended to be interpolated didactically into the curriculum.[2] One illustration of the potential for divorce between the educational and the political was the dissemination of progressive, child-centred doctrine in the United Kingdom through what was, even then, a centralised organisational hierarchy. Freedom in education became a matter of institutional dogma and orthodoxy within the typically segregated world of education rather than a stimulus for the exploration of new relationships between maturing individuals and the varied social institutions of democratic society. And this artificial disjunction between education and society facilitated the wholesale revision of educational purpose and method in Britain in the 1980s and a growing instrumentalism by the end of the century.

Similar instrumentalist trends, accompanied by more state intervention in education, have been evident in much of the developed world. Differences between education systems are nonetheless often considerably larger than might be expected, given the broad similarities between the cultures, technologies and political constitutions of the states in question. Core curricula are increasingly in evidence in European schools, though only very rarely has detailed content been given such legislative force as in the United Kingdom. The literature of different education ministries refers with growing consistency to the need to remain competitive in a global economy, to the need for adaptability, 'lifelong learning' and the requirements of a 'knowledge economy'. Nevertheless, cultural–historical variations and the differential development of educational institutions mean that direct comparisons are often likely to be invalidated by the sheer diversity of variables, particularly if they are intended to assist in a search for that chimerical objective: the 'best' educational policy.

On the other hand, certain contrasts are sufficiently marked to raise questions about cherished assumptions, even if the answers are unlikely to be straightforward. Of numerous initiatives mounted by British governments to improve educational standards, one that appears to have received the highest measure of endorsement has been the introduction of literacy and numeracy instruction in the early years of schooling.[3] And although compulsory education does not begin until a child reaches the age of 5, government has stressed the importance of pre-schooling and the need for assessment even at such early ages. Yet in Finland, long reputed to have extremely high levels of basic literacy and the highest-scoring country in the OECD's survey of literacy in eighteen developed nations (OECD, 2001), compulsory schooling does not begin until a child reaches the age of 7. Although about two-thirds of Finnish children now receive some pre-school education from the age of 6, this Scandinavian tendency to begin formal instruction late appears to indicate the disproportionate benefits of informal learning in the home in early childhood. Full-time home education is legally recognised as an alternative, but the overwhelming majority of children between the ages of 7 and 16 attend Finland's 4,300 comprehensive schools, eighty-six of which are in the private sector. After nine years of compulsory education students, who are usually between 16 and 19 years of age, may attend an upper secondary school to prepare for the matriculation examination that will determine their eligibility for further and higher education (Ministry of Education – Finland, 1999).

In the prevailing international climate of purposeful governmental direction, there is a tendency for educational freedoms to be granted almost by default: a legislative concession to reservations about state monopolisation of the induction of rising generations into their social milieux. Legislation in the United Kingdom has long recognised the legitimacy of private schools. Nevertheless, the intervention of the Secretary of State in the case of A.S. Neill's Summerhill School, discussed in Chapter 4, reveals the extent of official determination to ensure that independent establishments adhere closely to nationally prescribed standards, even though they may not receive public funding. With the exception of grant-maintained independent schools and state support for individual pupils in defined circumstances, this private sector has been available mainly to the wealthy and has consequently attracted the opprobrium of the political left as a bastion of class privilege and a source of social division. No doubt this identification of freedom of choice with wealth and superior social status reinforces the conviction of many professional educators that the state comprehensive school is the surest educational route to social inclusion. High and continuing levels of poverty, though, and a widening gulf between the richest and the poorest should be a warning against treating educational systems 'as instruments for the wholesale reform of societies which are characteristically hierarchical in their distribution of chances in life' (Halsey, 1972, p. 7). Ironically, the egalitarian ideals that still inspire comprehensive schooling in the United Kingdom have arguably facilitated a 'command and control' system capable of being transformed by a burgeoning vocationalism into an instrument of economic policy. And the clear danger is that instead of equipping young people to 'rejuvenate' the world, in the words of the great egalitarian, R.H. Tawney, that system will teach them only to 'grind corn for the Philistines and doff bobbins for the mill owners' (Tawney, 1961, p. 81).

A number of European countries provide generous levels of state support for independent education, but the Netherlands, in addition to providing state schools, fully finances a large private sector consisting of schools that may be established by like-minded groups of parents provided they meet basic statutory regulations and accommodate a minimum number of pupils. Public funding of school buildings, teachers' salaries, textbooks and other materials on this basis allows for forms of education expressing diverse religious, philosophical and pedagogic beliefs. This variety encompasses Christian, Moslem, Hindu and Jewish schools as well as others reflecting alternative educational philosophies and pedagogical approaches rather than religious beliefs: Montessori, Dalton, Jenaplan, Freinet and Rudolf Steiner schools are examples (Weeber and Ahlers, 1996). This policy is consistent with the original reservation of the Dutch government to Article 2, Protocol 1 of the European Convention, that the state should ensure that parents can exercise educational rights by appropriate financial measures (discussed in Chapter 4). Nevertheless, school education of some description is compulsory under 1969 legislation in the Netherlands and the freedom to establish new private schools has been constrained in recent years by the increasingly onerous criteria they must meet in order to achieve official recognition and funding. Parents choosing to educate their children at home are obliged to seek exemption from the law, sometimes by appealing to successively higher authorities, a requirement that severely limits opportunities for this kind of education and is held by a growing number of Dutch parents to be contrary to the provisions of the European Convention.

By and large, links between educational and political liberties tend to be recognised by law only in terms of those formal, external features that have developed over time within different states. Almost inevitably, this obscures important internal connections between individual liberties and democratic government. In the face of mounting pressures for international integration and for comparability of educational performances in different states in the name of economic efficiency, the possibility is that only the merest outward formalities of educational freedom will be observed. The influential OECD recognises the difficulties in drawing cross-cultural comparisons, though it is ambitious to develop measures to assess what it describes as the economic and social relevance of different approaches. That organisation's perspective on the international diversity of means and ends in education is unashamedly instrumentalist: 'it will soon be possible to see more clearly whether all this learning activity is producing more of the skills that are really needed for the knowledge economy and society' (OECD, 2001, p. 8). From the point of view of those most concerned with education as a means to personal enlightenment and democratic involvement, such aspirations must strike an ominous note, especially as a predominant aim of mass education in many societies has always been to fit people to their stations.

The Danish idea of educational freedom

The most notable exception has been Denmark, where the relationships between educational freedom, the enlightenment of individual minds and an ethos of political liberty are features of a proudly celebrated national tradition. There is an unusually explicit acknowledgement by government and its agencies of the internality of these relationships, as the quotation at the head of this chapter from an official Danish publication testifies. That includes a recognition of the fallibility of state authority and the need for clearly defined limits to its legal competence:

> Different schools reflect widely different educational approaches. Yet however great their differences, they are all agreed that it is not for the state or any other public authority to decide what is the correct educational approach or the correct way to run a school.
>
> (Carlsen and Borga, 1994, p. 17)

The legally recognised scope for educational innovation is not restricted to schools. Parents and guardians have a right to educate their children by other means, a principle enshrined in the Danish Constitution[4] as well as in laws relating specifically to education in that country. As a result of the special emphasis that has been placed on the foundational character of these rights, Denmark has an extremely diverse education system that inspires high levels of public confidence (Danish Ministry of Education, 1996, pp. 86–7). The outline, below, is not proposed in any sense as a blueprint because cultures do differ significantly, even when they are in such geographical and historical proximity as those of Britain and Denmark. Yet there are some aspects of the Danish experience that, I believe, raise matters of general significance. For example, it demonstrates that the availability of very varied alternative methods of educating young people is not inconsistent with commitments to social equality, inclusion and general prosperity, a common belief among educators committed to the 'comprehensive ideal' in the United Kingdom. Danish experience does not suggest that educational freedom is inimical to the achievement of sound basic standards of education, as that country's second-place ranking after Finland in the OECD's own assessment of adult literacy and under-achievement rates in developed nations indicates (OECD, 2001, pp. 49–50).[5] Nor, it seems, does Denmark's liberal and pluralist education policy encourage social divisiveness or discrimination against minorities, high levels of truancy or exclusions from school for bad behaviour. Of course, any or all of these benefits might be written off to the uniqueness of Danish culture. But, in any case, it would be foolish to pretend that the interrelationships between education and society could be reduced ultimately to measurable correlations between identifiable factors. Denmark's comparatively long history of educational liberalism can be described very plausibly as having had a significant impact on the outlook and culture of its people. That history, and its deep connections with a broader drive for social and political reform, warrants at least a brief examination.

The historical background

Danish educational liberalism emerged out of a grass-roots movement for land reform and constitutional reform that began in the late eighteenth century and culminated in 1849 in a non-violent revolution that established the previously absolute Danish monarchy on a constitutional basis. From a very early stage, demands for economic and political reform were closely identified with a drive for the education of peasant farmers and ordinary citizens that would enable them to participate more effectively in the life of their changing society. Agrarian reform stimulated a variety of co-operative 'people's' movements that gradually encompassed not only agricultural production but social activity, vocational training and the earliest forms of social health insurance. It was, as a government publication says, 'a self-assured rejection of central authority' which translated into the 'unquestioned principle in Danish political life that this sense of freedom should remain inviolate and, indeed, must be defended' (Danish Ministry of Education, 1996, p. 18). Perhaps the most seminal development of all, and one which was to establish a legacy of democratic 'ownership' in education, was the Danish *Folkehøjskole*, the Folk High School, the first of which was founded in 1844. These extremely liberal educational institutions proved so popular that by 1890 there were seventy-five of them. Steven Borish maintains that these schools and the movement to which they belonged influenced Denmark's route to modernisation as a whole despite the periodic crises and setbacks experienced by that small country:

> the Danes were able to come back from a series of national defeats and disasters to construct a society that perhaps more than any other in recent history resembles the ideal of Jeffersonian democracy.
>
> (Borish, 1991, p. 18)[6]

The 1892 Danish Education Act formally recognised the Folk High Schools as a component of the country's education system and they have remained an influential feature of it ever since. In 1996, according to the Danish Ministry of Education, there were a hundred of these institutions spread throughout the country, concentrating on subjects as diverse as literature, history, psychology, ecology and environmental protection, education, music, drama, sport, dance, art, photography, pottery and dressmaking (Danish Ministry of Education, 1996, p. 4). Nearly all Folk High Schools are residential, self-governing and supported by state subsidies. Some cater for young adults, others for senior citizens. During the early 1990s average annual attendance was about 60,000 – or around 2 per cent of Denmark's adult population. Courses usually vary between one to two weeks and four to eight months. However, apart from illustrating the centrality of these establishments to Danish life and education as a whole, data of this kind fail to convey the exceptional character of the Folk High Schools. They are required by law to provide an education that is general and broadening in character and, to preserve the integrity of this aim, they are legally prohibited from competing with other specialist educational establishments. They do not provide vocational training; they do not impose any form of assessment on their students; and they do not follow any prescribed syllabus or provide any form of certification. 'Lifelong learning', a recently adopted and rather hollow phrase in British educational and political rhetoric, had already been a living reality in Denmark's democracy for many generations and it has thrived on that rarest of political qualities: trust.[7]

Whatever the future of Denmark's Folk High Schools, their historical influence appears to have permeated the education system as a whole. The uniquely – and largely untranslatable – Danish concept of *folkeoplysning* conveys a sense of popular enlightenment and democratic empowerment which are almost entirely absent in the vocational emphasis that has been injected into the notion of 'lifelong learning' in more centrally directed educational regimes and, indeed, in the international community. The OECD, for example, describes it as a set of general competencies to equip learners to go on learning and adapt to new contexts in order 'to be of use in the labour market and in society more widely' (OECD, 2001, pp. 89–90). But the spirit of *folkeoplysning* is richer and deeper than this.[8] Denmark's famous 'Free School' movement, as well as the liberal state school system, owe a great deal to it and to the visionary programme of popular education inspired by Nikolai Grundtvig and Christen Kold during the process of nineteenth-century democratic reform.

Grundtvig (1783–1872), an ordained minister, brought to popular education a spirit of the Christian existentialism and individualism for which his compatriot and contemporary Søren Kierkegaard is more internationally famous. But another important influence on Grundtvig's educational philosophy, as briefly mentioned in an earlier chapter, was his experience of life at Trinity College, Cambridge, in the early 1830s and the spirit of equality and companionship between students and tutors he observed there: an ethos entirely lacking in most English schools of the time. What particularly impressed him was 'that the dialogue between them was open ended, continuous and intense', an insight that led him to the Millian conclusion that the traditional patterns of rote learning in schools can never produce the enlightenment that can emerge through dialogic engagement in real-life situations. And Borish indicates the wider implications of this insight for Grundtvig's educational and social philosophy:

[Grundtvig] was really insisting upon a mutual recognition that each institution, each power center, and indeed each individual could both teach and learn in a dialogue predicated on mutual respect. Furthermore, such dialogue would create in the long run a society with widened social and individual perspectives, constituting the type of fertile soil in which the experience of Enlightenment could best grow.

(Borish, 1991, p. 169)

Kold collaborated closely with Grundtvig, providing both theoretical endorsement of his ideas and a practical commitment that led to the establishment of both Folk High Schools for older students and Free Schools for younger ones. Their joint emphasis remained decisively on the primary educational task of encouraging the enlightenment of learners. Kold's insistence on teaching geared to 'children's needs and abilities' is a striking anticipation of the child-centred tradition of 1970s Britain. The significant differences, however, are that the two men established a child-centred tradition that survived into the twenty-first century and that it did so because the internal relationship between educational freedom and a free, democratic way of life was conscientiously preserved in their ideas and practice and given legal and constitutional expression. Despite the pressures of global economics, contemporary Danish education remains a tribute to that unified vision. It is symbolic of its influence that at the beginning of the last decade of the twentieth century, the Danish Minister of Education, Bertel Haarder, had received no formal schooling until he attended university.

An outline of the contemporary Danish education system

The legacy of Grundtvig and Kold is an immensely diverse education system in which individual rights and liberties are celebrated and safeguarded. Education between the ages of 7 and 16 is compulsory, though schooling is not. However, the proportion of parents availing themselves of the right to educate their children at home is tiny, about 1 per cent, and the alternative choices available to them are wide-ranging. The great majority (87 per cent) of children between 7 and 16 years of age attend their local authority state school, the *folkeskole*, as there is a typical Scandinavian disregard for the distinction between primary and secondary education. One consequence of this continuity of progression is that the *folkeskoler* tend to be fairly intimately connected with their surrounding communities, a characteristic accentuated by their typically small size (usually about 300 pupils) and average class sizes of nineteen. These schools do follow a national curriculum, though less prescriptive than those familiar in the United Kingdom. Detailed planning and implementation is largely a matter for individual schools (Human Scale Education, 2000).

A popular and growing type of educational establishment is the Continuation School, or *efterskole*, first established in the 1850s and now numbering about 250. Like the Folk High Schools, they are residential, accommodating on average eighty-five students in their late teens. These *efterskoler* are self-governing, non-profit-making trusts that provide a wide range of specialisms. Unlike the Folk High Schools, they now offer formally assessed one- or two-year courses of the kind provided by state schools but they tend to cater for students who might prefer to matriculate in a different, possibly more mature, residential environment. Funding is partly by the state, partly by local government and partly by parental contributions adjusted to take account of family income.

'Free Schools', or *Friskoler*, are a direct legacy of Grundtvig and Kold and have grown in popularity in recent decades as some smaller state schools have been closed in response to economic pressures. They are usually established by groups of parents and teachers and, under Danish law, receive state funding amounting to about 75 per cent of the costs of an equivalent state school. Although this means that parents generally pay modest 'top-up' fees, state benefits are available to families who cannot afford to pay them. As a result, the Free Schools are not seen as a middle-class alternative and enjoy considerable working-class support. About 12 per cent of Danish schoolchildren are now educated in just over 400 of these Free Schools, half of which are still committed to the democratic, child-centred tradition of their original founders. It is otherwise difficult to generalise about the ideals to which these schools aspire, as their fundamental purpose is to represent the great variety of beliefs among the population. There are, however, over fifty schools organised by religious groups, a few that cater for German-speaking minorities and about fifty very small *lilleskoler* run entirely by parents, usually of a left-of-centre political persuasion. Free Schools tend to be small, on average only half the already modest size of the state schools. Communities of between forty and sixty students are most typical, though a significant proportion of Free Schools are much smaller than this. An initial student body of sixty is the required minimum for state funding, though this will continue until the school population drops below twenty-eight. As a result, several schools open and others close

each year. With the exception of normal requirements for accountability in the spending of public money, the schools are self-governing
and are subject only to a liberally interpreted requirement to teach
Danish, English and mathematics to a standard broadly equivalent to
that provided by the state schools.[9] The Free Schools Association and
the Continuation Schools Association established a Free Teacher
Training College in the mid-twentieth century to provide appropriate
training in which democratic decision-making with students is strongly
emphasised (Human Scale Education, 2000).

Freedom, democracy and pluralism in Danish education

'Freedom' and 'democracy' are widely used and abused words in the
world at large. Consequently, it is useful to gauge the commitment of
the Danish Free Schools movement to these ideas in terms that are
common to most, if not all, of them. This is particularly relevant as
this comparatively small sector has exerted a powerful influence on
Danish education as a whole and because the ease with which Free
Schools can be established and funded makes them a readily available
alternative in the event of parental disenchantment with state schools.
In the following chapter, I will consider the burgeoning home education movement in English-speaking countries that has emerged as an
alternative to formal systems of schooling that parents and children
have rejected for various reasons. Interestingly, Denmark's Free School
tradition is a rather natural development of what was originally the
common practice of home education:

> The friskole has a long tradition in Denmark. It has grown from
> below for 150 years. The children's education is first and foremost
> a matter for the parents. The friskole has its roots in education at
> home. This option is not used much today, but it is still the funda-
> mental principle of freedom of education.
>
> (DFA, 1995, p. 8)

The Danish Friskole Association, which represents about half of
the Free Schools, is forthright in its defence of individual liberties and
minority rights as features of a mature concept of democracy.
Describing the Western European political tradition as one primarily
concerned with democratic majoritarianism, the Association asserts
the long-standing Danish tradition of respect for the rights of individuals and minorities, including legal protection and financial support
by the state as a rare national disposition. This is undoubtedly true,

though the historical emergence of democratic political systems was arguably more the practical consequence of assertions of individual and minority rights than of any belief in the infallibility of majorities. Thus, the Association points out, democratic states protect individual and minority rights but few go so far as to underwrite them with public funding in the way Denmark has. The point is not made in a self-congratulatory spirit but, as it were, to indicate the need to recognise openly and grapple with a recurrent and ineradicable dilemma of liberal democratic politics: minorities, families and individuals may be hostile to the system that sustains them.

> It is important to emphasize that the ideology [of a Free School] can be of a religious, political or pedagogical nature ... If one has the opinion ... that children should be educated to overthrow the existing society, one is also protected by the Friskole Act and can establish a school with this viewpoint.
>
> (DFA, 1995, p. 13)

The Association cites examples of revolutionary socialist groups who have established Free Schools and also a religious fundamentalist group which teaches its children that geological evidence contrary to the doctrine that the Earth was created 6,000 years ago is simply incorrect. In the light of more recent developments, it might also have cited the widely publicised case of a group aspiring to set up a state-funded Free School to teach according to National Socialist principles. These are the kind of rare 'hard cases' that are cited triumphantly by opponents of Danish educational libertarianism. But 'hard cases make bad law' and the Friskole Association represents the conviction that in the open, democratic contest of ideas in a free society, other values have the opportunity to prevail against dogmas and prejudices that would otherwise fester and perhaps grow beyond public scrutiny. On the other hand, the Danish policy of liberal impartiality meant that the German-speaking minority, relocated in Denmark by a 1920 adjustment to the southern border, received funding for German language schools on a par with state schools rather than Free Schools. The arrangement continued after the Nazi occupation of Denmark to the present, though these minority schools are now governed by the same legislation and funding arrangements that apply to Free Schools throughout the country.

Some may view this Danish respect for extreme educational diversity within the broad framework of a democratic constitution as a prelude to social divisiveness and economic inefficiency. But judgments about the conditions favouring either social cohesion or social division are impregnated with values and are not of a kind to be categorically supported or refuted. In any case, similar arguments could be marshalled against more conventional democracies. One argument against the sceptic is that Danish libertarianism has a considerable history, that it has co-existed with high and increasing levels of social welfare, and that Denmark has a distinguished humanitarian record. These and other such generalisations are inconclusive, but I suggest they are no more so than those that inspired, say, the catastrophic American drive for social efficiency through the wholesale imposition of managerialism in education described by Callahan (Callahan, 1962) or its more recent British version. The axiomatic principle, particularly for the Danes who constructed their radical version of liberal democracy, is the inalienable right of the individual human being, irrespective of the contingencies attending its protection. But even though the question of evidence is rather beside this point of principle, there are considerations that weigh against pessimistic appraisals of its implications and, as Borish claims, they are substantial in the case of Denmark.

Richard Estes of the University of Pennsylvania School of Social Work constructed longitudinal studies that were designed to establish a systematic series of indices for an operational model of world social welfare development covering more than a hundred of the world's nations for which sufficient data was available. Borish cites the results of Estes' *The Social Progress of Nations, 1984* and *Trends in World Social Development, 1988* (Borish, 1991, pp. 67–70) though these studies have continued since then, culminating in 2001 in *The World Social Situation, 1970–1995* (Estes, 2001). This research is based largely on data from the United Nations, the World Bank and the OECD that Estes used to construct forty-four indices of social well-being. They included literacy, health and welfare programmes, political participation, observance of women's rights, infant mortality, male and female life expectancy, proportional educational expenditure and measures of social and domestic violence over the periods in question. Although the study is extremely complex and has a variety of objectives of global significance, its present relevance is that Denmark has consistently ranked highest of all in Estes' 'social welfare league table' of the world's nations, compared, for example, to the United States which occupied the twenty-seventh position in 1995.

These conclusions are undeniably controversial because the data, no matter how accurate, are categorised according to values attributed to factors like the equitable distribution of wealth within national populations and the existence and scope of social welfare provision. These indices relate to political objectives that are deeply controversial in nations like the United States and Japan. But to whatever extent they are accepted as approximate measures of social and economic well-being – and, of course, they are widely accepted as such in many democratic states – Denmark seems to have survived its preoccupation with liberty remarkably well. And Danish educational freedom can hardly be shown to have been a liability on evidence of this kind. Borish suggests that the 'elegant research design' and copious statistical documentation of Estes' studies should bring into question contrary assumptions frequently made by citizens and leaders of some of the world's most affluent nations (Borish, 1991, p. 70).

In other words, vital questions about why and how we educate remain as salient as ever, as does an even more fundamental one: who is qualified to decide? The Danish answer is unambiguous: it is a matter for individual citizens and not for the state because a free, democratic way of life encompasses a multiplicity of purposes, many of which will be in mutual contention. Conceding so much to individual judgments and decisions might seem a high-risk strategy, requiring that 'spirit of adventure' that Pericles identified as the force motivating Athenian democracy. On the other hand, outcomes never can be guaranteed as the mediocre, controversial results of nearly two decades of educational revolution from above in the United Kingdom have shown.

Denmark is a very small country and it has not remained untouched by the feverish international preoccupation with the formulation and verification of supposedly desirable educational outcomes. An 'Evaluation Institute' has been established to monitor standards in all types of schools and colleges, though, for the time being, not the Free Schools. This development prompted Kim Hjerrild, the General Secretary of the Folk High School Association, to comment that 'in chasing after competitiveness and measurable results, we have thrown overboard fundamental education in citizenship' (Human Scale Education). Reservations of this kind do not disturb the official British conception of education in citizenship that promises to be an altogether more constrained and centrally directed affair. The search is on for the 'skills' required by the vaguely defined 'knowledge economy'. And even though the OECD acknowledges that 'there is no clear agreement on the definition and measurement of these skills' (OECD, 2001, p. 104) they are nonetheless prominent features in proposals for the education of future British citizens. But lack of clarity about objectives is no impediment to policy-making in a monolithic state organisation where institutional needs and interests display an almost invariable ambition to transform and subsume all others.

Such is the momentum behind the juggernaut of instrumentalism in education that the Danish model is unlikely to be adopted elsewhere. Human Scale Education, the British outpost of the European Forum for Freedom in Education, has campaigned for the introduction in the United Kingdom of legislation similar to that in Denmark (*ibid.*). A radical change of direction of this kind is highly unlikely where so much has been invested in the idea of central government as the guarantor of higher standards of educational attainment. But, as I shall argue in Chapter 9, there may be other ways of protecting educational and political freedoms and of approaching the ideal of a society that is genuinely committed to lifelong learning.

Educational freedom and educational attainment

The Danish case for educational freedom rests on a conception of the rights of citizens rather than claims about what, in modern terms, counts as measurable educational effectiveness. On the other hand, both the Danish position and the philosophical tradition of educational liberalism involve a conception of the intrinsic value of learning and qualitative assessments of the nature of learning and understanding. Yet arguments for rigorous state control in education are couched very much in terms of the need for demonstrable improvements in educational effectiveness. As a result, it seems appropriate to consider evidence of a quantitative kind for relationships between educational freedoms and educational standards according to officially recognised criteria.

It is difficult to generalise satisfactorily from experience in any single country, although individual 'case studies' may offer illumination. The 'argument from cultural difference' can always be invoked and substantial contrasts between national systems of assessment may be held to invalidate comparisons. However, some indication of a relationship might be gleaned from a study involving the federal states of America, all of which enjoy substantial independence in the formulation of education policy and, as a result, display considerable differences within the overall framework of a single culture.

The Education Freedom Index (EFI) constructed by Jay P. Greene of the Manhattan Institute for Policy Research ranks fifty American states according to five equally weighted measures: the availability of charter school options and of government-assisted private school options; the ease with which parents can 'home school' children, choose a different public school district by relocating, or send a child to a different public school district without changing residence. These measures were controlled for other factors in each of the states: median household income, spending per pupil on education, average class sizes and the percentages of ethnic minorities, for example. Now an index like this is highly politically charged, and, as Greene acknowledged, it is impossible to prove direct causal relationships between it and student performance. But essentially similar considerations apply in the case of official uses of standardised assessments as measures of the efficacy of educational provision. Common objections are that standardised measures ignore important qualitative issues or cannot be sufficiently sensitive to strategies for 'adding value' where social deprivation inhibits academic performance.[10] These objections, however, have rarely inhibited government enthusiasm for standardised testing. Greene chose the National Assessment of Educational Progress (NAEP) and America's widely employed standardised test scores (SATs) as recognised measures of educational achievement. He concluded that there is a strong positive correlation between state scores on the EFI and on student test performances. 'Put simply,' he argues, 'states with more education freedom have higher average student achievement.' Given the positive correlation between average family income and average student achievement, Greene maintains that for a state to achieve educational improvements comparable to a one-point gain on his index, state policy-makers would have to find ways of increasing average annual household incomes by $19,000. And, as though to decouple policies on educational freedom from what might be regarded as the most obvious form of political alignment, Greene points out that high-scoring states on his index may have either Democrat or Republican administrations (Greene, 2000, p. 16).

Citizens in many countries have grown accustomed to government claims to be the ultimate custodians of the quality of education. In the United Kingdom, in particular, this has involved unprecedented degrees of regimentation and assessment according to putatively objective standards. In the following chapter I will consider how far the most radical educational alternative of all, the rapidly growing home education movement, casts light on such official claims – and on the legitimacy of curtailments of educational freedoms in the cause of educational improvement.

8   A radical alternative

Home education

> The most Utopian thing about Utopia is that there are no schools at all.
>
> (John Dewey, quoted in Ryan, 1999, p. 121)

> In the United States today, the new thought moves to the tune of 'Back to Basics'.
>
> (Jacques Barzun, quoted in Barrow, 1979, p. 182)

Dewey's words imply that ideals must accommodate social realities. There is no such place as Utopia, by definition, even if some educationalists cherish the ideal of an unregimented education that enables children to learn in the non-custodial setting of their natural community. Barzun's words, by contrast, typify pragmatic American and British reactions in the late 1970s to the educational progressivism with which Dewey is associated. Those reactions generated some particularly harsh criticisms of the most radical variation on the theme of progressive education: the 'de-schooling' movement, represented by such figures as Goodman, Illytch and Reimer. In one contribution to that small but influential volume of essays entitled *Schooling in Decline*, Robin Barrow called for a step by step return to 'basics' in education in place of what he deemed to be the 'uncertain doctrine' of progressivism. His assessment of the idea of de-schooling was uncompromising:

> There is no empirical evidence (nor could be, since we are at present schooled), no logical coherence in the argument, and no obvious way of getting the plan off the ground in what are agreed by all to be, at present, anti-educational environments. De-schooling would lead to the antithesis of a useful education from society's point of view ... It is in effect an irresponsible proposal,

even more extreme than that of the progressives ... it has not been shown that ... there is any better way of trying to provide education than through schooling.

(Barrow, 1979, p. 192)

There are now large numbers of children in the world's democracies, particularly in English-speaking nations, who are not receiving education through schooling. In the United States, most notably, some partisan estimates place the figure as high as two million – and rising – though, as I will point out, lower official estimates also confirm that the numbers are very large and steadily growing. A substantial body of empirical evidence is now available and it demonstrates pretty conclusively that these children acquire a useful education in precisely the kind of terms that have been formally identified as such from society's point of view. This has been achieved in a remarkably straightforward way: by the individual decisions of citizens to assert their democratic rights and liberties. Disenchanted with official educational provision, significant numbers of parents have taken their children out of school – or have decided not to send them there in the first place – and educate them at home. Whether or not the justifications for doing this are logically coherent cannot easily be determined because, as one would expect, they vary from family to family. But if the arguments I have rehearsed in previous chapters are cogent, it should be no great surprise that knowledge and understanding can be acquired successfully in the absence of assessment-driven, pre-planned curricula, delivered to passive audiences by the obedient servants of hierarchical educational bureaucracies. Children *can* learn, and learn very well, in non-custodial surroundings, in an atmosphere of free inquiry and dialogue.

In his rather inconclusive introduction to the collection of essays which included Robin Barrow's (above), Gerald Bernbaum reflected that a resolution of the educational controversies of the late 1970s would not be easy. 'It is likely, however, that we will be required to agree upon what might constitute evidence, and to confront that evidence when we have it' (Bernbaum, 1979, p. 16). To the extent that effective learning can be measured by empirical research, the evidence *is* available. Unfortunately, there are powerful tendencies to disregard evidence that does not fit our preconceptions, and this is particularly true of large-scale institutions that exercise near-monopoly powers over significant sectors of social life. The evidence for the success of home education is there, but it has had little impact on official thinking about ways forward towards the holy grail of a 'learning society' or, for that matter, ways of achieving steadily rising educational standards.

Home education is becoming increasingly common in Britain, Australia and New Zealand. Information about numbers is sparse for mainland European countries, though most recognise a legal right for parents to educate children at home. Germany forbids home education; attendance at a school is a requirement of Dutch law though the state is committed to the full funding of approved private schools chosen by parents. Greece permits home education only for children with 'special needs'. In Denmark, as already noted, the constitutional right of parents to educate at home is balanced by generous government funding of 'Free Schools' and it is consequently fairly rare. Austria enforces a national curriculum on home educators and children are tested on it annually. The 'home education' movement in North America, however, represents a massive haemorrhage of parental support for public (state) education and is consequently a rich source of information about this phenomenon. Families in the USA and Canada have won legal recognition of their right to educate children outside the formal education system despite what has sometimes been determined official opposition. And although laws, as well as the attitudes of politicians and education officials, vary from state to state in these federal systems, home education has achieved widespread recognition and endorsement. The Pennsylvania State Senate (in Resolution 68, March 2001) and the Governor of Texas (in a Proclamation, April 2001) proclaimed 'Home Education Weeks' in the early months of 2001, while the New York State Senate was considering legislation that would radically de-regulate home education. By contrast, Michigan was the last state of the Union to drop a requirement that home educating parents should have teacher certification. But in May 2001 a Bill to impose mandatory testing on 'home schoolers' in that state was defeated after intensive lobbying by members of the increasingly influential Home School Legal Defence Association (House Bill 4521 of the Michigan legislature, May 2001).

This international trend should command the attention of all educationalists and politicians, not only because of its scale but, as I have said several times, because the average home educated student meets and far surpasses the standards of performance achieved within the formal state-education system, according to officially recognised assessment criteria. Growing recognition of the irreversibility of this development is symbolised by the United States Senate Resolution (Resolution 183, 19–09–99) calling on the then President to recognise the movement's achievements. That symbolic gesture was followed by the subsequent federal administration's promotion of measures to exempt home educators from federal control under the Elementary and Secondary Education Act. Reputable tertiary educational institutes have also proved increasingly willing to admit home educated students. These institutions include the élite Harvard University, which appointed an admissions tutor with the specific remit of considering applications from these students. Moreover, the absence of a commitment to state funding implies marginal but growing savings on conventional educational expenditure – in contrast to the position, previously considered, of private educational initiatives in some European countries. That might, of course, appeal to those on the political right who seek reductions in public expenditure and taxation, but it might equally appeal to those desiring more appropriately targeted expenditure to tackle the most extreme forms of educational and social deprivation. Regardless of questions of parental motivation, the phenomenon of home education raises profound but neglected questions about the nature of learning and teaching, the validity of assessment regimes and desirable forms of interplay between state institutions and families in the education of children and young people.

'De-schooling': the evidence

According to some estimates, about 1,900,000 young people were being educated at home in the United States as a whole in the school year 2000–1, a number that is also estimated to be growing steadily each year. An official estimate by the US Department of Education's Office of Educational Research and Improvement suggested that at an earlier period, 1995–6, the number was about 700,000, compared to an assessment by Ray for 1996–7 of a figure of 1.2 million (Lines, 1999). However, that report added that although Ray's estimate was considered to be high, the government estimate reflected considerable difficulties in gathering information of this kind and was probably low as a result. Subsequent assessments from various sources suggest that the number of home educated children continues to grow rapidly year by year. Despite the problems of eliciting precise information from a large number of independent education authorities in more than fifty diverse American states, it seems clear that home education is a well-established and growing sector of education in that country. And, by any reasonable standard, it works very well.

In a series of surveys over a number of years, Ray found that home educated children scored, on average, far above the nationally recognised norm, or 50th percentile, in all areas of the usual school curriculum. The standardised test scores of these children were on average at or above the 80th percentile (Ray, 1997).[1] Other studies, of which there are now very many in different states of the Union, register typical average test scores among the home-learners above the 80th percentile for reading and above the 70th percentile for mathematics. Nor is the research confined to curricular matters. 'Problem behaviour scores' have been found to be lower among the home educated than among their school-educated peers, findings consistent with other studies suggesting superior social adjustment, personal confidence, emotional stability and participation in various social activities beyond the home. In addition, the demographic characteristics of home educated students and their families have been investigated and analysed in great detail.

Motives for educating children at home include, of course, philosophical objections to positivist and behaviourist reductions of learning to statements about measurable outcomes. This is a position for which there are cogent defences. One is that over-identification of home education with schooling through the administration of standardised, officially endorsed tests debases its broader aims and might create opportunities for bureaucratic control. But quite apart from the traditional American predilection for quantitative research, there are significant advantages in statistics of the kind that are now widely available on this subject.[2] In particular, data is presented in language and concepts that are familiar in formal, state education. Evidence that is 'on all fours' with that routinely used to measure educational achievement and school effectiveness by governments has provided home educating families with the means of defending their legal rights against the frequently hostile actions of education authorities. Official opposition in the United States and Canada led to the formation of the Home School Legal Defence Association, a body which has developed the expertise necessary to mount legal defences for families in different states with varied statutory educational provisions. The HSLDA commissioned what, by 1998, was the single largest ever survey and testing programme for students educated at home in the United States – and, for that matter, anywhere else in the world. It was carried out under the direction of Dr Lawrence M. Rudner of the University of Maryland, Director of the ERIC Clearinghouse on Assessment and Evaluation, which is sponsored by the US Department of Education. Rudner was formerly a classroom teacher and, as he remarked pointedly, was father of two children attending public schools. This study involved sophisticated analysis of data relating to student achievement on officially recognised, standardised tests and a wide variety of demographic characteristics of young people and their families in every state of the Union.[3] Rudner cautioned that the report expressed his own views and not necessarily those of the Home School Legal Defence Association that had grant-aided the project.

Rudner's conclusions are of particular interest for several reasons. His sample of home educated children was very large: 20,760 children aged between 6 and 18 years in 11,930 families. The results of his survey were subjected to very detailed statistical analysis, and he clearly did not have an ideological commitment to home education. Another interesting feature of this survey was that it distinguished systematically between young people who were home educated and those in private or Catholic educational institutions as well as those in the public (state) school sector. This latter sample involved the test results of 137,000 students in public, private and Catholic schools. On academic achievement, Rudner admitted that even on his own conser-vative analysis, levels among home educated students, the majority of whom had never attended a school, were well above those of their public/private school peers in every subject and in every grade, demon-strating 'exceptional scores and exceptional grade-to-grade gains':

> Within each grade level and each skill area, the median scores for home school students fell between the 70th and 80th percentile of students nationwide and between the 60th and 70th percentile of Catholic/private school students. For younger students, this is a one year lead. By the time the home school students are in 8th grade, they are four years ahead of their public/private school counterparts.
>
> (Rudner, 1998, p. 26)

Rudner confirmed a finding by Ray in 1997, from a study of over five thousand home-schooled students, that the longer the period spent in home study, the greater the gain in performance. However, Rudner's cautious approach also led him to warn, among other things, that because of the sheer number of uncontrollable variables in such a study, his report could not be regarded as a conclusive demonstration that home education is superior to private or public school education, that public schools are failing, or that home education is superior to school education. Other findings were that the overwhelming majority of home educating parents were in traditional marriages; that average income levels for these families were considerably higher than national average incomes; and that nearly one quarter of the families had one parent who had held a teaching certificate. However, an analysis of data relating to 7,607 home educated students failed to identify a significant correlation between achievement and parental teaching qualifications (*ibid.*, p. 22), a finding which confirms an earlier study by Ray, in the United States and Canada, that youngsters whose parents were certified teachers did not, on average, outperform those whose parents had no such qualification.[4] (It seems that evidence of this kind led to the removal of requirements for home educating parents to be teacher-certified, Michigan being the last state to take this step, as noted above.) Despite cautious interpretations of the data and reservations concerning superior parental income, motivation and marital stability, Rudner reached the inescapable conclusion that 'those parents choosing to make a commitment to home schooling are able to provide a very successful academic environment' (*ibid.*, p. 27). This is extremely powerful evidence from the point of view of those wishing to defend the rights and liberties of home educating families.

Several further points arising from Rudner's survey should be emphasised. The United States' low standing on international measures of basic literacy, for example, might encourage the view that anything must be better than the system of public schooling prevailing in that country. Apart from being an unjustifiably sweeping condemnation of American public education, that view needs to be qualified by Rudner's findings concerning the superiority of outcomes for the home educated compared to those in the private/Catholic school sector. 'Median composite scaled test-scores' for the latter were significantly higher than for the nation as a whole. For the home educated they were even higher (*ibid.*, p. 16). These conclusions were summarised by the ratios between median scores for public schools (239), private/Catholic schools (257) and home 'schools' (276). America certainly does provide examples of excellence in education. If there is any temptation to identify them with the private rather than the public educational sector the broad conclusion remains: home education is a very adequate alternative by that standard, too.

Rudner's analysis also indicated that young people who had been home educated for the whole of their academic life performed more successfully than those who had been educated at home for only a few years. Average rates of improvement for the home educated accelerated with time and the gap between these students and their school-educated peers widened. Parental income and educational level were eliminated as factors that correlated significantly with lifelong home education. In other words, the significant relationship is directly between student achievement and lifelong home education (*ibid.*, p. 19). On the other hand, Rudner did find a significant positive correlation between higher levels of home-student achievement and levels of parental education, children of college graduates outperforming those whose parents lacked such qualifications. But the performance of home educated students whose parents did not have higher educational qualifications was nevertheless much higher than that of students in public schools: in the 65–69th percentile range (*ibid.*, p. 23). And while television viewing occupied less of the average home educated student's time, achievement correlated negatively with the amount of time spent in this way. A particularly interesting finding was that fewer than one in ten home educated students followed 'a full-service curriculum program' encompassing teaching materials, lesson plans and tests in subjects like language, social studies, mathematics and science. Nor did Rudner find any significant differences in achievement by gender in his sample (*ibid.*, p. 25).

This absence of gender differences in the educational attainment of children educated at home has been confirmed by a three-year study by a researcher at the University of Durham of one thousand home educating families in the United Kingdom (Rothermel, 2000). Among other interesting findings in this study, apart from levels of attainment above the national average and well-developed social skills, was an unexpected contradiction of a common assumption about education and social class. Rothermel found that children whose parents would normally be classified as belonging to the lower end of the social scale tended to progress more rapidly than their middle-class, home educated counterparts. As in American studies, about one quarter of parents taking part in this national assessment programme had been trained as teachers. According to Rothermel, some of these parents found their training to have been helpful, others that it was a hindrance – and yet others that their training made communication with local education authorities easier. Of the reasons parents gave for deciding to educate their children at home, over half involved concerns about class sizes in schools, 'bullying' and discontent with the present state of school education. About one-third cited 'child-centred' reasons relating to the individual needs and choices of their children or to their own moral and philosophical beliefs.

One of the most prominent British advocates of home education is Professor Roland Meighan of Nottingham University, who estimated that more than 50,000 British children were being educated at home by the year 2000. Meighan has suggested that in the face of overwhelming evidence of its effectiveness, the appropriate question concerning home education is no longer a matter of 'does it work?' but 'why does it work so well?' Parents who make the decision to allow their children to learn at home are often surprised at its success. 'Home based education effectiveness research demonstrates that children are usually superior to their school-attending peers in social skills, social maturity, emotional stability, academic achievement, personal confidence, communication skills and other aspects' (Meighan, 1995). Meighan summarises a number of answers to these questions that resonate strongly with some of the themes explored in earlier chapters of this book. In particular, it is worth recalling Mill's epistemic individualism, his scepticism concerning the legitimacy of didactic teaching and Popper's conception of the growth of knowledge through encounters with problems, interpreted by Burgess as 'the logic of learning'. And, of course, there is the ancient Socratic injunction to 'follow the logic of argument wherever it leads' (to which Mill and Popper were heavily indebted) rather than to adhere slavishly to ready-made programmes, formulae and techniques.

Classrooms, Meighan points out, involve restricted and predominantly one-way communication between teachers and pupils, whereas the opposite applies in the home situation. Schools traditionally involve regimentation and other features of collectivities like uniform pedagogic approaches, standardised curricula and assessments and age-matched cohorts that are inhospitable to the idiosyncrasies of personal mental development and are largely uncharacteristic of life beyond the school. At home there is a premium on self-directed and co-operative learning, informal communication in familiar language and an absence of peer pressure to conform to established stereotypes. Families who commence home education by adhering to formal methods of teaching or learning often find themselves drawn gradually into more informal modes of learning by the 'logic' of their domestic situation:

> It is actually hard for a school as currently organised to match an alert, organised and energetic family. Only a few schools even get near it, as I was able to observe as I went from studying home educating families to supervise students in school and back again for over ten years.
>
> (Meighan 1995)

Implicit in the institutional organisation and the now highly formalised procedures of schooling is a theory of knowledge, the authoritarianism of which is at odds with the historical processes that have driven the growth of knowledge: a sense of intellectual independence; the development of critical ways of thinking as a result of argumentative discourse; a committed search for solutions to problems posed by traditional explanations of the world and how it works. The successes of the modern home education movement suggest that this simple paradigm shift from school to home has enabled young people to tap into these primary sources of effective learning much more effectively than have the numerous initiatives by governments to improve standards in schools.

Trends in home education

Confronted with the weight of evidence for the effectiveness of informal, home-based educational activity, many professionals in the field of education are inclined to defend conventional schooling with the 'socialisation' objection, a remark of Meighan's amply borne out by personal anecdote. This objection has been anticipated and at least partly rebutted by the kind of research into the social adjustment and personal qualities of home educated children mentioned above. Nevertheless, judgments of this kind are inevitably value-laden and it is arguable, for instance, that it is simply wrong to rate formal measures of social adjustment and personal maturity above the existential realities of peer contact. Alternatively, there is the argument that the resolutely isolationist learners who shun lesser mortals might attain greater heights than their more sociable fellows and achieve greater personal fulfilment as a result. There are plenty of historical examples of this kind, none more notable than the irascible and paranoid Newton. Nevertheless, references to the darker side of genius will not impress those who see education as very largely a matter of the induction of a child into its social environment. It would be a mistake, however, to see the typical home educated child as the isolated victim of fanatical, hot-housing parents. The choice of this kind of education is very often largely or entirely at the child's own behest and very typically involves rich and diverse forms of social contact.

As the movement has grown, so too has the impulse to identify opportunities for collaboration between families, for joint expeditions to centres of learning like museums, wildlife sanctuaries, libraries, lectures and places for outdoor activity. This trend has been greatly encouraged by the development of electronic communications. A brief review of the web-pages of organised groups of home educating families in many parts of the world will confirm this growing trend towards collaboration, joint initiatives and communal activities between the children themselves. One of the obvious virtues of this kind of development is that it is voluntaristic and it usually involves random mixtures of adults and children of different ages and social conditions. Peer relationships of a fundamentally different kind to those experienced in school are established, and they not only bear a closer resemblance to the child's natural community, they *become* part of the child's natural community. Meighan refers to the strength of bonds between children of different ages and siblings, a development usually precluded by age-segregation in formal schooling. At the same time, vast amounts of educational material for home educators is available on websites for general use, as well as suggestions for activities and regularly updated news reviews. Undoubtedly, though, these collaborative initiatives have often been stimulated by the real or perceived need of individual families to defend their educational projects against a hostile officialdom. The highly effective nationwide lobbies established by the Home School Legal Defence Associations of the United States and Canada have been emulated on a smaller scale by the Australian Home Education Research and Legal Information Network, a 'loosely organised collective of home educators who are concerned about the current trend of heavy government intervention and regulation of home education' (HERLIN website, 1998).

As might be expected, government attitudes to home educators vary from state to state and from one school district to another, resulting in different patterns of co-operation, conflict and official insistence on levels of monitoring and supervision. The same is true at county and regional levels of the rapidly growing home education movement in Britain that I will consider shortly. It is true, of course, that a proportion of parents make the decision to withdraw their children from school, or not to register them there, in order to isolate them from a variety of social influences. In the United States, in particular, fundamentalist religious convictions often precipitate such decisions and, in extreme cases, these may well involve a conscious decision to isolate the child from all and any influences other than those determined by particular religious beliefs.[5] This, however, raises the very basic civil libertarian consideration that moral disapproval of certain kinds of belief and practice is not of itself sufficient justification for interfering with personal liberties. Evidence of some kind of demonstrable harm to the interests of children on a case-by-case basis would be required, the situation already established by laws for the protection of children's physical, psychological and moral rights and interests.[6] These laws may, of course, be exploited unreasonably by official opponents of home education.

My present point is that the weight of evidence concerning the academic achievements and personal qualities of home educated young people strongly indicates that there can be no persuasive *general* argument against the practice on grounds of demonstrable harm or disadvantage. Indeed, it might be rather easier to demonstrate the reverse: that conventional schooling frequently exposes children to bullying, drug abuse, racial and gender prejudice, and that it is in these settings that greater vigilance is required. I have already noted the astonishing failure of many British local authorities to maintain records of the school performance of children in their care, a situation exposed by the educational press and tackled by government and local authorities only at the beginning of the present century. Such neglect is symptomatic of wider concerns about the welfare of 'looked after children', a disturbingly high proportion of whom leave school with few, if any, qualifications and subsequently drift into unemployment, homelessness, prostitution, drug abuse and crime. The vitally important matter of establishing a framework for the protection of children's rights should be the task of a specialised Children's Rights Commission, independent of government and its agencies, with authority to scrutinise both official and unofficial approaches to the treatment of children and young people.

Home education is now highly organised. In the United Kingdom, the earliest collaborative venture was the formation of the now well-known organisation, Education Otherwise, by a small group of families in 1977. Its title reflects the statutory responsibility of parents to ensure that their children receive a suitable education at a recognised school 'or otherwise'. Membership has grown steadily with the increase in numbers of home educating families, providing support and advice through a nationwide network of contacts as well as through literature and electronic media. The Home Education Advisory Service (HEAS), a registered charity, produces a handbook, a quarterly bulletin and information and suggestions about actual and potential educational resources, the public examination system, the law and special educational needs. In London, a centre called The Otherwise Club provides opportunities for regular contact between families educating children outside school and runs workshops and other group events for its members. Some groups cater specifically for Christian, Muslim and Jewish families educating, or wishing to educate, their children at home. Others are informally organised local groups of families who arrange outings, social events and joint educational initiatives. Education Now, a promotional body closely identified with Roland Meighan, disseminates ideas about non-authoritarian, democratic forms of education and encourages developments in education which enable learners to define their own personal curricula in partnership with others.

This list is indefinitely long, but the foregoing examples convey some sense of the proliferation of activity among home educating families. Some will, of course, operate in isolation from others from choice or from financial or geographical necessity. Precise numbers are difficult to ascertain because mistrust of official attitudes certainly discourages many families from registering their intention to home educate, especially where local education authorities have a record of hostility to alternatives to schooling. However, it should be noted that the motivation of many of these families has nothing to do with a desire to isolate their children. As Rothermel found, the decision frequently registers disillusionment with aspects of conventional schooling and aspirations to enrich the experience of education and fashion it according to the child's personal interests and aptitudes. Many parents would welcome positive recognition and support by education authorities if this could be distinguished in practice from a supervisory role that, by the nature of their rejection of the schools system, they feel would be unjustifiably intrusive. And a new pattern of voluntary co-operation between education authorities and parents might just provide the modest beginning of an incremental reform of education systems that really would achieve revolutionary improvements in standards and eventually foster something that could be described credibly as a 'learning society'.

A case in point: joint action by home educators

A concrete example should help to identify some important issues surrounding home education and relate broad generalisations to the particular experiences of home educating families. One of the most vigorous of these groups in Britain, Schoolhouse Home Education Association, is based in Dundee, Scotland. Established by a group of parents in 1996, it became a registered charity. Within a few years, and partly as a result of the high media profile it maintained, the Association had become sufficiently well known and respected to be quoted in local authority circulars as a source of reliable advice and information. Schoolhouse describes its broad aim as that of offering:

> information and support on a Scotland-wide basis to parents/carers who seek to take personal responsibility for the education of their children; families who have chosen or are

contemplating education outwith school for various reasons; and those who wish to safeguard the right of families to educate in accordance with their own philosophy and, most especially, with due regard to the wishes and feelings of their children.
(Schoolhouse Home Education Association, 2000, p. 3)

Other objectives include the promotion of community responsibility for children's education and the encouragement of children, themselves, to participate actively in making decisions about their education. A distinctive feature of Schoolhouse policy is its campaign for active state support for home education. Scottish legislation imposes a legal duty on parents to ensure a suitable and 'efficient' education for their children and, the association argues, the state should therefore provide support for those who require it in order to fulfil those legal responsibilities.

By the beginning of the new century, significant numbers of individual cases were being referred to Schoolhouse by both statutory and voluntary agencies. Enquiries by home educators, prospective home educators, lawyers, journalists, politicians and voluntary organisations reached well over a thousand in 1999/2000, an increase of about 50 per cent on the previous year. The largest increase came via electronic mail, Internet links and the group's own website, an interesting illustration of the potential for information technology to add new dimensions to the idea of home education. A majority of these enquiries were from actual or prospective home educators in every local authority area in Scotland, but particularly from those areas where education authority attitudes were unfavourable or hostile to home education and where disputes had arisen as a result. The commonest of these issues involved difficulties parents had experienced in withdrawing their children from schools, bullying, and what parents felt to be the unmet or inadequately met special needs of their children. A proportion of enquiries related to the Scottish examinations crisis of 2000 that I discussed in Chapter 5. In addition to contacts with over two hundred voluntary and other bodies, more than seventy came from home education organisations, some from other European countries like Germany, Switzerland and Sweden, and others from as far afield as Japan and America.

In addition to the more formal roles of providing information and support and lobbying on behalf of home educators, Schoolhouse has organised a wide range of social activities for members including conferences, 'family days' at different Scottish locations, as well as group picnics, sales of work and other fund-raising events. Its activities are broadcast by means of regular newsletters and, consistent with its aim of promoting self-directed learning by children, a lively periodical called *Schoolhouse Times* is written, illustrated, edited and produced collaboratively by home educated children of different ages. One issue contained an enthusiastic account of a march on the new Scottish Parliament in September 2000 by the association and its supporters, including some members of the Parliament. The aim was to draw attention to their case for legislative reform to achieve a harmonisation of Scottish law with that of England and Wales to allow parents to withdraw their children from school without first having to obtain local authority consent.[7] Schoolhouse failed in that objective, but the example typifies the high political profile that the association has adopted and helps to account for other successes it has achieved in its relationships with central and local government.

Official responses to home educators

Schoolhouse has addressed problems of a kind encountered by home educating parents generally as well as in Scotland, where the education system had been largely independent of the rest of the United Kingdom even prior to the establishment of the devolved Scottish Parliament in 1999. One of these problems has been the continuing opposition of elected representatives in some areas of Scotland to the whole idea of home education. Another has been the tendency among some education officers to try to insist that families adhere to structured methods of teaching. This demand, apart from being beyond their legal powers, does not take account of the general aversion to formally structured teaching and learning among demonstrably successful home educating families. It is also symptomatic of the powerful hold of an authoritarian theory of learning on the imagination of many educational professionals. And these attitudes and prejudices must account for the extraordinary catalogue of unjustified official intrusions by education officials in the affairs of parents and their children uncovered by a survey in 2000 of twenty-seven of the thirty-two Scottish local authorities' approaches to working with home educators.

The report of that survey by the Scottish Consumer Council estimated that although only 300 cases of children being educated in their homes were officially recorded, the real number was closer to 4,000. Many local authorities were 'exceeding their powers by placing barriers in the way of families who exercise this legitimate choice', and the discrepancy between the official and estimated numbers was largely attributable to the fact that 'many families never inform local authorities of their decision to keep their children out of schools because they have no confidence in councils acting in their interests' (Welsh, 2000, p. 11). According to the report, many children experienced mental health problems as a result of being forced to attend school in an atmosphere of conflict between their parents and the authorities. Even when families asserted their right to educate children at home, they often faced demands by officials for entry to their homes to assess educational provision, though there was no statutory right or duty for them to do so. Other education officers tried to insist that home educators should adhere to the official '5–14' curriculum guidelines even though they were not even legal requirements for Scottish schools.[8] Only two of the twenty-seven councils surveyed did not prescribe these guidelines as definitive of sound home educational procedure. Although there were examples of good practice and instances of positive support, poor and misleading advice was frequently given to parents by local authority staff who had received no training about home education or the laws relating to it. One of the disturbing consequences of the requirement for parents to obtain the consent of the education authority to withdraw their children from school was that if long delays led them to pre-empt an official decision, they faced the possibility of criminal proceedings or referral to a 'children's panel'. The SCC commented that this involved an undesirable blurring of the distinction between education and social work. As the report also pointed out, confusion reigns over the interpretation of the statutory requirement for parents to ensure that children receive efficient education suitable to their ages, abilities and aptitudes, whether in school 'or by other means'.

One of the conclusions of the SCC report which accords closely with the view of Schoolhouse is that a positive, supportive approach by local authorities to home educators could obviate many of these difficulties: that the ideal of partnership should replace the interventionist approach adopted by many of these authorities, suspicious as they are of home educators and predisposed to assert a supervisory role in relation to them. The question must be whether a combination of partnership and supervision is feasible in relationships between individual citizens and their children on the one hand and hierarchically organised bureaucracies under political direction on the other. There are reasons for believing that a genuine, effective partnership could be achieved only if a clear separation between these functions of support and supervision is achieved.

Following the SCC report, the Scottish Executive Education Department invited education authorities to make submissions concerning the appropriate content of official guidance on home education provided for by statute.[9] An initial response by Scottish Directors of Education and the Convention of Scottish Local Authorities revealed a largely negative mindset about home education, despite its acknowledgement of the legal right of parents to make such educational provision for their children.[10] Some education officers were sceptical that home educators could 'provide adequately for the breadth and depth of the curriculum, tuition, social development, achievement and progress that can be provided in a school'. The local authority response also incorrectly interpreted the statutory duty of parents to provide 'efficient education to their children which is suitable to their age, ability and aptitude' (Education Scotland Act 1980, s. 30) as requiring local education authorities to 'monitor' home education. The document expressed frustration at the absence of a statutory right of access to the home for this purpose and argued that 'there are compelling grounds for amending the current legislation' relating to home education. 'One potential difficulty,' it was claimed, 'is that there are really no grounds for refusing home education unless issues of child protection emerge. Some councils will find themselves dealing with families whose lifestyle is unconventional' (*ibid.*).

A further difficulty envisaged by the local authorities was the absence in the legislation of a definition of what a 'suitable' education would be. Local authorities would base their monitoring framework on a mainstream curriculum that was precisely what many home educating parents had rejected. This, and the fact that some local authorities had challenged such unstructured approaches in the courts and lost, deprived them of clear criteria concerning 'acceptable home education' and the ability to assess whether a child might be 'at risk' (*ibid.*). And although the document acknowledged Article 2, Protocol 1 of the European Convention and the Human Rights Act 1998, it interpreted it as meaning that parents have 'the right to have a say in certain aspects of educational provision' rather than, in the words of that Article, 'the right ... to ensure that such education and teaching is in conformity with their own religious and philosophical convictions'.

To some extent, the document accepted the inevitability of a growth of home education and urged the Scottish Executive to consider working with local authorities to establish a 'virtual school' that built on distance learning approaches used in countries like Australia and New Zealand. But there is a danger that such positive initiatives, which certainly would meet the wishes of many home educating parents, might be altogether vitiated by official insistence on rigorous monitoring and testing to a curriculum designed for the very different context of the school. That would not only fly in the face of the kind of abundant evidence already cited in favour of individualised curricula in which the child plays a creative part; it would undermine the very liberties that the human rights legislation was intended to protect.

A very real practical consideration is that a determined, interventionist approach would have the immediate effect of driving home education still further underground – of adding additional numbers to the estimated thousands who already fail to register their children with education authorities. Moreover, the apparent enthusiasm of local authorities to adopt a supervisory role in this context should be set against their record in supervising the education and general welfare of children who are officially in their care. At precisely the same time that the issue of guidance on home education was being considered, the Scottish Executive was just beginning to take steps to remedy some of the notorious defects in educational provision for 'children looked after away from home by local authorities' (HM Inspectors of Schools and the Social Work Services Inspectorate, March 2001). That report acknowledged that those children were 'at a particular educational disadvantage', that a majority leave care with no formal qualifications, and that there was a lack of clarity about the roles and responsibilities among professionals who have responsibility for the children. Demands for the establishment of a Commissioner for Children's Rights arose out of just such long-standing and tragic defects in the supervisory role of government. The creation of trust and confidence between education authorities and families disenchanted with formal schooling requires the deliberation of an expert and independent agency. *If* a system of monitoring is considered to be a necessary safeguard for the right of the child to education, it should be compatible with internationally agreed principles for the protection of human rights. It should not set up standards that are unrealistic in relation to what formal schooling *actually* accomplishes for most children. It should be independent of the formal schools system and should make the fullest possible provision for taking account of the expressed wishes of individual children rather than impose some official interpretation of their 'entitlement'.[11] In short, a conscientious reassessment of educational rights and liberties is needed. As Katerina Tomasevski, Special Rapporteur to the United Nations High Commission on Human Rights, said:

> The objective of getting all school-aged children to school and keeping them there until they attain the minimum defined in

compulsory education is routinely used in the sector of education, but this objective does not necessarily conform to human rights requirements. In a country where all school-aged children are in school, free of charge, for the full duration of compulsory education, the right to education may be denied or violated. The core human rights standards for education include respect for freedom. The respect of parents' freedom to educate their children according to their vision of what education should be has been part of international human rights standards since their very emergence.

(08–04–99)

9   Ways forward

Towards a learning society

> The true test of intelligence is not how much we know how to do, but how we behave when we don't know what to do.
>
> (Holt, 1964, p. 163)

Most educators would agree that the influence of family background is the single most consistent reason for the success or failure of children in school. In the 1970s, Halsey cited evidence suggesting that the home was twice as significant as the neighbourhood and the school put together in this respect (Halsey, 1972, p. 10). That report stressed that educational deprivation was a function of 'the total structure of society'. Pre-schooling, Educational Priority Area status for certain communities, and the establishment of community schools were partial solutions which needed to be accompanied by measures to address historically entrenched economic and cultural inequalities. The unyielding nature of educational deprivation had been demonstrated by the much-advertised failure of the American programme of 'compensatory education', leading to the acrimonious 'nature versus nurture' debate of the early 1970s.[1] The 'Head Start' scheme had not had a substantial, long-term impact on children's intellectual and social development according to the Westinghouse Report, and one review of a thousand intervention programmes identified only twenty-one studies suggesting clear evidence of success, but then only involving small-scale projects and very small numbers of children (*ibid.*, pp. 19–30).

On the other hand, Halsey detected signs of greater success in American measures to counteract educational disadvantage by changing the kind of relationship between schools and communities. The report considered the alternative strategy of deploying resources to make an impact on 'the child's experience in the home' rather than concentrating them in the formal education system. The Nashville pre-school project and the Bloomingdale family programme prioritised parental involvement and were said to have led to 'measurable changes in parental behaviour and attitudes towards education, and even produce[d] IQ gains amongst parents as well' (*ibid.*). Those sceptical about the integrity of this concept of general intelligence perhaps may take this to mean that parents appeared to benefit in educational terms from participation in their children's education. Other experiments included 'free schools' that, according to the report, had demonstrated how members of minority groups could run schools effectively, and 'schools without walls' that utilised resources available in the community like libraries, museums and research institutes. But the overall British strategy recommended by Halsey was one that would encourage parents to join in the educational process. 'To foster the partnership between home and school it is necessary to move in both directions – to take education into the home and to bring parents into the school'; and a key proposal was the appointment of 'educational home visitors' on the analogy of the health visitors familiar in the National Health Service (*ibid.*, p. 191).

Educational Priority Areas and their ideal of family and community participation were partly reinvented in the 1990s as Education Action Zones but these, as I observed in Chapter 2, placed a premium on the involvement of private enterprise. The mantra of parental involvement was invoked, but was destined to have little influence on how decisions were reached about the curricular framework – that was already laid down by statute and in government policy, permitting little flexibility. Indeed, political priorities seem to have asserted themselves above all others in the form of ministerial demands for success rates measured as performance on national tests. The experiment foundered partly on the reluctance of private enterprise to demonstrate the required vision and to provide the anticipated resources. Public mention of these once proudly heralded zones subsequently blended into the amorphous background noise of educational jargon.

Contrasting visions

The idea of educational home visitors, or family tutors, could be developed in different ways, depending on the willingness of the state to resource such an idea and upon the scope of this vision of education. John Adcock has sketched out a future in which an elaborate system of home tuition and distance-learning support replaces the schools system more or less in its entirety (Adcock, 1994). And this kind of scenario is one among a number of options for future educational development outlined as 'tools for reflection' by the Organisation for Economic Development and Co-operation (OECD, 2001, pp. 122–33). The latter report offered six alternative scenarios on a continuum between a 'robust bureaucratic schools system' in which vested interests resist fundamental change despite continuing problems about resourcing schools, and a 'meltdown scenario' of crisis-level teacher shortages and falling standards. Between these extremes are other conjectured situations. In one of these, schools achieve new standards of excellence as 'learning organisations', utilising information technology and the resources of private industry to drive a 'lifelong learning for all agenda'. In another, the 'de-schooling' scenario, widespread dissatisfaction with the inflexible, bureaucratic nature of the schools system leads to new forms of private, voluntaristic and community funding arrangements. Here, distinctions between the roles of teachers, students, parents and the community in education break down, producing diverse responses according to perceived needs. The OECD report does not consider the formal or informal decision-making processes by which these different scenarios might be realised in any detail. Nor, by the nature of its econometric remit, does it relate this range of future possibilities to those fundamental questions about educational and civil liberties in democratic societies.

I referred again to the Halsey Report because its findings have perhaps even greater relevance now that the radical alternatives of home education and family networking have emerged spontaneously as features of the educational landscape, especially in America. Potential for a gradual convergence between home life and formal schooling that respects the rights and choices of children and parents has now been greatly enhanced by the advent of that movement. But it is only a potential. A fault-line between informality and regimentation distinguishes these two experiences of education. Programmatic teaching is a comparatively rare, frequently abandoned, feature of learning in the home. But under the influence of political imperatives for demonstrable success, it has become increasingly characteristic of institutional methods. The idea of effective learning in the absence of pre-specified curricula and assessment regimes is greeted with suspicion and incredulity by many education professionals.

Pondering the self-perpetuating cycle of deprivation, Halsey quite properly questioned 'the rights of the state, through its agencies, to intervene in the relation between parents and children'. Even then, the possibility of incremental movements towards a voluntaristic rather than an interventionist stance by governments must have seemed remote in the near-complete absence of spontaneous educational initiatives by families. It is, after all, rather characteristic of the history and ethos of education in Britain that educational reform is seen, even from liberal perspectives, in terms of 'top-down' initiatives within a framework of centralised decision-making and ultimate legal compulsion. The attitudes of some Scottish local education authorities that I discussed in the last chapter are symptomatic of this general preoccupation with control and it is probably the greatest single obstacle to effective co-operation with families. It certainly seems to have been a significant factor in driving underground a large proportion of home educating families who might otherwise have provided the occasion for interesting experiments in educational diversification.

That patronising view of the limitations of what parents and children can contribute to education without careful supervision manifests itself in their exclusion from matters relating to curriculum content and design, in the introduction of fundamental changes in the declared aims of schooling, and in the controversial redesign of examination systems with minimal public debate. It is hard to exaggerate the consequential alienation between families and schools, even though many appear untroubled by it or unaware of it. But it is important to recognise how generations of compulsory schooling have produced an obstinate popular conviction that education is something that happens to people at a particular stage of their young lives, irrespective of their wishes; that it is done to them by other people in buildings designated for that purpose; that educational under-achievement reflects shortcomings in that closed system and its personnel.[2] That is the essence of alienation and no amount of rhetoric about participation and community involvement will change it significantly – at least until the assumptions that there is a 'best way' of educating and institutional machinery best suited to find that way are seriously questioned. Against the background of such assumptions, the aspirations of untrained parents who opt to educate their children outside the schools system appear to be dangerous steps into the unknown. Their remarkable achievements seem so counter-intuitive that the authorities' reaction is often an insistence on the superiority of their system in the face of inconsistent or contradictory evidence.

Of course, there are those educationalists of established reputation, like David Hargreaves, who anticipate and advocate radical and far-reaching reforms to achieve diversity in education. A key question is just how that change is to come about; *who* is to manage it? Another politically influential writer, Tom Bentley, has provided an extremely detailed account of what 'learning beyond the classroom' might look like (Bentley, 1998). His vision is one of schools and colleges as the 'hubs' of widespread learning networks that reach deep into communities, exploiting their educational resources in unprecedented ways. Schools, for instance, would have new roles as 'neighbourhood learning centres' (*ibid.*, p. 72). Bentley, like Halsey before him, addresses alienation and social deprivation as a priority. In doing so, he provides important reminders of the rich resources that exist outside educational institutions among the organised public as well as the kind of initiatives provided by breakfast and homework clubs, summer schools and collaborative study-support projects by youth organisations and local employers.

Perhaps because one of his principal concerns *is* social deprivation, Bentley's accent is strongly on what he regards as 'real life' knowledge and skills in everyday situations, in employment and on the challenges posed by 'the new world of work' and the 'knowledge economy'. He sees the need for a shift in thinking beyond a narrow traditional school curriculum, but in reality the shift he recommends is towards at least as narrow a conception of the role of education in society, as something overwhelmingly concerned with fitting individuals to the predicted shape of things to come. For example, 'direct feedback and assessment on the relevance of active learning projects to the world of work could play a much greater part in the assessment of learning' (*ibid.*, p. 149). One way in which he envisages this being done is through the involvement of local business volunteers from employer organisations in the process of evaluation. These assessors, Bentley acknowledges, would require some training and 'understanding of the goals of education', a curiously elliptical statement that simultaneously embraces both the idea of authoritatively established educational goals and a sense of their limited relevance to real-life situations.

Something that is missing, and this is characteristic of his analysis as a whole, is an account of the source from which these revolutionary changes will spring. One is almost tempted to assume that behind the progressive transformation will be government and its agencies, maintaining what Bentley describes by means of a number of organic metaphors as 'a balance between order and chaos' (*ibid.*, pp. 176–7). However, he expressly rejects the idea of a 'chain of institutional command and control' while appearing to acknowledge human agency more as the sum of forces that will sustain a predetermined future than as a matrix of independent forces that will actually shape a future. And this conclusion is rather strikingly borne out by a paragraph in which Bentley casually welcomes a developing political view that 'the old polarities between left and right' are 'no longer helpful'. The new challenges are about achieving more effective government without raising

taxes, achieving sustainable global economic development and reconciling individual aspirations with collective needs and resources (*ibid.*,
p. 172) – as though such questions were not the very essence of so
many unresolved left–right political issues. More importantly, it is as
though these issues did not encompass radically incommensurable
views about the relationship between individuals, their society and an
expansionist global economy that is widely regarded as outstripping
effective democratic control.

Of course, Bentley's vision of learning beyond the classroom is a
personal one. But that does not diminish its significance because it has
much in common with contemporary government policies and with
one future scenario portrayed by the OECD in its previously
mentioned report (OECD, 2001). Bentley denies that he is putting
forward a blueprint, but it *resembles* a blueprint nevertheless: a fairly
detailed plan for the wholesale reform of education according to a
particular view of its relationship to social and economic life. And in
this respect he typifies the instrumentalist trend in educational policy-
making. There is little to suggest that a primary function of education
is to equip people with the means to assess their society and its values
critically and to act independently to achieve their own objectives,
rather than to meet a demand for economically versatile employees.
Many of the features of citizenship education recommended by the
Crick Report (QCA, 1998) are anticipated, with a strong bias towards
local community involvement by young people. Knowledge and understanding of political and legal institutions and 'concepts such as
democracy and freedom' are elements, but unelaborated elements, of
this citizenship curriculum. Moreover, they are projected as subjects to
be taught and learned rather than as principles guiding what Bentley
calls 'the progressive transformation of education'. Illytch is recalled as
an untimely prophet of de-schooling and the 'learning web', but in
Bentley's version the ends seem to be largely pre-ordained even if the
means have changed. Personal choice about alternative learning-routes
is emphasised but it would be under what turns out to be pervasive
scrutiny by unidentified but implicitly near-infallible authorities:

> From the age of four or five, records of progress would be
> collected and in an integrated, IT-based portfolio of achievement,
> regularly updated and reviewed, which would stay with the student
> right through into adulthood. As well as expert assessments, it
> might eventually include self-assessment, video-recordings of
> project presentations, written work and a number of more stan-
> dardised assessment results. Over time, this portfolio would

provide detailed evidence of progression and attainment, able to offer complex, sophisticated and clear evidence of what a student has and has not been able to do.

(ibid., p. 183)

Individual learning would thus cash itself as the comprehensive objectification of a person. This, alone, implies a certain conception of society and the individual's place within it, even if the scenario is less than explicit about who the custodians of this social order would be. Emphasis has moved decisively away from learning as enlightenment, the Danish idea of *folkeoplysning*, to the instrumental means of matching people to putative social requirements, irrespective of how those are defined.

It is worth recalling that, in reality, these requirements are far from clear, let alone legitimate educational priorities. Apart from those traditional areas of employment where specialised skills have usually been necessary and are well defined, employers seem to be vague about what general skills they require, mentioning basic literacy and numeracy most frequently with the frequent addition of 'inter-' and 'intra-personal' skills.[3] Yet it was on the basis of such vague generalities, as well as the indistinct notions of a 'learning society' and a 'knowledge economy', that a whole raft of educational innovations were introduced in the 1990s. Moreover, determined efforts were made by governments to bridge the divide between education and training, largely by equating education with skills-training and manipulating assessment regimes to reflect this dubious identification. One of these innovations was the ill-fated reform of the Scottish examinations system that I discussed in Chapter 5. Another has been the attempt to graft features of remedial education on to the curriculum as a whole in the form of 'key' or 'core' skills.[4] Nothing quite illustrates the folly of dispensing with philosophical considerations for ostensibly pragmatic reasons as clearly as the wholesale commitment to these reputedly 'generic' skills and their indifferent, sceptical, even hostile reception by students, employers and universities (Hodgson *et al.*, 2001).

However, my present point is not about the specifics of these unfortunate episodes in educational policy-making but the manner in which decisions are reached and implemented. It reflects the monolithic nature of an education system in contrast to the multiplicity of interests, aspirations and potentialities of society at large. Innovations of the kind I have mentioned demand huge investments of time, effort and public money. They reflect ideological and political commitments that are condensed into policies affecting the futures of a society's young people by a complex institutional hierarchy. Inevitably, policy decisions reflect judgments by those institutions of what is possible within existing resources and management structures, of their implications for funding and staffing and their potential impacts on target populations and on society more generally. And these ramifications are labyrinthine, of course. Governments stand in a similar relationship to those they represent in educational and vocational matters as they do to the industry and commerce of a nation. Recent British governments have advertised their limitations as leaders in the latter context, though there is still no sign that they might issue such a self-denying ordinance in the case of education.

A problem arises for those, like Bentley and Hargreaves, who advocate educational diversity without at least equally emphasising means of diversifying the articulation and representation of interests. This is that the ideological and electoral momentum behind government commitments to manage social and educational change might continue to produce a series of large-scale, uncontrolled experiments to subsume that diversity within a single, controllable system. The revision of assessment regimes, involving tight pre-specification of learning outcomes and increasing use of internal, modular assessment, is one example. Change has been radical and abrupt enough to cast serious doubt on how the new system relates to the one its replaces. How, in other words, do student abilities measured by the new regimes compare with those measured by the tried and tested regimes they replaced? A quainter illustration of the all-embracing aspirations of British governments was the task assigned by the Qualifications and Curriculum Authority to a Forum on Values in Education and the Community in 1996, to determine 'whether there are any values on which there is common agreement in society' (Bentley, 1998, p. 59).

Of course, there are many commonly agreed values. But when one gets beyond consensus about generalities like the virtues of tolerance and respect for others, the need arises for an imposition of order on chaos, for arbitration about substantive meanings – and with it, the possibility of trespassing on rights of individual belief and free expression. Among the controversies following the newly elected Labour government's announcement in 2001 of a policy to encourage specialisation in secondary education was one that highlighted the invidious nature of centralised control of a process of diversification. The government envisaged an increasing number of establishments specialising in such subjects as modern languages and technology. There would also be more 'faith' schools. But the newly appointed Education Secretary hastily repudiated suggestions for 'ethnic' schools catering for the educationally underprivileged Afro-Caribbean community as divisive and, in doing so, peremptorily asserted the state's authority to decide the distinction between a 'faith' and a 'culture'.[5] Alternatively, those campaigns against government proposals to repeal Section 28 of the Local Government Act, prohibiting the promotion of homosexual relationships as 'pretended family relationships', indicate the extent of popular British habituation to the state's monopoly in determining educational ends, means and morals.

A dominant theme in educational thought has been the quest for the best possible form of education. There is nothing wrong with discourse concerning proper ends and means in education, of course, and this book inclines strongly towards a certain view of optimal conditions for effective learning. At a purely practical level, there may be no 'best' method in education. As Meighan has argued, children and adults learn in highly individualised ways and respond differently to any single approach. However, problems are created in centralised institutions by the need to prioritise certain conceptions of ends and means as matters of public policy. It might be argued that this is a perfectly justifiable democratic process. That, however, involves a particular conception of democracy as government by élite minorities whose interpretation of public goods is legitimised by the fact that they are elected periodically on the basis of broad manifesto commitments.

A radical alternative, perhaps, to the kind of educational diversification Bentley anticipates, and certainly to the current situation in the United Kingdom and other countries, is James Tooley's idea of 'education without the state' (Tooley, 2000). This might be called a radical-right vision of a society liberated from centralised state control through the privatisation of all aspects of education. There would be no direct state provision, state funding would cater only for the most deprived sections of society, regulation of private educational provision would be minimal and access to the system by educational enterprises would be correspondingly easy. An 'educational market' would ensure direct accountability to the 'consumer' and equilibrium between demand and supply.

Central to Tooley's privatisation argument is the idea that large consequential reductions in taxation would compensate families for the additional costs of paying for their children's education. This scenario might be regarded as a logical extension of Bentley's bland assertion of the need for 'more effective government without raising taxes' (*ibid.*). Indeed, it might even be regarded as the ultimate destination of the British education system in the light of recent rejections by government of 'ideological' arguments against public–private initiatives in educational provision and the proposed introduction of specialisation in the state comprehensive school system. Tooley is clear, though, that what he recommends is more than partnership with the private sector; it is wholesale adoption by it of most educational responsibilities.

In a number of respects, Tooley and other 'privatisers' seem to be on strong ground. The welter of top-down initiatives, many of which have had no demonstrable success and have been couched so densely in jargon that they must have been all but unintelligible to the public at large, has diminished the argument that state provision ensures political accountability. Arguments for the superiority of existing forms of government supervision of education cannot be beyond dispute, given existing levels of under-achievement and the official failures to safeguard the interests of vulnerable children catalogued in previous chapters. There is, of course, a fundamental case for the redistributive role of the state, and this is closely bound up with the question of equal opportunities to exercise basic human rights. But the redistributive principle has been challenged increasingly by government fiscal policies and emphasis on more precise targeting of welfare benefits to those in greatest need, something that Tooley does not challenge. In any case, it could be argued that educational expenditure is severely distorted by conventional institutional arrangements. To take an extreme example, Rudner calculated that the average expenditure on educational resources by the thousands of highly successful home educating families he studied was about $400 a year, a figure far below the per-capita cost of school education anywhere (Rudner, 2000). And, finally, any principled resistance by governments to the wholesale commercialisation of education can only have been weakened by their deference to the international market economy.

All of these arguments and the counter-arguments involve deep ideological commitments and divisions and will not be resolved in *a priori* fashion. In the meantime, education systems continue to change and adapt through a combination of principle and pragmatism. The comprehensive privatisation scenario might be anticipated as an outcome of present trends, though the tenacity with which even 'deregulating' governments have sought to control education makes this unlikely. There is a greater possibility of a piecemeal drift towards a government-controlled, private educational market serving only officially defined educational objectives in a semblance of public accountability. In that case, market forces would lose most of whatever liberating potential they might otherwise be claimed to have; the participation of parents and children would be restricted to the choices exercised by the consumers of pre-packaged products. Of course, the veneer of broader educational purpose would remain, but another possibility suggested by precedent is that its pattern could be determined by the urge to promote social cohesion through the inculcation of whatever core values government manages to identify. In any event, a large and continuing role for government in education seems inevitable for the foreseeable future, and despite all these anxieties, for many it has at least a potential for genuine democratic accountability and respect for individual liberties.

Learning to let go

Concerns about inequalities in a diversified system are hardly borne out by experience. Denmark shows that educational freedom does not, itself, imply social exclusion or inequality, while the United Kingdom's comprehensive school system has, *itself*, done little or nothing that can be demonstrated to have reduced social inequalities. On the other hand, there are conscientiously held but mutually inconsistent views about these and all other aspects of education that could not be encompassed by any blueprint. A dynamic is needed that will lead to incremental accommodations between the numerous interested parties – between individual citizens and the state; between parents and children; between homes and schools; between government and private enterprise – a dynamic that will permit gradual and sensitive reallocations of resources in response to emerging needs and established rights. I have already suggested that such a dynamic is already available in the home education movement that, in the United Kingdom, accounts for an estimated 50,000 children and possibly many more. My argument is not that a scenario involving children learning in the isolation of their homes should be taken as a generalisable model, though part of it certainly *is* that the legitimacy of that kind of education should be acknowledged forthrightly in principle, as it is in Denmark. It is important that there should be more generous official recognition that home educators are pioneering forms of learning that have been effectively ruled out by the ever increasing formalisation of state schooling. Home education is rapidly evolving into a highly diversified and informal system of networks in which adults and children of different ages, backgrounds and interests collaborate and create their own learning opportunities, and make sophisticated use of modern information technology, of libraries, community centres, museums, art galleries and nature reserves.

What the movement lacks in the United Kingdom and certain other democratic countries, though, is consistent, formal recognition by government that it is a legitimate expression of the civil rights laid down in the European Convention/Human Rights Act 1998. Too much depends on variable interpretations of these rights by local authorities, and on the scope this permits for official attitudes towards home educators to range from the positive and supportive to the hostile and obstructive. There is also a possibility that the child's right to education in this and other international instruments, such as the Convention on the Rights of the Child, might be interpreted in ways inconsistent with the fundamental right of parents to ensure that the state respects their religious and philosophical convictions.

This is not to diminish the importance of measures to safeguard the rights of children. It is, however, to dispute the justifiability of allowing partial interpretations that effectively reformulate children's rights and entitlements as parental obligations to send them to school or to submit to monitoring and supervision by local education authorities if they do not. The overwhelming evidence, it is worth repeating, is that home educating families are more successful in general than schools and education authorities and that children thrive in that educational setting. Consequently, many parents argue that the protection of children in respect of their rights to education is of a piece with their rights to safety and security in general, a position endorsed by court decisions in the United States.[6]

Nevertheless, concerns will remain about the possibility of seriously deviant practices by a minority of parents. Although these would arguably occur irrespective of where a child is educated, this anxiety might prove insistent enough to be felt to warrant special measures to safeguard children. In that event, the construction of an appropriate framework for protecting children's educational rights should be a matter for an independent Children's Commission that would review the available evidence impartially. Hopefully, it would recommend that any system of monitoring should, itself, be independent. In any event, this still-small sector of the educational enterprise deserves to be accorded the recognition that it has in Denmark: as an expression of the basic duty of parents to educate their children, and as a cornerstone of a liberal and democratic education system that provides wide-ranging choices. Significantly, perhaps, by securing and perpetuating that right, as well as by providing for further tiers of independent education, Denmark actually has very few home educated children. It also has a sensitive mechanism for registering individual family preferences, as the recent shift towards Free Schools in response to the closure and amalgamation of smaller state schools demonstrates.

The obvious alternative to an exaggerated preoccupation with what might go wrong would be the adoption by government and local authorities of constructive, differential approaches to home educators, to recognise that their motives are very diverse and often far from hostile to official involvement, as distinct from intervention. Indeed, many argue for more generous resourcing by education authorities, the introduction of elements of 'flexi-schooling', home tuition and accurate advice on all aspects of education. And it is in this area of co-operation that so many unrealised possibilities for educational improvement are located, not least that ambition of Halsey's to dismantle the barriers between homes and schools by converging from both directions at once. Success, however, is predicated on the adoption by government and its agencies of a rather unfamiliar principle: management without control.

An advantage of home education initiatives is that their small scale in relation to the formal education system lends itself to incremental developments that do not imply significant additional funding. Indeed, if only a modest proportion of the per capita costs of educating children in schools were transferred directly to supporting their educational activities at home, resources could be released for other educational priorities. Ultimately, and without large-scale financial commitments by government, the options available could range from orthodox schooling, through a variety of forms of 'flexi-schooling', distance learning and periodic tuition to fully independent versions of home education. It is important to recognise the extent to which home educators already co-operate in educational and social activities and in identifying and utilising existing resources in the community. In addition, home education has become a global phenomenon and information and communications technology provide world-wide resources for learning at home and in community institutions as well as in schools. Relatively modest investments would be required to upgrade public libraries, community and sports centres as family learning centres where combinations of informal and formal learning take place. And the exciting prospect is that, by these means, education could become a genuine lifelong activity for anyone, regardless of age or station in life.

Educational resources

One of the virtues of Bentley's vision of education beyond the classroom is that it draws attention to the huge range of actual and
potential resources in the community that might be more effectively
harnessed for educational purposes. His emphasis is on community
involvement that would reinforce vocational competence and citizenship rather than the more academic aspects of education. But the
latter are essential features of our intellectual inheritance and of the
repertoire of the effective citizen. Regardless of the excesses of some
'domain' theories of the kind I discussed in Chapter 6, the traditional
academic disciplines represent (though all too often in fossilised form)
a heritage of critical inquiry that has transformed human consciousness and understanding of the world. Educational under-achievement
and political apathy amount to a disinheritance. The critical traditions
belong to everyone, a heritage that is intimately connected both with
the historical emergence of democracy and with the awareness that
citizens need for effective participation in contemporary democratic
societies. There is a distressingly common tendency to confuse tradition with obsolescence: to associate democratic participation with the
merely vocational and the communal; to consign the 'academic' to
those who are judged intellectually capable of looking after themselves; to find practical alternatives for the rest – the majority, indeed.
The crucial educational task of the future will be to make the critical
traditions accessible to everyone: to rescue them from textbooks,
timetables and tests.

A vital lesson of the home education movement seems to be that
free inquiry and discursive relationships with intellectual peers do not
result in diffuse understanding and an absence of disciplinary rigour.
Indeed, the reverse seems to be true to a remarkable extent, though
there remain important questions about access to specialised expertise.
And this is more abundant than might be supposed. Every small town
has its scientific, artistic and historical societies, its photographic and
astronomical societies, its organised groups of naturalists and environ-
mentalists. These relatively informal voluntary bodies include many
individuals whose disciplinary expertise and qualifications compare
very favourably with those of many professional educators. Yet they
are usually involved in formal educational activity sporadically,
marginally or even not at all. Many academically able students qualify
for university education without even being aware of the existence of
this local pool of expertise in the very disciplines they have chosen to
study. This is another indication of the alienation of education from
society at large. Yet others are the huge obstacles to consistent educa-

tional participation with and by these organisations posed by over-crowded, prescriptive school curricula, a relentless succession of formal assessments and the pervasive requirements for bureaucratic supervision. And although these obstacles may be too formidable for the average school to surmount, the pioneering activities of home educating families might be just what could stimulate a new pattern of relationships between that voluntary sector and the segregated world of education. And this is to say nothing of the educational contribution by many expert statutory agencies that might follow a thorough appraisal of their scientific, technical and human resources for such a task.

By degrees, the universal right to be educated has mutated into a universal obligation to be assessed, and it is easy to forget that these are, in fact, quite distinct objectives. It is theoretically possible for a person to acquire a very thorough education without ever being formally examined, and this was undoubtedly true of the education of many distinguished historical figures. However, the need to maintain standards in our institutions and the unavoidable requirement to ensure levels of ability and aptitudes appropriate to various callings in life make some assessment essential. But the point has now been reached where the core experience of nearly all schoolchildren is that of being assessed continuously from the earliest ages until their final liberation from formal schooling. This is especially true of young people in Britain, who are probably the most intensively tested anywhere in the world. One well-advertised consequence of this is the high level of stress among schoolchildren, reports of increasing levels of mental illness and, of course, the even more widely publicised stress experienced by teachers and its probable connection with severe staff shortages. These are serious problems in their own right, but the tacit identification of learning with the outcome of testing and the pressures on the educators to teach to tests must be one of the most destructive forces at work in contemporary schooling. It is entirely inimical to the ideal of a society in which people are motivated to embark on 'lifelong learning'.

In fact, for most people that aspiration is probably destined to be realised, at best, as the practice of continuous industrial re-training that has long been familiar, particularly in Scandinavia. Of course, the continuing possibility of acquiring new vocational skills and improving the adaptability of employees as a result is a socially desirable thing in its own right. The point is that as a model for educational policy it is extremely damaging because it substitutes for the open-ended ideal of a creative citizenry the much narrower aim of matching the training of citizens to those future social and economic needs which are regarded as predictable. There is a great difference between working to live and living to work and, as John Holt's words at the head of this chapter should remind us, the gulf between acquiring the know-how to carry out assigned tasks and the education needed to equip a person for life in an unpredictable world is about coping with the unfamiliar and the unexpected. This is especially true in the current climate where the configurations of the world of work are taken as constants on which policy must be based rather than the results of choices exercised by consumers in a culture which is inherently unpredictable – but nevertheless modifiable by rational agents.

Education and the citizen

In certain old industrial areas of the United Kingdom, folklore records how, when their shifts had ended, steelworkers would once queue to attend Workers' Educational Association lectures on politics, economics and philosophy. Some of these tales are apocryphal, but the remnants of well-stocked libraries in miners' institutes testify to the spontaneous urge of significant numbers of working people to educate themselves to play a more decisive, responsible role in their societies. Of course, those were the days when formal educational opportunities were severely limited for the great majority of people and poverty was deeper and more widespread. There was a widely shared vision of a just, equitable society that could be achieved by developing the intelligence of ordinary men and women. Education and political empowerment were directly connected in popular imagination – at least in significant sections of it. Other perspectives on the education of ordinary working people were more pragmatic. In 1918, at the close of the Great War, the Federation of British Industries had opposed any extension of the age of compulsory schooling as a threat to the availability of labour. An issue of the *Daily News*, quoted by Tawney, expressed outrage at this casual assertion of the instrumental role of the majority of the nation's children:

> This, then, is the subtle discovery that, as they pore over the lessons of the past three years, inspires the Federation of British Industries' bright hopes of a more profitable future. There are classes who are ends and classes who are means – upon that grand original distinction the community is invited to base its educational system. The aim of education is to reflect, to defend, and to perpetuate the division of mankind into masters and servants.

How delicate an insight into the relative value of human beings and of material riches! How generous a heritage into which to welcome the children of men who fell in the illusion that, in their humble way, they were the servants of freedom!

(Tawney, 1966, p. 49)

The *autodidact* is a rare figure nowadays; there is less apparent need for self-education; the state has taken over responsibility for learning – if not from the cradle to the grave, at least for several decades of the average person's lifetime. Many, though by no means all, of the old inequalities of opportunity have been eliminated in primary, secondary and tertiary education. So it is all the more ironic that official solutions to crisis in that system are seen so readily in terms of their estimated contribution to the labour force and the skill requirements of a capricious global market economy. It must be possible to do better. In the more relaxed educational atmosphere of the 1970s, Halsey envisaged a gradual, two-way accommodation between homes and schools as an important contribution to raising educational standards and tackling social exclusion. The germ of a solution is already there but the crucial task is to establish the mutual confidence that will enable it to flourish and grow in an atmosphere of freedom.

Conclusion

Education and democracy

> ... what excuse shall we give (not for the public, but for ourselves as
> scientists and educators) to account for the fact that most of the public
> appears not to have caught up with Nicholas Copernicus and Galileo
> Galilei?
>
> (Durant *et al.*, 1989, pp. 11–14)

The past four hundred years have transformed human conceptions of
the world and our place in it, and the last century saw the advent of
nuclear, space and digital technology. It is now possible to telephone a
friend, anywhere on the face of the planet, from a place so remote that
no one had even seen it a century ago – and to tell them your precise
position to within a metre or less. This kind of explosive development
of science and technology has led to what politicians like to describe as
'the knowledge economy'. We are told that we live in a 'learning
society'. Consequently, it comes as an unpleasant surprise to learn that
about ten years from the end of the twentieth century, two out of three
British people in a representative sample were unable to tell researchers
investigating the public understanding of science that the earth 'goes
round' the sun in one year. It was this finding that prompted Professor
Durant's soul-searching question, above.

There are those who argue that such arcane knowledge is irrelevant
to the 'real' needs of ordinary people, though heliocentrism is more
than an isolated brute fact and actually provides the conceptual background for understanding many other features of the world: the
distribution of climatic regions, flora, fauna and varying patterns of
agriculture – and much more. However, we are all affected by bacteria
and viruses and the public understanding of that distinction revealed
in Durant's survey was also very limited. It seems a reasonable infer-
ence from such findings that large majorities of people will have little
or no grasp of scientific and technological issues like nuclear power

generation, atmospheric pollution or nutrition. Yet these are only a few of the large issues relevant to everyone, however the 'real world' is defined. This places a very considerable onus on the wisdom and good faith of elected representatives to act on behalf of the majorities who elect them. It raises basic questions about the standards of judgment required by democratic electorates if they are to exercise any kind of rational control over the social processes that determine the course of their lives and those of their children. We all exist in the penumbra of rational, scientific culture, taking our cues from others more conversant with particular fields of activity and areas of knowledge. In a highly specialised society this is inevitable; the physicist bows to the specialised knowledge of the physiologist and vice versa. There are, nevertheless, standards of rational appraisal according to which we can reach fairly reliable if tentative conclusions, whether they are about political and commercial pressures which might bias a government minister's interpretation of specialist advice, or the extra-scientific implications of genetic research. But these examples and many others presuppose reasonable levels of understanding, dispositions to keep abreast of developments and, at the very least, communicative abilities that involve a great deal more than the mechanical ability to decode the written word.

Education *is* in crisis from almost any point of view. We hear most frequently that school-leavers lack the basic 'skills' required by that burgeoning global 'knowledge economy', though I have argued that the problem runs far deeper than that. It is implicated in dangerously superficial ideas about what knowledge is, how it is acquired and why it is to be valued. Nevertheless, few statistics are quite as startling as one that is periodically cited as indicative of the modern 'skills deficit'. About one-quarter of the populations of some of the world's most advanced technological societies lack the ability to read the trades section of a telephone directory accurately or to understand simple notices on public display.

The latter example brings to mind a telling contrast. According to the Roman writer, Suetonius, the emperor Caligula maliciously ordered that laws, written in a tiny script, should be posted at a height that made them unreadable to the public, who were thus more easily convicted of law-breaking. Of course, Suetonius' own account might have been malicious, but his point concerned Caligula's despotic behaviour; widespread literacy among the Roman population was taken as understood. But nearly half a millennium earlier than that, most citizens of democratic Athens were probably literate. The ancient world provides an Archimedian point beyond our modern, rather myopic perspectives on education that should help us to expose some of the more fundamental issues about teaching and learning. One of these is the absence of a consistent relationship between standards of education among a general population and the sophistication of the technological basis of their society. Another is the absence of a consistent relationship between basic standards of education and effective democratic participation. 'Social inclusion' is not a simple concept and there are no guaranteed ways of achieving it. Its implicit identification by political leaderships with what the OECD describes as 'the competencies demanded in the knowledge economy' is seriously, even dangerously misleading.

Despite significant variations in the educational systems of western industrialised states, there has been a trend towards greater government intervention in most of them. This has been particularly marked in the United Kingdom, where the traditional distinction between education and vocational training was officially repudiated with the merger of formerly distinct branches of government in the Department for Education and Employment. The 'unique importance' of this fusion, according to the then Labour Secretary of State, David Blunkett, lay in the new department's 'responsibility for ensuring that the UK has a well-functioning labour market'.[1] It is deeply ironic that a whole generation of young people who had passed through primary and secondary education in the UK and America, preoccupied as these countries have been with techniques of industrial efficiency in schools, should have mean literacy scores which are in the lowest third of eighteen of the world's most economically developed nations (OECD, 2001, p. 49). For those of us sceptical about the idea of profound innate educational differentials it is difficult to find words to articulate the disturbing contrasts with which we are often confronted. On the one hand, a child has learned at home to read effortlessly and with pleasure by the age of five. On the other, a fairly typical late-teenage product of eleven years of formal schooling stumbles over a single, simple sentence.

Content and method in education are dictated by democratically elected governments according to the perceived imperatives of a global economy that is commonly acknowledged to be beyond effective democratic control.[2] The mantra of 'social inclusion' is consequently invoked as an ideal to inform government strategies for the achievement of ends which are not in their gift. Gaps between rich and poor persist and even widen; poverty and deprivation remain common features even in advanced western economies. Yet schoolchildren are scorned or even victimised by their peers for failing to wear popularly sanctioned designer labels on garments manufactured in third-world sweatshops, marketed by global enterprises. Disillusionment with traditional politics, particularly among the young, has become a major concern of governments and educationalists. In place of the ideal of participatory liberal democracy we have, increasingly, what a recent American administration called 'market democracy', a system in which popular preferences are infallibly recorded in the form of mass consumer choices. The problem is that, *as consumers*, we take what is on offer and rarely play more than a remote and subordinate part in deciding what is to be offered. As increasingly isolated individuals in a mass society, we register preferences capriciously, making 'lifestyle choices' which are not mediated by reasoned debate or creative participation in defining personal and social ends. The ends are set for us, in education no less than in economic matters. In this environment, 'social inclusion' becomes a matter of uniformity of treatment rather than active participation and decision-making. Education, as officially conceived, has ceased to be the solution to these modern problems; it threatens to become one of them. It is something designed by government and its agencies in language which is becoming ever less intelligible to many educationalists, let alone to the learners to whom it is 'delivered'.

The numerous UK government measures to raise educational standards in recent years suggest desperation rather than resolution. Chris Woodhead counted more than sixty in four years and dismissed all but the national literacy and numeracy strategies as having been largely a waste of time. Many were flagship initiatives like the Education Action Zones, designed to build on the new relationship between industry, commerce and education. Yet ironically this plague of 'initiativitis' contributed to the high levels of stress already apparent in the teaching profession as a result of the rigors of an inspection regime supervised by Chris Woodhead. Virtually every claim that standards improved as a result can be countered by the sceptical argument that changing methods of measuring standards vitiate that conclusion.[3] Woodhead's retrospective view of four years as Chief Inspector of Schools is perhaps the most surprisingly negative of all. Years of educational restructuring in Britain suggest that the system is incapable of sufficiently radical reform from within: that what is required is a major initiative from without, a reclamation by ordinary citizens of the education which is their fundamental right and, particularly, their children's right.

In developed western societies we live within a framework of internationally agreed human rights and freedoms. These include, quite fundamentally, educational rights and freedoms because this alone is how a culture that respects democratic liberties is transmitted from one generation to another. I have argued that despite variable and often restrictive interpretation by different states, these rights and freedoms are rooted in a dialectic between human rationality and the fallibility of epistemic, and thus all, authority – a principle which accounts for the explosive growth of knowledge in modern times and sanctions liberal democratic forms of government. This is admittedly an *a priori* argument but a positive relationship between liberty and learning by individuals and communities should nevertheless be borne out by experience. Of the many individual initiatives that can plausibly be said to have done this, the growing international home education movement provides an especially compelling challenge to educationalists and politicians to review basic educational principles. It also provides an opportunity for them to pioneer new and varied modes of educational partnership with citizens and their children on a voluntary rather than a compulsory basis which might significantly improve trust and confidence between lay people and professionals.

Support by education authorities for family learning and resource centres based on libraries and other places of community activity is likely to be the most realistic way forward towards a genuine learning society. It would help to heal the divisions between home and school which have led so many parents to relinquish all responsibility for their children's education to an ever more inscrutable and managerially convoluted system. It should certainly enable some parents to resume their own, incomplete education by offering them learning opportunities untainted by the humbling experience of revealing their ignorance in yet another classroom.

A principled objection to educational freedom and diversification that applies particularly in the United Kingdom is that it might be seen to militate against 'the ideal of comprehensive education' to which many educationalists subscribe. The attraction of this ideal must be obvious to anyone who aspires to a future of greater social equality and mutual tolerance. This is, of course, against the historical background of a viciously segregationist system that defined more than half the population of 11-year-old children as failures to be consigned to a very basic education with the prospect of eventual vocational training. Apart from the counter-objection that many people may not agree with this ideal for whatever reasons, and do not wish their children to be constrained by it, there are additional considerations. One is that the United Kingdom government policy of introducing subject-specialisation in possibly as many as half the comprehensive schools in

England reintroduces a form of segregation by ability or aptitude. Another is that the comprehensive ideal, in the institutional form in which government sought to realise it, has yielded to a servile vocationalism which removes much of its original justification.[4] And that was surely to maximise the opportunities for all children to gain access to the rich intellectual and cultural traditions of a free democratic society.

One other principled objection to freedom in education has a direct bearing on the all-important rights of children and has been rehearsed, as I have pointed out, by a number of local education authorities opposed to education beyond the school. Children have an indisputable right to education. They also have a right to protection against seriously deviant parental beliefs and behaviour. But it certainly does not follow that schools or education authorities are the appropriate agencies to ensure the observance of those rights. Such a conclusion is implied partly by existing levels of educational under-achievement in the state schools sector. It is made even more compelling by the widespread failures of education authorities to maintain records of the educational performances of children officially in their care and, in the most disturbing cases, failures to ensure the physical and emotional integrity of many 'looked after' children.[5] These long-standing deficiencies have been generally acknowledged and seriously tackled only in the twenty-first century. This fact, alone, is indicative of deeply ingrained systemic failures to comprehend and respect the most basic rights of children, rather than periodic lapses by overstretched services. I have suggested that the centrality of educational rights to human rights in general requires an agency independent of government to safeguard them, that planning and implementing measures for the protection of children's rights and liberties as a whole should be a matter for an independent and generously resourced Children's Rights Commission.

There are, of course, many initiatives that could liberalise formal education from within. Proposals for citizenship education involving children in their communities could, if liberally interpreted, offer valuable ways out of the increasingly closed society of the school, into the more open atmosphere of democratically organised society. This could be a source of genuine educational enrichment, especially if the principle were extended to include recognition of the vast range of resources of expertise, enthusiasm and goodwill among the organised public. Obstacles to such a revolution from above are unfortunately already apparent in the manner in which proposals of this kind are cast in the Procrustean mould of assessment-driven, pre-specified curricula and 'learning outcomes', the immense investment of governments in that approach, and the consequent logistical problems of introducing real change. There is a need for enlightenment from outside sources to encourage incremental accommodations between the formal and informal education sectors. And that could be provided only by examples set by independent citizens and their children. The logistics of education are subordinate to those rights and fundamental freedoms that the idealists of the Enlightenment identified as the proper ends of education.

> A government cannot have too much of the kind of activity which does not impede, but aids and stimulates individual exertion and development ... the worth of a State, in the long run, is the worth of the individuals composing it; and a State which postpones the interests of *their* mental expansion and elevation, to a little more of administrative skill, or of that semblance of it which practice gives, in the details of business; a State which dwarfs its men, in order that they may be more docile instruments in its hands even for beneficial purposes – will find that with small men no great thing can be accomplished; and that the perfection of machinery to which it has sacrificed everything will in the end avail it nothing, for want of the vital power which, in order that the machine may work more smoothly, it has preferred to banish.
>
> (Mill, 1965a, p. 360)

Notes and references

1 Introduction

1 A notable example was the protracted agonising by government and its appointed consultees over the appropriate wording of official guidelines to convey the value of marriage and its alternatives following an unsuccessful attempt to repeal Section 28 of the Local Government Act 1988. This section prohibited local authority employees, including teachers, from promoting homosexual relationships as 'pretended family relationships' and was widely regarded as discriminatory.
2 Resolution 183 of the United States Senate, 19–09–99.
3 Human Scale Education, the British branch of the European Forum for Freedom in Education, advocates the adoption of educational legislation similar to that of Denmark, and the Third Sector Schools Alliance was formed in England to campaign for state funding of educational alternatives reflecting various religious and philosophical beliefs.
4 As I will point out in later chapters, there is little agreement about what these are among employers and some scholars even dispute the possibility of generic skills.

2 New buckets under old leaks?

1 *You and Yours*, BBC Radio 4, 14–10–99.
2 For a slightly fuller account of some of these criticisms, see Chapter 6 and notes.

3 Why educate? Society, the individual and education

1 An early example of Mill's continuing hostility to dogma and didacticism is in Mill, 1946, pp. 28–40.

4 Ours to reason why? The human rights issue

1 European Commission on Human Rights, Strasbourg, May 2000.
2 Ofsted. Ref. 144/99/Ind.
3 Complaints 4 and 6 by the Secretary of State for Education and Employment in his Notice of Complaint to Summerhill School.

4 See, for example, Burgess' argument that 'the traditional organisation of formal education is inimical to learning' (Tyrrell Burgess, *The Philosophy of Karl Popper and the Improvement of Educational Practice: the Implications of Popper for Formal Education*, paper presented to SERA, 24–09–98).

5 Statement of Intent between the Secretary of State for Education and Employment and Mrs Zoe Redhead, Summerhill School, agreed following the Independent Schools Tribunal, 23–03–00.

6 Report of the inquiry into Summerhill School, Leiston, Suffolk, in January 2000 by a group of independent experts following the adverse report by Ofsted inspectors. The independent inspectors, who had no previous connection with Summerhill School, included heads of two very different independent schools, two experienced school inspectors and others with senior positions in universities and enterprise: Stuart Ainsworth, Dr Ian Cunningham, Dr Harry Gray, Derry Hannam, Jill Horsburgh, Colin Reid, Dr Michael Rosen. Their report is available at: http://www.selfmanagedlearning.org.

7 A recent opinion poll of 500 parents in the *Guardian* newspaper (29–02–00) found that 91 per cent were happy with the quality of their children's schooling.

5 What price freedom? Economy and effectiveness in education

1 For example, see the wording of Section 2(1) of the Standards In Scotland's Schools Act 2000.

2 For example, the *Herald*, 07–04–01, p. 1.

3 A study on behalf of the Nuffield Foundation by the Institute of Education reinforced doubts about the cogency of this idea of key skills as well as of the practicalities of implementing them throughout all levels of the curriculum (Hodgson *et al.*, 2001).

4 Siegel cites an argument by Gene V. Glass against criterion-referencing and a counter-argument by Michael Scriven in favour of 'needs assessment' (Siegel, 1988, pp. 118–21).

5 Response of the London Association for the Teaching of English in 1988 to proposals by the Task Group on Assessment and Testing, established by the Secretary of State for Education. Quoted by Keith Kimberley in *New Readings: Contributions to an Understanding of Literacy* (Kimberley *et al.*, 1992).

6 A year after the exams debacle, proposals were being considered by government and teachers' unions for reductions in the burden of external marking by restricting it to papers by candidates who would have been most likely to achieve external examination passes under the original system, an idea that led the *Times Educational Supplement for Scotland* to ask in its editorial column:

> have we now reached the stage after almost 10 years of frustrating reform where we can conclude that Higher Still was an overly complex failure, that attempts to bridge the academic and vocational divide were doomed and that the SQA was completely unnecessary?
>
> (*TESS*, 08–06–01, p. 24)

6 Learning, teaching and learning to learn: some epistemological perspectives

1 Ian Stronach, research professor, Manchester Metropolitan Institute of Education, reported in *THES*, 13–04–01, p. 8.
2 Phil Hodkinson, Professor of Lifelong Learning, Leeds University, reported in *THES*, 13–04–01, p. 8.
3 Jack Goody and Ian Watt identify the emergence of the 'democratic' alphabetic script as a key factor in the diffusion of ideas and the origin of a disposition to compare and evaluate ancient oral traditions with a new scepticism (Goody and Watt, 1963, pp. 304–45). Matthew Lipman, a pioneer of 'philosophy for schools' has explained the Greek enigma as the emergence of 'spontaneous communities of enquiry' though this does tend to beg questions about the sources of that spontaneity which Goody and Watt addressed.
4 See, for example, essays on this and related topics in Wertsch, 1989.
5 Galileo's thesis is exemplified by his 'Letter to the Grand Duchess Christina' in 1615 (Goodman, 1973, pp. 27–49).
6 Popper's most sustained treatment of this theme is in his *The Open Society and Its Enemies* in which he explores the threat to the critical, scientific traditions and democratic institutions posed by a return to ancient totalitarian modes of thought.
7 This issue, with its resonances of Plato's doctrine of reminiscence in the *Meno*, is a fundamental contradiction between Piaget's 'constructivism' and Chomsky's 'innatism', as Jerry Fodor pointed out in a symposium comparing and contrasting the two opposed schools of thought (Piattelli-Palmarini, 1980).
8 For example, Voneche and Bovet argue that by removing the ambiguities in class-inclusion tests which may ask children 'are there more red flowers or more flowers?' in an assemblage, the experimenter has removed the logical problem posed by the original form of the experiment (Voneche and Bovet, 1982, p. 89).
9 Darling traces this relationship between the philosophical case against 'progressivism' and the political climate which led to the increasing involvement of government in British education, observing that '[t]he introduction of the National Curriculum (by a government pledged to reduce government power) represents an extension of government power almost unimaginable to those working in the education service before the 1980s' (Darling, 1994, p. vii).
10 John McPeck follows Oakeshott in this respect, though his argument is in the context of the more recent debate about 'general skills' of critical thinking that I addressed on an earlier occasion (Brown, 1998). McPeck cites Oakeshott's theory of domains of knowledge and Wittgenstein's metaphor of 'language games' in support of his sceptical thesis against generic skills. But the idea of language games does not provide support for a theory of domain-specificity. Wittgenstein explicitly disavowed any wish to identify boundaries as he considered the task irrelevant to his metaphorical intent and, in any case, impossible in terms of the very conception of language and logic he was propounding (Wittgenstein, 1968, PI 76, 130, 131).
11 Mill's hostility to this idea was articulated most ferociously in his attack on Auguste Comte's Platonic vision of oligarchic government by a 'rational

clerisy' and his concomitant belief that the role of teachers is simply to inculcate rather than justify 'rational' doctrine to their pupils. Mill summarised his refutation of Comte with the acerbic comment that 'M. Comte ... does not imagine that he actually possesses all knowledge, but only that he is an infallible judge of what knowledge is worth possessing' (Mill, 1965c, pp. 178–81).

12 Sceptics who dispute the idea of 'truth' face the difficulty of explaining the status of their own assertions. They also underestimate the reliance of an intelligible contrast between truth and its alternatives on the fact that we do know some truths despite the ever present possibilities of illusion, deception or hallucination.

13 This italicised phrase is the title of a paper by Richard Bailey in which the author also urges that Popper's maxim that 'we learn from our mistakes' should be recognised as a fruitful source of inspiration for alternative educational approaches (Bailey, 1998).

14 Popper emphasised the role of written language in developing and recording a linguistic 'third world' of ideas and associated problems as the necessary objects for rational criticism (Popper, 1972, pp. 120–2). Jack Goody and Ian Watt elaborated on the contribution of the easily accessible alphabetic script to sceptical inquiry in Greece. Unlike the oral traditions of tribal societies which succumb to 'structural amnesia', reflecting and reinforcing present beliefs and social realities, literate societies amass records which stimulate critical comparisons between past and present and facilitate argumentative discourse about varying beliefs and standards, a situation illustrated by records of controversies among the pre-Socratic Greek philosophers (Goody and Watt, 1963, pp. 304–45).

7 How others do it: some international alternatives

1 As I observed in Chapter 6, this question of prioritisation between the individual and the social divided Piaget and Vygotsky on the manner in which the child accommodates to the social nexus, the latter stressing the incoherence of any account of higher mental functions that disregarded the mediating role of culture from the first onset of language.

2 A recent manifestation of this tendency was the introduction of 'citizenship education' into the UK curriculum, replete with the apparatus of 'learning outcomes' and 'generic skills'.

3 In the opinion of former Chief Inspector of Schools, Chris Woodhead, published in the *Daily Telegraph* of 1 March 2001, of more than sixty government educational initiatives, only these literacy and numeracy strategies achieved significant improvements.

4 'All children of compulsory education age have the right to free education in the *folkeskole*. Parents or guardians who can themselves provide an education comparable to that normally demanded at the *folkeskole* are not obliged to have their children educated at the *folkeskole*' (paragraph 76, chapter 8, Danish Constitution).

5 The mean literacy scores (as measured by the International Adult Literacy Survey) of young Danes who had completed upper secondary education were second only to those of their Finnish counterparts out of eighteen countries surveyed. The United Kingdom was thirteenth and the United States seventeenth. 'Under-achievement rates', defined as the proportion

of upper secondary completers judged 'by experts' according to their performance on literacy tasks to lack minimum levels of competence for everyday life, told a similar story, though in this case the United States was eighteenth out of the eighteen countries surveyed.

6 Borish's book, in addition to a wealth of information about the relationships between Danish education and society, contains first-hand accounts of his experiences in three very different Folk High Schools.

7 There is an unfortunate postscript to the story of the Folk High School. Student numbers dropped in the latter decades of the twentieth century, reflecting declining numbers in the population of young adults in the 18–25 age range. International pressures have also placed a premium on formal educational qualifications, and local government funding has been partly diverted towards alternative courses providing exam-based qualifications. There were about ninety-five of these establishments at the beginning of the twenty-first century and many were beginning to consider the introduction of formal assessment as a defensive measure.

8 The Danish Research and Development Centre for Adult Education, a private, state-funded institution, was established in 1983 partly to provide additional support for *folkeoplysning*.

9 As Free Schools are generally set up in conformity with the philosophical, religious, pedagogical or other orientation of parents and teachers, they can and sometimes do select pupils according to parental conviction. However, selection according to wealth is limited by the state support available to parents on lower incomes and, in practice, self-selection according to conviction usually means that schools simply accept pupils as they come. In any case, the fundamental principle of this kind of educational freedom is that dissenting parents may set up their own schools or educate their children at home.

10 This was a major objection by many professional educators to the adoption by UK government of 'league tables' for school performances based on the outcomes of nationally standardised forms of assessment.

8 A radical alternative: home education

1 Ray openly supports and advocates home education, though his copious research in the United States and Canada over more than a decade is cited frequently by less committed scholars and includes data gathered by researchers in universities from different states of the Union.

2 The Internet is a major source of information about all aspects of home education, including academic research on the subject. See, for example, the Holt Associates *Growing Without Schooling* website, which lists research papers dealing with such subjects as student achievement, social skills, teacher certification of parents, college admission and the future employment prospects of home educated students.

3 The Iowa Tests of Basic Skills (ITBS) were used for younger students and Tests of Achievement and Proficiency (TAP) for older students in both the home educating, public and private sectors. Demographic data was gathered by a questionnaire distributed to home educating parents.

4 From the point of view of the HSLDA this was significant information as a number of education authorities had insisted on parental teaching quali-

fications as a condition of permitting them to educate their children outside the school system.

5 Public education in the United States is, of course, explicitly secular. Hamilton expresses concern about a trend towards narrow religious sectarianism among some families, though she also argues that the 'Christianisation' of state schools in the United Kingdom by the Education Reform Act 1988 was a disturbing development and possibly a violation of international treaty obligations concerning human rights (Hamilton, 1995, pp. 337–42).

6 A court ruling in the state of Idaho, for example, held that the burden of proving that home educating parents were in breach of their statutory duties fell on the prosecuting authorities and the situation was no different to that in the case of other alleged offences against juveniles. (See note 6, Chapter 9.)

7 The Education (Scotland) Act 1980 provides for the education of children, 'in accordance with the wishes of their parents' on condition that they ensure 'suitable instruction and training and the avoidance of unreasonable public expenditure' (Section 28(1)) and for parents to educate their children 'by other means' than regular school attendance (Section 30). The Act differs, however, from legislation applying to England and Wales. Where a child has attended a public school on one or more occasions, parents may withdraw them from school only with the consent of the relevant Scottish education authority, though that consent 'shall not be unreasonably withheld' (Section 35(1)). There is no statutory limit on the time an education authority may take while considering to grant or withhold that consent. It is the belief of many home educating parents in Scotland that unreasonable delays are involved as a result and, despite vigorous lobbying by home educators, the Scottish Parliament did not take the opportunity to repeal this clause relating to consent when it passed the Standards in Scotland's Schools Act 2000.

8 The '5–14' guidelines for the Scottish schools' curriculum, unlike the statutory national curriculum in England and Wales, are notionally optional and flexible, though the original emphasis on this has declined with the increasingly directive role of the schools inspectorate.

9 Section 14 of the Standards in Scotland's Schools Act provides that 'Scottish Ministers may issue guidance as to the circumstances in which parents choose to educate their children at home; and education authorities shall have regard to such guidance'.

10 Joint ADES/COSLA draft response to Scottish Executive consultation on guidance on home education, September 2000.

11 The Standards in Scotland's Schools Act pays homage to the Convention on the Rights of the Child by providing for consultation by schools with their students, though in a context where virtually every aspect of schooling, including the curriculum, is determined by government policy and is consequently not subject to significant amendment.

9 Ways forward: towards a learning society

1 This debate was revived for essentially the same reasons twenty years later with the publication in America of *The Bell Curve* by Charles Murray and Richard Herrnstein, and consequent claims about the inevitable ineffec-

tiveness of 'affirmative action' to improve the intellectual development of sections of society facing the supposedly inflexible obstacle of low, genetically determined IQs.

2 One disturbing measure of the gulf between family and school has been an increasing incidence of abuse and violence by parents towards teachers.

3 The OECD notes that so called 'workplace competencies' tend to be distinguished in public debate from what is taught and learned in traditional education. But, as previously noted, there is little agreement about what these competencies are. UK employers, for instance, valued 'communication skills, learning ability, problem solving skills, team work and the capacity for self-management' above technical, ICT or numeracy skills in the recruitment of graduates (*ibid.*, pp. 100–4).

4 The draft of a study for the Nuffield Foundation of the role of 'key skills' in the UK's *Curriculum 2000* urges 'a shift in thinking' by government and its agencies on the grounds that an important component of it, the Key Skills Qualification, was based too narrowly on remediation, that it created assessment burdens, and that it was almost universally rejected by students and selective schools and, consequently, widely disregarded by universities (Hodgson *et al.*, May 2001).

5 The Secretary of State for Education, Estelle Morris, speaking during a BBC radio interview for *The World at One* news programme, 21–06–01.

6 For example, Welker *v.* Independent School District of Boise City, Idaho (25 May 1990): 'the burden does not shift to the defence [i.e. the home educator] to affirmatively defend, or prove compliance, since the full panoply of criminal procedural due process applies to juvenile prosecutions'.

Conclusion: education and democracy

1 These words from a speech by David Blunkett were quoted and condemned by his former Chief Inspector of Schools, Chris Woodhead, as 'depressing, narrow and utterly misguided' in an opinion column in the right-wing *Daily Telegraph* newspaper of 28–02–01.

2 A cogent demonstration of this point was provided by the financial crisis engendered in the UK in the early 1990s, partly as a result of huge international movements of capital by the speculator George Soros, whose subsequent verdict was: 'There is a widespread presumption that democracy and capitalism go hand in hand. In fact the relationship is much more complicated. Capitalism needs democracy as a counterweight because the capitalist system shows no tendency towards equilibrium' (Soros, 1998, p. xxvii).

3 Duke Maskell, for instance, has claimed that 'standards' have become unintelligible and that they have become 'cripplingly low' (*THES*, 23–03–01).

4 UK government proposals to encourage specialisation in these schools are, in any case, seen by many as inimical to the ideal, the tarnished image of which was not helped by the description 'bog standard comprehensive' offered by the official spokesman who announced this further initiative.

5 The Waterhouse Report of February 2000 published seventy-two recommendations for the protection of children in care against physical and sexual abuse, chief among which was one for the appointment of an inde-

pendent children's commissioner for Wales. As mentioned in Chapter 4, the UK government in 1999 had opposed a similar proposal on the grounds that existing services were adequate to ensure that children's 'voices are heard'.

Bibliography

Adcock, J. (1994) *In Place of Schools: a Novel Plan for the 21st Century*, London: New Education Press.

Anderson, J. (1963) *Studies in Empirical Philosophy*, London: Angus and Robertson.

Andrews, J.N. (1990) 'General thinking skills: are there such things?' *Journal of Philosophy of Education*, 24, 1, 71–9.

Anthony, W. (1979) 'Progressive learning theories: the evidence', in G. Bernbaum (ed.) *Schooling in Decline*, London: Macmillan.

Aristotle (1966) *The Politics* (trans. T.A. Sinclair), Harmondsworth: Penguin.

Arnold, M. (1966) *Culture and Anarchy* (ed. J.D. Wilson), Cambridge: Cambridge University Press.

Association of Directors of Education in Scotland and Convention of Scottish Local Authorities (September 2000) *Joint ADES/COSLA Draft Response to Scottish Executive Consultation on Guidance on Home Education*, Edinburgh: ADES/COSLA.

Bagehot, W. (1963) *The English Constitution*, London: Fontana.

Bailey, R. (1998) *Knowledge and Criticism – Popper's Non-Authoritarian Epistemology*, paper to the Scottish Educational Research Association.

Barrow, R. (1979) 'Back to basics', in G. Bernbaum (ed.) *Schooling in Decline*, London: Macmillan, pp. 182–203.

Beck, F.A.G. (1964) *Greek Education 450–350 BC*, London: Methuen.

Benedict, R. (1971) *Patterns of Culture*, London: Routledge and Kegan Paul.

Bentham, J. (1948) *Principles of Morals and Legislation*, New York: Hafner.

Bentley, T. (1998) *Learning beyond the Classroom: Education for a Changing World*, London: Routledge.

Bernbaum, G. (ed.) (1979) 'Schooling in decline', in G. Bernbaum (ed.) *Schooling in Decline*, London: Macmillan, pp. 1–16.

Bonnet, M. (1995) 'Teaching thinking and the sanctity of content', *Journal of Philosophy of Education*, 29, 3, 295–309.

Borish, S.M. (1991) *The Land of the Living: the Danish Folk Highschools and Denmark's Non-Violent Path to Modernization*, Nevada City, California: Blue Dolphin Publishing.

Boyle, D. (1982) 'Piaget and education: a negative evaluation', in S. Modgil and C. Modgil (eds) *Jean Piaget: Consensus and Controversy*, New York: Praeger, pp. 291–308.

Bridges, D. (1993) 'Transferable skills: a philosophical perspective', *Studies in Higher Education*, 18, 1, 43–51.

Brown, K. (1998) *Education, Culture and Critical Thinking*, Aldershot: Ashgate.

Burgess, T. (1998) *The Philosophy of Karl Popper and the Improvement of Educational Practice: the Implications of Popper for Formal Education*, paper presented to the Scottish Educational Research Association, 29–09–98.

Burston, W.H. (ed.) (1969) *James Mill on Education*, London: Cambridge University Press.

——(1973) *James Mill on Philosophy and Education*, London: The Athlone Press.

Callahan, R.E. (ed.) (1962) *Education and the Cult of Efficiency*, Chicago: University of Chicago Press.

Carlsen, J. and Borga, O. (1994) *The Danish 'Folkehøjskole'*, Copenhagen: Royal Danish Ministry for Foreign Affairs, Secretariat for Cultural Relations.

Chalmers, A.F. (1980) *What is This Thing Called Science? An Assessment of the Nature and Status of Science and its Methods*, Milton Keynes: Open University Press.

Chomsky, N. (1972a) *Problems of Knowledge and Freedom: the Russell Lectures*, London: William Collins Sons.

——(1972b) 'On the nature, use and acquisition of language', in *Mind and Cognition* (ed. W. Lycan) Oxford: Blackwell, pp. 627–45.

——(1992) *Language and Mind*, New York: Harcourt Brace Jovanovich.

CIE, *International A Level and Advanced Subsidiary Qualifications* at http://www.cie.org/q_and_s/gce_a/gce_a.htm. Accessed 01–05–01.

Cole, M. (1989) 'The zone of proximal development: where culture and cognition create each other', in J.V. Wertsch (ed.) *Culture, Communication and Cognition*, London: Cambridge University Press, pp. 146–61.

Collingwood, R.G. (1946) *The Idea of History*, Oxford: Clarendon.

Council of Europe (1995) *Convention for the Protection of Human Rights and Fundamental Freedoms*, Strasbourg: Secretariat to the European Commission on Human Rights.

Danish Friskole Association (DFA) (1995) *The Danish Friskole: a Segment of the Grundtvigian–Kold School Tradition*, Faaborg: Danish Friskole Association.

Danish Research and Development Centre for Adult Education (1988) *New Approaches to Adult Education in Denmark*, Copenhagen: Danish Research and Development Centre for Adult Education.

——(1993) *Adult Education in Denmark and the Concept of 'Folkeoplysning'*, Copenhagen: Danish Ministry of Education, Department of Adult Education.

Darling, J. (1993) 'The end of primary ideology?' *Curriculum Studies*, 1, 3, 417–26.

——(1994) *Child-Centred Education*, London: Paul Chapman.

Davydov, V.V. and Radzikhovskii, L.A. (1989) 'Vygotsky's theory and the activity-oriented approach in psychology', in J.V. Wertsch (ed.) *Culture, Communication and Cognition*, London: Cambridge University Press, pp. 35–65.

Department for Education and Employment, *The Standards Site* at http://www.standards.dfee.gov.uk/. Accessed 23–02–01.

——*A to Z – Citizenship Education* at http://www.dfee.gov.uk/a-z/CITIZEN-SHIP_EDUCATION_ba.html. Accessed 10–03–01.

Dewey, J. (1974) *John Dewey on Education* (ed. R.D. Archambault), London: University of Chicago Press.

Donaldson, M. (1990) *Children's Minds*, London: Fontana.

Donaldson, M. and Elliot, A. (1982) 'Piaget on language', in S. Modgil and C. Modgil (eds) *Jean Piaget: Consensus and Controversy*, New York: Praeger, pp. 157–66.

Durant, J.R., Evans, G.A. and Thomas, G.P. (1989) 'The public understanding of science', *Nature*, 340, 11–14.

Education Otherwise, *Home-education Research* at http://www.education-otherwise.org/publications/eoleaflets/research.htm. Accessed 20–05–01.

Ennis, R.H. (1962) 'A concept of critical thinking', *Harvard Educational Review*, 32, 1, 81–111.

Estes, R.J., *The World Social Situation 1970–1995: Professional Challenges for a New Century* at http://caster.ssw.upenn.edu/~restes/jak2.html. Accessed 13–06–01.

Farrow, M. (2000) Correspondence by Head of Policy, CBI Scotland, *Times Educational Supplement*, 05–05–00.

Foreign Office (1999) *Human Rights*, Foreign and Commonwealth Office and Department for International Development Annual Report for 1999, London: Foreign and Commonwealth Office and Department for International Development.

Foster, J. (1974) *Class Struggle and the Industrial Revolution: Early Industrial Capitalism in Three English Towns*, London: Weidenfeld & Nicolson.

Frankfort, H., Frankfort, H. A., Wilson, J. and Jacobsen, T. (1968) *Before Philosophy*, Harmondsworth: Penguin.

Gerwitz, S. (December 2000) 'Bringing the politics back in: a critical analysis of quality discourses in education', *British Journal of Educational Studies*, 48, 4, 352–70.

Gibbons, A. (2001) Letter, *Times Educational Supplement*, 27–04–01, p. 23.

Gleick, J. (1994) *Genius*, London: Abacus.

Goodman, D.C. (ed.) (1973) *Science and Religious Belief 1600–1900: a Selection of Primary Sources*, Milton Keynes: Open University Press.

——(1979) 'Galileo and the Church', in *The Conflict Thesis and Cosmology*, Milton Keynes: Open University Press.

Goody, J. and Watt, I. (1963) 'The consequences of literacy', *Comparative Studies in Society and History: an International Quarterly*, 5, 304–45.

Greene, J.P. (2000) 'The Education Freedom Index', *Civic Report*, 14, September, at http://www.manhattan-institute.org/html/cr_14.htm.

Hagen, E.E. (1962) *On the Theory of Social Change*, Illinois: The Dorsey Press.

Halévy, E. (1952) *The Growth of Philosophical Radicalism*, London: Faber & Faber.

Halsey, A.H. (1972) *Educational Priority: EPA Problems and Policies*, London: HMSO.

Hamilton, C. (1995) *Family, Law and Religion*, London: Sweet & Maxwell.

Harber, C. and Meighan, R. (1989) 'The democratic school', in C. Harber and R. Meighan (eds) *Education Now*, Derbyshire: Educational Heretics Press.

Hare, W. (1995) 'Content and criticism: the aims of schooling', *Journal of Philosophy of Education*, 29, 1, 47–60.

Hargreaves, D. (1997a) 'Guru predicts classroom exodus', *Times Educational Supplement*, 30–05–97, p. 11.

——(1997b) 'A road to the learning society', *School Leadership and Management*, 17, 1, 9–22.

Harris, D.J., O'Boyle, M. and Warbrick, C. (1995) *Law of the European Convention on Human Rights*, London: Butterworth.

Hirst, P.H. (1974) *Knowledge and the Curriculum: a Collection of Philosophical Papers*, London: Routledge and Kegan Paul.

——(ed.) (1983) *Educational Theory and its Foundation Disciplines*, London: Routledge and Kegan Paul.

HM Inspectors of Schools (2000) *Education for Work in Schools*, Edinburgh: The Scottish Executive.

HM Inspectors of Schools and the Social Work Services Inspectorate (March 2001) *Learning With Care: the Education of Children Looked After Away from Home by Local Authorities*, Edinburgh: The Scottish Executive.

Hodgson, A., Spours, K. and Savory, C. (2001) *Broadening the Advanced Level Curriculum: Institute of Education/Nuffield Foundation Research Report No. 4. Improving the 'Use' and 'Exchange' Value of Key Skills: Debating the role of the Key Skills Qualification within Curriculum 2000*, London: Institute of Education, University of London.

Holroyd, C. (1989) *Problem Solving and the Secondary Curriculum*, Edinburgh: Scottish Council for Research in Education.

Holt Associates, *Growing Without Schooling* website at http://www.holtgws.com/research.htm. Accessed 05–01.

Holt, J. (1964) *How Children Fail*, Harmondsworth: Penguin.

Home Education Research and Legal Information Network (HERLIN) website at http://homeschool.3dproductions.com.au/legal/index.html. Accessed 13–05–01.

Hooykaas, R. (1977) *Religion and the Rise of Modern Science*, London and Edinburgh: Scottish Academic Press.

Human Scale Education (HSE), website at http://www.hse.org.uk/. Accessed 13–05–01.

——(Autumn 2000) *News*, Bath: HSE.

Humboldt, W.v. (1969) *The Limits of State Action*, edited J.W. Burrow, Cambridge: Cambridge University Press.

Hyland, T. (1993) 'Competence, knowledge and education', *Journal of Philosophy of Education*, 27, 1, 57–68.

Inglis, B. (1972) *Poverty and the Industrial Revolution*, London: Panther Books.

Ingram, A. (1994) *A Political Theory of Rights*, Oxford: Clarendon Press.

Kaseman, L. and Kaseman, S. (1995) 'Testing our freedom: goals 2000, vouchers, and charter schools', *Home Education Magazine*, January/February, 'Taking Charge' column, available at http://www.home-ed-magazine.com/INF/FREE/free_2m.v.chtr.html. Accessed 08–01.

Kimberley, K., Meek, M. and Miller, J. (eds) (1992) *New Readings: Contributions to an Understanding of Literacy*, London: A. and C. Black.

Kluckhohn, C. and Leighton, D. (1960) *The Navaho*, London: Oxford University Press.

Kuhn, T.S. (1970) *The Structure of Scientific Revolutions*, Chicago and London: University of Chicago Press.

Lawrence, E.S. (1970) *The Origins and Growth of Modern Education*, Aylesbury: Pelican.

Learning and Teaching Scotland (LTS) (2000) *Education for Citizenship in Scotland*, Dundee: Learning and Teaching Scotland.

——(2001) *The Global Dimension in the Curriculum*, Dundee: Learning and Teaching Scotland.

Lines, P.M. (1999) *Homeschoolers: Estimating Numbers and Growth*, US Department of Education: Office of Educational Research and Improvement.

Lipman, M. (1991) 'Squaring Soviet theory with American practice', *Educational Leadership*, May, 72–6.

Locke, J. (1913) *Some Thoughts Concerning Education* (ed. R.H. Quick), Cambridge: Cambridge University Press.

——(1991) *John Locke: An Essay Concerning Human Understanding (An Abridgement)* (ed. J.W. Yolton), London: Dent.

Lowe Boyd, W. (December 2000) 'Editorial: what counts as educational research?' *British Journal of Educational Studies*, 48, 4, 347–51.

Lyons, J. (1970) *Chomsky*, London: Fontana/Collins.

MacDermott, J.J. (ed.) (1981) *The Philosophy of John Dewey*, Chicago and London: University of Chicago Press.

McPeck, J.E., Norris, S.P. and Siegel, H. (1990) *Teaching Critical Thinking*, New York: Routledge.

Maskell, D. (July 1999) 'What has Jane Austin to teach Tony Blunkett?' *Journal of Philosophy of Education*, 33, 2, 157.

Mays, W. (1985) 'Thinking skills programmes: an analysis', *New Ideas – Psychology*, 3, 2, 149–63.

Meighan, R. (1995) 'Home-based education effectiveness research – and some of its implications', *Education Now*, 47, 3, available at http://www.education-otherwise.org/publications/eoleaflets/research.htm.

——(Spring 2000) 'Home based education: not 'Does it work?' but "Why does it work so well?" ', *Topic*, 23, available at http://www.geocities.com/Heartland/1400/hbe.html.

——*Roland Meighan's Theme Pages* at http://www.gn.apc.org/edheretics/EHT012.htm. Accessed 13–05–01.

Merton, R.K. (1979) 'Puritanism, pietism and science', in C.A. Russell (ed.) *Science and Religious Beliefs,* Sevenoaks: Hodder & Stoughton/Open University Press, pp. 20–54.

Mill, J.S. (1946) Letter to *The Monthly Repository*, known as 'On Genius', in *Four Dialogues of Plato* (ed. R. Borchard), London: Watts.

——(1963) *Essays on Politics and Culture: Civilization* (ed. G. Himmelfarb), New York: Anchor Books.

——(1965a) *Essential Works: On Liberty* (ed. M. Lerner), New York: Bantam.

——(1965b) *Essential Works: Autobiography* (ed. M. Lerner), New York: Bantam.

——(1965c) *Auguste Compte and Positivism*, Michigan: Ann Arbor Paperbacks.

——(1968) *Utilitarianism* (ed. M. Warnock), London: Fontana, pp. 251–321.

——(1984) 'Inaugural address delivered to the University of St Andrews', in *Essays on Equality, Law and Education (CW)*, vol. XXI (ed. J.M. Robson), Toronto: University of Toronto Press.

Ministry of Education – Denmark (1996) *Facts and Figures: Education Indicators Denmark 1996*, Copenhagen: Danish Ministry of Education.

Ministry of Education – Finland (1999) *Education in Finland*, Helsinki: Finnish Ministry of Education.

——(2000) *Education and Research 1999–2004. Development Plan*, Helsinki: Finnish Ministry of Education.

Molnar, A. (1996) *Giving Kids the Bu$iness: the Commercialization of America's Schools*, Boulder, Colorado: Westview Press.

Morris, N. (1972) 'State paternalism and laissez-faire in the 1860s', in B.R. Cosin (ed.) *Education: Structure and Society*, Middlesex: Penguin, pp. 281–91.

National Educational Research Forum (NERF), website at http://www.coidigital.net/nerf/index.html. Accessed 01–05–01.

Neill, A.S. (1975) *Summerhill*, Harmondsworth: Penguin.

Newell, P. (2000) *Taking Children Seriously: a Proposal for a Children's Rights Commissioner*, London: Calouste Gulbenkian Foundation.

Nuovo, V. (ed.) (1997) *John Locke and Christianity*, Bristol: Theommes Press.

Oakeshott, M. (1933) *Experience and its Modes*, London: Cambridge University Press.

——(1967) *Rationalism in Politics*, London: Methuen.

Organisation for Economic Co-operation and Development (OECD) (2001) *Education Policy Analysis*, Paris: Organisation for Economic Co-operation and Development.

Paterson, L. (2000) *Crisis in the Classroom: the Exam Debacle and the Way Ahead for Scottish Education*, London and Edinburgh: Mainstream Publishing.

Paul, R. (1990) 'McPeck's mistakes', in I. Scheffler, V.A. Howard and J.E. McPeck (eds) *Teaching Critical Thinking*, New York and London: Routledge, pp. 102–11.

Phillips, D. (1982) 'Perspectives on Piaget as philosopher: the tough, tender minded syndrome', in S. Modgil and C. Modgil (eds) *Jean Piaget: Consensus and Controversy*, New York: Praeger, pp. 13–30.

Piaget, J. (1970) 'The stages of the intellectual development of the child', in P.L. Wason and P.N. Johnson-Laird (eds) *Thinking and Reasoning*, Middlesex: Penguin, pp. 355–64.

Piattelli-Palmarini, M. (ed.) (1980) *Language and Learning – the Debate between Jean Piaget and Noam Chomsky*, London: Routledge and Kegan Paul.

Plato (1966) *Protagoras and Meno*, Middlesex: Penguin.

——(1967) *The Republic*, Middlesex: Penguin.

Plowden, B. (1967) *Children and Their Primary Schools. A Report of the Central Advisory Council for Education (England). Volume 1: Report*, London: HMSO.

Popper, K.R. (1961) *The Poverty of Historicism*, London: Routledge.

——(1963) *Conjectures and Refutations*, London: Routledge and Kegan Paul.

——(1966) *The Open Society and Its Enemies. Volume 1*, London: Routledge and Kegan Paul.

——(1969) *The Open Society and Its Enemies. Volume 2*, London: Routledge and Kegan Paul.

——(1972) *Objective Knowledge*, Oxford: Clarendon Press.

——(1977) *The Logic of Scientific Discovery*, London: Hutchinson.

Priestley, J. (1904) *Memoirs of Dr Priestley*, London: H.R. Allenson.

Putnam, H. (1992) *Renewing Philosophy*, London and Cambridge, Mass.: Harvard University Press.

Qualifications and Curriculum Authority (QCA) (1998) *Education for Citizenship and the Teaching of Democracy in Schools (The Crick Report)* at http://www.qca.org.uk/ca/subjects/citizenship/crick_report_1998.pdf. Accessed 2001.

Rawls, J. (1973) *A Theory of Justice*, Oxford: Oxford University Press.

Ray, B.D. (1991) *A Nationwide Study of Home Education: Family Characteristics, Legal Matters, and Student Achievements*, Washington: National Home Education Research Institute.

——(1997) *Home School Research Summary – and a New Study*, at http://www.nheri.org/.

Richards, C. (2001) Correspondence to *Times Educational Supplement for Scotland*, 27–04–01, p. 14.

Rieber, R.W. and Carton, A.S. (eds) (1987) *The Collected Works of L.S. Vygotsky, Volume 1*, New York: Plenum Press.

—— (eds) (1993) *The Collected Works of L.S. Vygotsky, Volume 2*, New York: Plenum Press.

Rothermel, P. (1999) 'A nationwide study of home education: early indications and wider implications', *Education Now*, 24, Summer, at http://www.jspr.btinternet.co.uk/Research/Newspaper/ednow.htm.

190   Bibliography

——(March 2000) 'The Third Way in education: thinking the unthinkable', *Education 3–13*, 1, 28.

——(2000) *A Critical Evaluation of Home Education and Its Broader Implications*, paper presented at European Educational Research Association, Edinburgh, 20–23 September.

Rudner, L.M. (1998) 'Scholastic achievement and demographic characteristics of home school students in 1988', *Educational Policy Analysis Archives*, 7, 8, at http://www.alternative-learning.org/v7n8.html.

Russell, C.A. (ed.) (1979) *Science and Religious Belief: a Selection of Recent Historical Studies*, Kent: Hodder & Stoughton.

Ryan, A. (1999) *Liberal Anxieties and Liberal Education: What Education is Really For and Why It Matters*, London: Profile Books.

Scheffler, I. (1973) *Reason and Teaching*, London: Routledge and Kegan Paul.

Schoolhouse Home Education Association (2000) *Annual Report 1999–2000*, Dundee: Schoolhouse Home Education Association.

——, website at http://www.schoolhouse.org.uk/html/. Accessed 05–01.

Scottish Consultative Council on the Curriculum (SCCC) (1998) *Higher Still*, Edinburgh: Higher Still Development Unit.

Scottish Consumer Council (SCC) (2000) *Home Works: Local Authorities' Approaches to Working with Home Educating Parents in Scotland*, Edinburgh: Scottish Consumer Council (11–07–2000).

Scottish Office Education and Industry Department (SOEID) (1998) *Parents as Partners*, Edinburgh: SOEID.

Siegel, H. (1988) *Educating Reason: Rationality, Critical Thinking and Education*, New York: Routledge.

——(1990) 'McPeck, informal logic and the nature of critical thinking', in I. Scheffler and V.A. Howard (eds) *Teaching Critical Thinking*, New York and London: Routledge, pp. 75–85.

——(1991) 'The generalizability of critical thinking', *Philosophy and Theory*, 21, 1, 18–30.

Siegel, L.S. and Hodkin, B. (1982) 'The garden path to the understanding of cognitive development: has Piaget led us into the poison ivy?', in S. Modgil and C. Modgil (eds) *Jean Piaget: Consensus and Controversy*, New York: Praeger.

Skorupski, J. (1991) *John Stuart Mill*, London: Routledge.

Slater, J. (1999) 'Briefing analysis: a strange kind of loving', *Times Educational Supplement*, 05–03–99, p. 23.

Smith, D.W. (1965) *Helvétius: a Study in Persecution*, Oxford: Clarendon Press.

Smith, F. (1992) *To Think: In Language, Learning and Education*, London: Routledge.

Soros, G. (1998) *The Crisis of Global Capitalism: Open Society Endangered*, London: Little, Brown.

Swann, J. (1998) *A Popperian Theory of Learning and Teaching*, paper to the Scottish Educational Research Association, 29–09–1998.

Tamburrini, J. (1982) 'Some educational implications of Piaget's theory', in S. Modgil and C. Modgil (eds) *Jean Piaget: Consensus and Controversy*, New York: Praeger, pp. 309–25.

Tawney, R.H. (1961) *The Acquisitive Society*, London: Fontana.

——(1966) *The Radical Tradition*, Harmondsworth: Penguin.

Third Sector Schools Alliance (1998) 'Briefing note', *Update,* 2 (July).

Tiles, J.E. (1990) *Dewey*, London: Routledge.

Tooley, J. (1998) *Educational Research: a Critique. A Survey of Published Educational Research*, London: Office for Standards in Education.

——(2000) *Reclaiming Education*, London: Cassell.

Vernon, P.E. (ed.) (1970) *Creativity*, Harmondsworth: Penguin.

Voneche, J. and Bovet, M. (1982) 'Training research and cognitive development: what do Piagians want to accomplish?' in S. Modgil and C. Modgil (eds) *Jean Piaget: Consensus and Controversy*, New York: Praeger, pp. 83–94.

Vygotsky, L. (1978) *Mind in Society: the Development of Higher Psychological Processes*, Cambridge, Mass.: Harvard University Press.

——(1989) *Thought and Language*, Cambridge, Mass.: MIT Press.

Weeber, F. and Ahlers, J. (1996) *Going to School in the Netherlands*, Zoetermeer: Ministerie van Onderwijs Cultuur en Wetenschappen.

Weil, G.L. (1963) *The European Convention on Human Rights: Background, Development and Prospects*, Leyden: A.W. Sythoff.

Welsh, J. (2000) *Home Works; Local Authorities' Approaches to Working with Home Educating Parents in Scotland*, Glasgow: Scottish Consumer Council.

Wertsch, J.V. (ed.) (1989) *Culture, Communication and Cognition*, Cambridge: Cambridge University Press.

White, Michael (1997) *Isaac Newton: the Last Sorcerer*, London: Fourth Estate.

Whorf, B.L. (1959) *Language, Thought and Reality*, Cambridge, Mass.: MIT Press.

Williams, R. (1963) *Culture and Society*, Harmondsworth: Penguin.

Wittgenstein, L. (1968) *Philosophical Investigations (PI)*, Oxford: Blackwell.

Wolf, A. (2000) 'Trying to box clever', *Times Higher Education Supplement*, 31–03–00, p. 39.

Woodhead, C. (2001) 'Blair and Blunkett have not delivered. The children have been betrayed', *The Electronic Telegraph* at http://www.telegraph.co.uk/ Issue 2106.

Index